T0072781

LIVE LIKE
A MILLIONAIRE
(WITHOUT HAVING
TO BE ONE)

LIVE LIKE A MILLIONAIRE (WITHOUT HAVING TO BE ONE)

VICKY OLIVER

Skyhorse Publishing

Skyhorse Publishing books may be purchased in bulk at special
discounts for sales promotion, corporate gifts, fund-raising, or
educational purposes. Special editions can also be created to
specifications. For details, contact the Special Sales Department,
Skyhorse Publishing, 307 West 36th Street,
11th Floor, New York, NY 10018 or info@skyhorsepublishing.com.

Skyhorse® and Skyhorse Publishing® are registered trademarks of
Skyhorse Publishing, Inc.®, a Delaware corporation.

Visit our website at www.skyhorsepublishing.com.

10 9 8 7 6 5 4 3 2 1

Library of Congress Cataloging-in-Publication Data is available on file.

Cover design by Rain Saukas

Print ISBN: 978-1-62914-753-6
Ebook ISBN: 978-1-63220-032-7
Printed in China

CONTENTS

TWENTY MUST-HAVE ITEMS TO LOOK LIKE A MILLIONAIRE

1. One pair of sunglasses that hides majority of face for instant celebrity appeal.
2. One gadget (cell, iPhone, iPad, Samsung Galaxy Note) to prove your time is very valuable.
3. One underwire bra (only if you're female; guys, you're off the hook).
4. Dunkin' Donuts coffee securely hidden inside a thermos with a Starbucks logo.
5. One copy of *Vanity Fair* to show you're part of the literati.
6. One watch fob, monocle, or other item that is painfully out of touch with modern sensibilities.
7. More than 1,000 Facebook friends (only 100 of whom you have actually met). A Twitter following is also helpful.
8. One pet that is a bit more unusual than a dog or cat.
9. One scarf in the colors of the university you wish you had attended.
10. One signet ring. (If you had to change your initials at some point, all the better.)
11. One copy of *The Wall Street Journal* to show you understand heady financial matters.

12. One ticket stub to a cultural event within the last year.
13. One key chain with charm signaling sport of choice, i.e., tennis, horseback riding, skeet shooting, etc.
14. Something in your pocket that's a historical curiosity.
15. One passbook savings account with at least $5 left after all expenses are paid.
16. Good hair.
17. Better shoes.
18. An eye for art. (Not confusing Jasper Johns with Jackson Pollock is a good start.)
19. A sincere desire to break some fashion rules.
20. Brass balls, gumption, and confidence galore.

FIVE OBSERVATIONS ABOUT MONEY

Penge er mere veltalende end et dusin medlemmer af Folketinget.
Money is more eloquent than a dozen members of parliament.

—Danish proverb

Geld is niet alles, maar het is ver vooruit wat er op de tweede plaats.
Money isn't everything, but it's way ahead of whatever is in second place.

—Dutch proverb

Geld regiert die Welt.
Money rules the world.

—German proverb

Et genus et formam regina pecunia donat.
Money, like a queen, gives rank and beauty.

—Latin proverb

מיט געלט אין דיין טאש איר זענט איר קלוג און איר ביסט שיין און איר זינגען גוט צו
With money in your pocket, you are wise and you are handsome and you sing well too.

—Yiddish proverb

LIVE LIKE A MILLIONAIRE (WITHOUT HAVING TO BE ONE)

HOW TO LIVE LIKE A MILLIONAIRE (ON A STIPEND)

We all know that "money is power." The wealthiest few get invited to glitzier parties, live in swankier homes, and attract more lucrative deals than the rest of us.

But why should the best perks accrue only to those able to afford them? Don't we all deserve to live the luxe life?

Just imagine how grand life would be if the posh club memberships, sophisticated yacht parties, and sojourns to Martha's Vineyard, Nantucket, and Southampton were no longer the exclusive province of the fabulously rich but were, in fact, within reach.

This book will show you how to wing it till you *cha-ching* it—by spending what little money you do have wisely and making a positive investment in yourself. It will help you gain the trappings of luxury—even if you're six generations removed, not just from Kevin, but from *anyone* who brings home the Bacon. You'll learn how to look, dress, speak, and live like a millionaire so that you, too, can enjoy the same privileged lifestyle. You just won't have to spend like a millionaire.

There are entire stores filled with chichi clothing. There are

Do you dream in green?

countless ways to pamper, party, and globetrot—all while sampling the world's finest luxuries. But if you have to worry about how much it all costs, then this is the right book for you. It will help redistribute the perks that come with the power of money, so that we can all get more of what's coming to us (for a great deal less).

IF YOU CAN DREAM IT, YOU CAN LOOK IT

This book describes eighteen separate aspects of looking and living like a millionaire even if you aren't one. Each chapter begins with a fictional scene, which sets the stage for the true-life advice and tips that follow.

As we travel together through these chapters, you will meet some friends and learn what to do (and, indeed, what not to do). Hopefully, some of the suggestions will work for you, whether your aim is to dress for success at the workplace, court the wealthy for business purposes, meet a financially eligible someone, or simply to secure a better social life. (Millionaires throw excellent parties.)

Budgeting, prioritizing, skimping, and stretching a dollar will all

Or do you dream in black and white?

be explored as tactics to achieve the fabulous lifestyle without taxing your bank account. Following these suggestions may even help you see more green, but it won't be with envy. You may well ask: What does it mean to be a "millionaire" today? After all, it's been several centuries since we were first awed by that rich title. Indeed, a million dollars is not what it used to be. Some people think ten million dollars in assets isn't enough to be considered a millionaire by today's standards. There's the housing to pay for, not to mention the help, the private schools, the twice-yearly trips to Europe—it all adds up!

To me, the word "millionaire" describes a mind-set that can't be pinned to an absolute number. The phrase "a person who's well off enough to feel comfortable" could easily substitute (but, alas, didn't make for a catchy title).

CONFESSIONS OF AN OUTSIDER

I first learned about the class system in the United States when I was six years old. At the time, I attended a private all-girls school in New York City. Upon hearing why my mother missed Parents' Day that year, a friend in my class crinkled up her tiny pug nose and said, "Your mother has to work? God, you *must* be poor."

It was at that moment that I recognized that, while the little girl's statement was harsh, it was technically accurate. I *was* the poorest kid that wasn't on scholarship in that particular class. While many of my friends lived in expansive prewar apartments along Park and Fifth Avenues, I lived in a personality-free postwar building directly across the street from an inn where brawls were commonplace and someone had recently been shot with a pistol. At my school, being relatively poor made me feel like an outsider peering in.

I grew up "not quite as privileged," but learned how to make do. I went to all the same varsity games and dances as my classmates but had to buy my own attire. My parents didn't have the money to buy me nice clothing. (At any rate, their version of "nice" was something made of velveteen from the *Sears Roebuck* catalog.)

In the process of growing up around the über-rich without

being part of the tribe, I formed all sorts of ideas about how to get away with being relatively poor in a rich person's world. Those experiences shape this book (and will spare you the pain of having to learn by trial and error the way I did).

Before I became a professional, full-time writer, I had a career in advertising. I started as a receptionist and eventually rose to creative director at a series of ad agencies in New York City. Working in advertising, crafting copy for some well-loved corporate brands, helped me form some indelible opinions about personal branding and how to use it to get ahead in life.

It is my hope that this book will show you how to brand yourself as a success—even if your bank account currently suggests otherwise. Money may not buy happiness. But having it—or the appearance of it, anyway—*will* provide access. By branding yourself as successful even before you are a success, I believe you will achieve it all the faster. In business, you'll rub elbows with industry leaders, moguls, and tycoons. In the social arena, you'll meet the barons of society.

Until then, I am pleased to take the journey with you . . . What? You're wearing that?! I'm terribly sorry, but you are going to need to change first. Oh, don't worry about me. I'll go find a smart jacket to wear and put on some lipstick, and I'll catch up with you in Chapter One.

THE TEN LAWS OF MATERIAL SUCCESS
(Or How to Dress the Part on a Pauper's Salary)

You've always considered it a stroke of bad luck to bump into anyone important before ten o'clock in the morning. Today is no exception.

As the office elevator door opens, your supervisor strolls out onto the landing, looking as if he stepped out of a very upscale men's store catalog. Tall, dark, and dapper, he's the golden boy of the company. Meanwhile, you look as if you tumbled out of bed or a thrift store.

His tailored navy suit has such panache. Your orange-and-brown plaid shirt with the hole in the right elbow is not as stylish.

His immaculately cuffed wrist shoots out in front of the heavy, closing elevator door and narrowly prevents it from crushing

you into smithereens as you scoot past him into the empty cabin.

"Nice outfit!" he says, grinning at your ratty plaid shirt and wrinkled gabardine pants.

"Thank you," you say, grateful that you have a supervisor like Mr. Bucks who can see past your humble threads to recognize all of the vital contributions you make to the firm.

"But I can't send you to the clients wearing that."

"It's casual Friday!" you say in your defense.

"True," he laughs, "but there's nothing casual about our clients."

"The meeting's in half an hour," you say,

still hoping you'll persuade him to change his mind.

"No worries," he says, eyeing your plaid shirt as if it's a hand-me-down whose previous owner might have been a leper. "I'll just send Cindy to the meeting instead." *Ouch!*

As the elevator door slams on your dreams for speedy advancement, you ask yourself how you're supposed to dress for success on the stipend that passes as your salary. Isn't that a catch-22 or a paradox or something?

Alone in the elevator, you ask for divine inspiration.

First, you pray to the shopping gods.

"Wait until the sales," the gods retort. "Big discounts the day after Christmas, July 4, and Labor Day."

Next, you beseech the Lotto gods. But they just tell you to take a number.

You mull over the advantages of shoplifting, yet worry that a stint in jail might well take your status in the wrong direction.

What does a person have to do to look successful, you wonder. *Rob a bank? Indulge in credit card fraud? Take up with a Sugar Daddy or Momma?*

THE TEN LAWS

First, the good news: In a world where social standing is determined primarily by perception, there is a way to dress the part on a pauper's allowance. And you don't even have to take up with the criminal element to do it.

However, dressing for success on a shoestring will require a leap of faith. You will need to give up all shopping preconceptions and vow to follow the path of sartorial enlightenment.

Here, for your shopping enrichment, are the Ten Laws of Material Success. Master them, and learn how to spend what little money you have wisely, by making a proactive investment in yourself.

LAW ONE: DON'T LOSE YOUR SHIRT ON EPHEMERAL PURCHASES

Do you have a passion for fashion? Cool your ardor. Fashion is fickle and its whims, fleeting. Many

designs are created with planned obsolescence in mind. The average Bic pen lasts longer than this year's hot boots.

Follow every passing fashion, and you can lose your shirt (and it won't even be "in" next season). As Quentin Crisp once remarked, "Fashion is what you adopt when you don't know who you are," while Coco Chanel said, "Fashion fades, only style remains the same."

When your budget is as constraining as a girdle, you'll get more stretch out of a style that will see you through season after season. Opt for classic pieces over trends, and start by building your wardrobe in one- or two-color palettes. Choose items that will mix and match with everything so your limited funds will go further.

Fashion is ephemeral. Style endures. Now that you're a whiz at hanging onto your shirt, it's time to mosey on to Law Two.

class acquisition strategy! Middle-of-the-road prices beget middle-of-the-road cuts with middle-of-the-road stitching, buttons, and seams. Middle of the road means it's not made well enough to be considered "uptown" or luxe, and it's too costly to be considered "downtown" or cool. Your clothing will never amount to more than a mediocrity. How sad.

But middle-of-the-road mind lock is a tough habit to break. We all carry around price lists in our heads for what things should cost. We are like contestants on a virtual game of *The Price Is Right*, our brains conditioned to seek clothes that match our preconceived notions.

When this type of thinking threatens to prevent you from achieving your ambitions, tell yourself that you are "stuck in the middle." If that doesn't work, make a date with yourself to test-drive Law Three and Law Four.

LAW TWO: DIVORCE YOURSELF FROM MIDDLE-OF-THE-ROADISM

How much does a pair of pants set you back? $100 or $150? Even less perhaps? Stop pursuing this middle-

LAW THREE: RIDE THE ESCALATORS WITH APLOMB

Middle-of-the-road thinking is a stranglehold. Break out of the rut. Stroll into an upscale department store. Ride the escalator up to the most expensive floor. Take a deep breath. Then give yourself permission to try on the designer items that you feel you could never afford in your lifetime. The point isn't to buy them, so don't succumb! Simply survey them. You are training your eye to recognize quality.

Feel the superior drape of the fabric and observe how the colors glisten. Run your hands along the seams. Recognize the tight, almost invisible stitching. Check out the superior buttons and perfectly crafted buttonholes. Notice the even hems and flattering cut.

Then, remember to take OFF the clothes while you read Law Four.

LAW FOUR: FOLLOW THE ONE-THIRD RULE

You can't look the part without a generous clothing allowance. However, since you don't have one, you will have no choice but to reallocate your resources. Buy one-third as many clothes as you do now, but spend three times as much on each item.

Instead of buying multiple pairs of pants at middle-of-the-road prices, resolve to invest in *one* pair of luxe, 100% wool black Armani pants and wear them everywhere. Apply the same logic to each item in your wardrobe. Buy one $2,000 suit and never take it off, if need be. But don't squander one penny on trendy items or impulse purchases.

I recently bought two pairs of Armani pants at 40% off at Bergdorf Goodman. The tailor spent half an hour pinning each leg. He knelt before me on the beige tufted floor of my dressing room while I modeled my new acquisitions in the full-length mirror and said, "No, let's try it a quarter of an inch shorter." Now that made me feel rich!

Apply the One-Third Rule to the purchase of any and all accessories. A pair of designer shoes crafted of fine Italian leather will last for ten years. With TLC and tons of shoe polish, a pair of cowboy boots could even outlive you. It really makes sense to invest a lot more money per item so that the fine craftsmanship, cut, and stitching will be apparent to the most casual onlooker, and forgo the cheap chic specials, bargain basement finds that are really no bargain, and sales of ravaged seconds.

Clothing is an investment. Choose wisely, and you will wear the items with pride for years, even decades. Buy the best; throw out the rest. You'll look a couple of tax brackets richer. And, once cleared of clutter, your closet will breathe a huge sigh of relief.

"What if you spend $500 per suit and buy four suits?" my glamorous friend Alexis asked over a glass of wine at a New York hotspot. She used to work at a law firm so has an inquisitive mind when it comes to details.

"No. Buy one $2,000 suit," I said.

"Not four suits for $500 each?" Alexis said, nervously glancing down at her own white silk jacquard suit.

"$2,000," I said. "Go for it."

You are now primed for Law Five.

LAW FIVE: STAY OUT OF THE OUTLETS

Some shoppers swear by the outlets. These bargain hunters believe they are on the great American treasure hunt. If they travel long distances and diligently scavenge through racks of outlet merchandise, the rewards will be bountiful. These discounter denizens think they'll unearth a delicious designer item, in the height of fashion, at a fraction of the cost. What a find!

But is it? Consider: Today, 90 percent of the merchandise sold in outlets is manufactured specifically *for* the outlets. The Coach handbag in an outlet is not the same model that's for sale in a department store. Its non-discounted cousin may be sturdier, have superior stitching, or softer leather. The outlet merchandise is less costly but lower in quality. And if it is the real thing, it's only there because people with money didn't like it enough to buy it. Here again, most of the time, you get what you pay for. Out, out, stay out of the damned outlets!

LAW SIX: CONSIDER SWAPPING BLACK FOR WHITE

You have to be exceedingly wealthy to wear white. Think about it: One tiny sweat stain and the garment is no longer white. And every time you dry-clean the vestment, it turns a little yellower.

At parties in the Hamptons, everyone wears white. You, on the other hand, won't even be able to afford to take the Jitney out to the Hamptons if you squander all of your money on white clothing.

White is like a brand-new car. Take it out of the lot, drive it around the block, kick the tires once or twice, and it's already depreciated. As an investment, white is a disaster.

If you can afford to buy only one suit, it should be black for women and charcoal gray or navy blue for men. Step over to the dark side, and at least you won't be taken to the cleaner's every time you go to the dry cleaner's!

There's a reason black is associated with sin. Black forgives a lot of debauchery. Did you wash down three eggnogs instead of two at the Christmas fest? Cheat on your diet with half-and-half this morning instead of 1% milk? Have you packed on ten pounds due to spousal anxieties? Meet Black—your new best friend.

Black hides ten pounds on contact, looks stupendous with any color, and easily escorts you from a casual lunch with friends to a business meeting to an elegant evening affair without ever having to change. Few colors are as accommodating.

That said, wearing black can be tricky. Wools grip dye better than cotton, so when buying black trousers, sweaters, and suits, always opt for wool. (In the summer, you can buy lightweight wool that's almost as light as cotton but will preserve its serene black color far longer.)

Shades of black differ widely. Some black has a bluish undertone; some black has a brownish tint. When pairing black with black, it's best if the undertones also match. The harsh fluorescent glare in most department stores distorts colors.

Before buying, bring the black garments over to a window so that you can examine their undertones in daylight, or bring a flashlight with you when you shop so you can see the undertones more clearly. (If a salesperson asks why you're using a flashlight to inspect the clothes in broad daylight, you may want to pretend you don't speak English.)

Newsflash: Salespeople will generally tell you whatever they think you want to hear. But seeing *is* believing.

In matters of clothing, not to mention love, opposites attract. This is especially true for pairings between textures. For sartorial sizzle, the textures need to contrast with each other, particularly when the two items are a perfect color match. A heavily textured black sweater paired with a smooth black pant looks divine.

You might also partner a soft, black cashmere sweater with a black pleated pant. If both pieces are cut from the same cloth, the way most suits are, pay special attention to the shirt or sweater under the jacket. If the entire ensemble is black, the sweater should have a noticeably different texture.

Now that you've gotten the hang of all black-on-black rules and regulations, it's time for some color therapy. Pick a color, any color, as long as it makes you look resplendent. Learn more by studying Law Seven.

LAW SEVEN: FIND YOUR COLOR OF MONEY

There are seven colors in the rainbow, each with an infinite number of shades. According to feng shui, which analyzes color properties as they relate to one's home, purple, green, and gold are "prosperity colors," while white, metallic silver, and black are "creative life cycle" colors that can jumpstart one's career (which can also lead

The exception that proves the rule—this woman looks glorious dressed head to toe in orange.

blue, researchers determined that it conveys pluck without being somber. While many have sung the blues in the corporate world, blue is the uniform of power suits. Blue is associated with intelligence, stability, unity, and conservatism. Pale blue is thought to be calming.

Red. During the McCarthy era, "Better dead than red" was the slogan associated with purging communism. Today, red has

to prosperity). Always remember that the richest color is the one that makes your hair look lustrous and your skin radiant. Pick one or two colors to work with plus one neutral color to offset them, such as black, gray, or brown.

Blue. Political candidates may be quick to promise "change," but they're slow to change the color of their blue ties. That's because blue is a crowd pleaser—it's everyone's favorite color. After blue-skying long and hard about the color

redeemed itself. Celebrities receive red-carpet treatment. Red cars get stolen twice as often as other cars and cost more to insure. In China, red is the color of prosperity and is used to attract good luck.

Yellow. Folk rock legend Donovan called it "mellow yellow," but the color has a perky quality that's impossible to ignore. Who needs to see a psychiatrist when researchers believe the color yellow increases self-esteem and bolsters overall well-being? Closely associated with the sun, yellow is a vibrant color that brings good cheer. In Japan, yellow represents courage.

Orange. Some critically acclaimed television shows would have you believe that "Orange is The New Black." But orange is still orange. Scientific research has confirmed it: People who sit in orange rooms become moody and morose. Orange is the color of prison garb and highway litter patrol uniforms. However, while orange can be a tad aggressive, it also incites passion. It's a color on the cusp, in between summer and winter, and combines the properties of red and yellow to make fire. If you decide to model the bold shade, do so in the fall and use sparingly. Wear an orange scarf or a sweater—never screaming orange pants!

Green. If someone is "green," it means he's inexperienced. Green is also the color of jealousy, the green-eyed monster. (Should your project receive the green light, competitors will seethe, green with envy.) Green shamrocks are considered lucky, especially on St. Patrick's Day.

Today, green stands for environmentally friendly. It's a popular color with all sorts of companies, proving that sometimes money does grow on trees.

Closely associated with nature, green symbolizes growth and renewal. Some people look glamorous in green and others resemble

mermaid wannabes or frogs rather than princes. If green doesn't work with your coloring, keep the shade far away from your face or use only as an accent color. A navy scarf with a skinny green stripe will work, and you only need wear it if green is sprouting in popularity among the well-heeled in your area.

Find the color that makes you look alive and feel happy. And then resolve to build your wardrobe around that color. Did you know that listening to your friends could save you oodles of money every time you shop? No really, it can, as Law Eight attests.

Law Eight: Follow a Compliment

A compliment is a gift, but that doesn't mean it's easy to accept. By "compliment," I refer to a phrase, offered freely, that is meant to convey how spectacular you look.

Compliments from friends and others who have no desire to sell you anything are the only expressions of praise that count. On principle, you should screen out all fawning commentary from employees, shop clerks, insurance salespeople, car salesmen, or others striving to curry your favor. Does

someone who's out to win you romantically *insist* that you look absolutely darling in a particular outfit? Consider tossing it or giving it away to thrift immediately. (Love really is blind.)

These caveats aside, most sartorial praise is sincere. If you stroll into an event wearing a crimson sweater and more than three people approach you to rave about how gorgeous you look, chances are excellent that you really do look amazing and that you've stumbled on a flattering shade for your skin tone.

Don't forget to say "Thank you." You are thanking your admirer for saving you piles of money the next time you shop. Because now you're going to do the intelligent thing and follow that compliment all the way to a department store.

We all need to hear positive fashion feedback—if for no other reason than to help us find our best colors. Following a compliment means refusing to act embarrassed when you hear one because then people will sense that and laud you less often. Never dissuade anyone from giving you a compliment!

If your crimson sweater receives rave reviews, then be sure to take *that* sweater with you the very next time you shop. Perhaps you can find a vest or a pair of earrings or a scarf in the same shade. (It's worthwhile to actually bring the garment with you, as opposed to trying to match it in your mind's eye. Trust me, the mind's eye is no Picasso when it comes to matching color samples.)

Once you've purchased a few items in the colors that make you shine, you'll need a mini lesson on throwing the elements together. Never fear. Law Nine is here to help.

LAW NINE: YOU DON'T HAVE TO BE A POLICEMAN TO WEAR A UNIFORM

Policemen, nurses, judges, and young ladies at some all-girls schools are lucky to wear a uniform every day, as doing so keeps clothing costs and decision making minimal. But just because you don't literally wear a uniform doesn't mean you can't imagine that you're wearing one.

For a female associate at a law firm, the uniform may involve several classic two-piece suits and ten mix-and-match separates. For a male partner at a dot-com, the wardrobe might be markedly different, entailing multiple black jackets, black chino pants, and black T-shirts.

The idea is to think of your clothing as a collection and consider how many pieces your collection would hold if there were strictly enforced limits. If each item that you purchase is one in a fixed group, and you can never surpass the limit, you will buy with care instead of rashness. You'll tend to pair your clothes so they can work together to create new and flattering combinations. And your clothes will look sensational. I like to refer to this as "shopping your own closet." Before you go out and buy something new, make sure that you have thoroughly shopped your closet. It's just like real shopping—minus the extravagant outlays that make strong Visa cards faint.

Before I get dressed for a special event, I create a list. It's not a list of the stuff I want. It's a list of the stuff I have.

I write down every clothing item I own. My list isn't long, so the task isn't arduous. Looking at my clothes on paper in this way often gives me fresh ideas on how to match the tops and bottoms for maximum flair, bottom to top. Sometimes, the greatest treasures are the ones we already own.

LAW TEN: REFUSE TO BE A DRONE

Fashion isn't any fun unless you can be creative with it. Now that you're as uniformed as a soldier on the front lines of fashion, it's imperative to violate the standard in some way that expresses your own personality. You are not a fashion robot. You are a breathing, living creature with thoughts, joys, loves, hates, hurts, and scores of pet peeves. Express a tiny bit of who you are through the prism of some accessory that is undeniably You.

Maybe it's a piece of jewelry that brings you back to a trip to Morocco that was intensely enjoyable. Perhaps it's that funky sweater in a vibrant color you used to wear back when you were single and carefree. Or a leather jacket that screams "hipster" while the rest of your outfit whispers "banker."

It's the moment of truth. Go find a full-length mirror.

Peer at the image reflected therein. Could you double as a mannequin at the Armani store? Try substituting red argyle socks for the regulation black silk. Or slip on a vest that breaks the monotony with a dynamic pattern. Women can express themselves through earrings, nail color, scarves, hats, gloves, belts, and jewelry. For men, personality is best aired through ties, belts, vests, socks, and watches.

When you break the mold, you announce to the world that you are not a slave to fashion. (There's nothing "rich" about being a slave to anything.) You are your own man. Or woman. You have your own signature style—you know who you are. You respect the rules, but you also know that sometimes they are meant to be broken and shaped to your will.

Always strive for a tiny bit of imperfection. Then, you'll not only look rich, you'll look like something even better: yourself.

GET YOURSELF OUT THERE

Now that you're all dressed up, you need

someplace to go. Your invitations to world-class art museums, charitable galas, and cocktails at seven in the billiards room await.

You may not be able to jet across the country for a fancy shindig, but you can jump over a few puddles in pursuit of premiere guest list status in your hometown.

EMBRACE THE MORAL OF THE PURPLE HERMÈS TIE (AVOID KNOCKOFFS)

My friend Alec recently told me a story about a purple Hermès tie he bought as a birthday present for his stepfather.

I adore Alec. He has a heart of gold. Still, this year, his wallet was full of ones instead of hundreds. Believing in the myth of magical bargains, Alec ordered an Hermès tie from eBay. After opening the orange box, Alec inspected his purchase.

The design was reminiscent of the classic Hermès style without being exactly right. There was a repeating pattern of—what were they anyway? The width seemed narrower than anything Hermès had manufactured in recent years and the color, more muted. To its credit, the tie did have an Hermès label stitched into the back in roughly the correct location. But:

The tie came in the wrong box.

The tie was the wrong color.

The tie was the wrong width.

The tie was the wrong price.

The tie wasn't an Hermès tie after all.

Other than that, the tie was absolutely fabulous!

Knockoffs often come in generic boxes.

Alec's mind reeled with a thousand questions about the curious neckwear, but then the phone rang, his wife walked in, and the kids started to clamor. A lawyer by profession and the antithesis of a fashionista, Alec quickly stuffed the gift back into the orange box and mailed it to his stepfather, not thinking anything more about the matter until his stepdad phoned him a few weeks later.

Apparently, Alec's stepfather had tried to return the tie for one in a different color at his local Hermès shop where he was promptly called into the back of the store and questioned about the knockoff for thirty minutes!

In the end, the store refused to take back the tie—that's what happens with counterfeit goods. They don't pass muster.

Moral: If something seems too good to be true, it IS too good to be true.

Don't get swindled by a knockoff that's trying to masquerade as the real thing. There is a time and a place for cheap imitations, which will be revealed in Chapter Two. But as a general rule, buy your Hermès ties from Hermès instead of from some vendor on the street (or online), and you'll walk away with the luxury good that you *think* you're paying for.

Lesson learned, you are now ready for Chapter Two.

A knockoff tie has no pedigree. Avoid one at all costs.

SKIMP ON THE ITEMS NO ONE WILL NOTICE

You never realized that vying for "easy money" could be this hard.

"Take 67," you say, staring into the video camera. "Hello, my name is Alex. If I win a million dollars, I will use the money to help foster world peace, end world starvation, and buy an Armani suit."

"CUT!" your friend Hadley screams.

"Why?" you say, "I thought that take had real promise."

"Don't say that bit about the suit," Hadley says with a toothy grin. "It makes you sound like an empty suit."

"To be an empty suit, I'd actually have to own a suit," you say.

"Suit yourself."

"If only."

"Maybe you're not allocating your resources properly," Hadley says, pulling an elastic band out her long, tawny hair and gently putting down the video camera on the one tissue-free area of the floor.

The videotape you're making is for the show on NBC called

Minute to Win It. In spite of the fact that it only takes "a minute," you've spent the last three hours and twenty-seven minutes trying to beat your best time record as you perform a stupid human trick over and over again in order to qualify for the show.

Your best friend Hadley has been taping, timing, and gently coaching you to telegenic greatness as you frantically yank tissues out of two boxes of Kleenex strategically placed by your right and left hands.

Now both of your wrists feel sore and there's white tissue paper littered all over your shaggy blue living room rug. What's more, you're not convinced that you have enough hand-eye coordination to perform this particular stunt well enough to be considered for *Minute to Win It* fame and fortune.

"Have you ever considered *The Price Is Right?*" Hadley asks.

"If I knew anything about prices, I wouldn't be in this financial mess," you say, picking up a tissue off the floor to mop the sweat off your brow. "Why?"

"You should try shopping with me at Duane Reade sometime," Hadley says.

"YOU shop at Duane Reade?"

Hadley comes from money. Her ancestors came over on the Mayflower or one of those boats.

"Of course I shop there!" Hadley says. "My parents are blue bloods. That means I inherited the cheapness gene, you know."

"And you really save money there? In a drugstore? What on earth do you buy?"

"Don't knock it till you've tried it."

And so it came to pass that you agreed to go shopping with the richest person you know at a discount drugstore chain.

Is your life glamorous or what?

JUST HOW BROKE ARE YOU?

Please take the following diagnostic. It should take but a minute.

Are you significantly poorer than your friends?

Do you have a job where you're expected to wine and dine clients, even though you never have enough money to wine and dine yourself?

Are you living from paycheck to paycheck?

Have you ever fantasized about taking a part-time job at a depart-

IF YOUR CLOTHING BUDGET IS THREADBARE, SAVE ON THE "VISIBLE INVISIBLES"

Skimp on the items no one will notice.

Save on all items that are visible to the naked eye but blend into the fabric of the whole. I call them the "visible invisibles": those items on your personage that are on display for the entire world to see but, for one reason or another, have become commodities. Since one type of visible invisible is barely distinguishable from the next, it makes a great deal of sense to pay next to nothing for them.

Skip brands, and go generic. Or purchase the visible invisibles at drugstore chains and mega wholesalers, such as Walmart. Or

Street fashion is always in fashion.

ment store purely to snag the hefty clothing discount?

Have you ever considered dating a Sugar Poppa or Sugar Momma—just for the clothing perk?

Did you answer "Yes" to at least one of these questions?

If so, the bad news is that you are beyond broke. But the good news is that you can still look absolutely fabulous. You will simply need to practice some budgetary restraint. And it's easier to do that with some items than others.

give street chic fashion a leg up and buy the items from a vendor whom you'll never lay eyes on again.

THE SEVEN TYPES OF VISIBLE INVISIBLES

The visible invisibles include four types of accessories, two types of clothing, plus one quote-unquote *luxury* service that's actually mandatory for any woman with a job.

Pinch pennies with gusto. Following is the full shopping list of stuff about which to act like a real skinflint. Spend as little money as you can possibly get away with on these items so that you'll have some cash left over to spend on more important things, such as your wardrobe essentials.

1. Items where you'd be hard-pressed to name a brand, such as reading magnifiers and pantyhose.
2. Outerwear that's immediately stripped from your body the nanosecond you get indoors, such as woolen scarves, gloves, and hats.
3. Items that you're destined to lose anyway, such as umbrellas.
4. High-end accessories that have become clichés among the *Ferragamo 400* (think Forbes 400, only more so) due to years of over-exposure on the gray market.
5. Workout clothes, especially if you exercise in a gym where no one important will ever see you.
6. Formal wear for women, such as cocktail dresses that everyone incorrectly assumes are as expensive as hell.
7. Manicures.

PRACTICE FASHION FRUGALITY WITH FLAIR

Does the prospect of cutbacks make you feel like a layoff victim even though you're gainfully employed? Console yourself with the knowledge that, by scaling back, you are starting to develop the mind-set of a millionaire. Many bona fide millionaires really *are* cheapskates, and there's no shame in adopting a certain frugality if you have aspirations to look the part.

There is an art to being frugal out of need rather than greed. There is also a certain magic to it. Just like David Copperfield and other masters of illusion, you can employ the principle of misdirection to steer people away from discovering your secrets.

Like a magician choreographing his actions, you can direct spectators to look only where you want them to and to see only what you wish them to see. In Chapter One, you learned to never cut corners on wardrobe builders (like suits). But there are other items in your closet that are mere afterthoughts. Always spend as little as possible on a clothing afterthought.

By spending a fortune on all major wardrobe items and saving a fortune on all minor wardrobe items, you'll learn how to prioritize your clothing, achieve a blended balance, look fabulous, and prevent yourself from going broke.

Always remember: You can live like a millionaire on a pauper's allowance. It's all in the way that you allocate the precious few resources you do have.

THE RAZOR-THIN LINE BETWEEN CLASS AND MASS

There is supposedly a line between "class" and "mass," but I prefer to think of it as a circle. A drop-dead gorgeous eyeglass design might start out on the drawing board of a designer working for a prestige brand, but if the look catches on, then the "masstige" brands suddenly perk up and take notice, and that design will be copied and recopied until it shows up on the reader magnifier shelf of Duane Reade.

Plenty of designer brands also contract directly with mass distributors. And finally, there are the high-end designers on the prowl for inspiration who busily snap photographs of what the average person on the street is wearing. One trend spotter's "ordinary Joe" is another's fashion muse.

Class and mass inhabit the same circle of influence. Each has an indelible impact on the other, and the same trends course through both at the speed of business.

The bottom line? If you can find virtually the identical luxury item at one-fifth of the price, it's your financial obligation to do so. Especially when the money you're *not* spending is on some throwaway accessory that no one's going to notice anyway.

So make haste. Get thee to Duane Reade. Or CVS. While you're on the hunt for the great American reading magnifiers, why not pick up some generic black pantyhose (but only if you're a woman).

You'd have to be a bank robber with a stocking over your head to distinguish the cheap brands from their pricier cousins; and weekly investments on items like pantyhose add up to a queen's ransom over time.

STREET SMARTS

In Manhattan, we are blessed. We never want for scarves, gloves, and hats. Not when there is a street vendor hawking these wares on every other corner. Granted, the quality of these woolens is poor, since the "wool" feels suspiciously like the by-product of an acrylic sheep. But at least the price is right: $10—even less if you're a clever negotiator.

It certainly never hurts to try. Haggling is a skill on par with acting, except that you don't have to memorize any lines. But, just like acting, haggling becomes easier with practice. If at first you don't succeed in driving down the price, try, try again. At the very least, you'll be sharpening your bargaining skills for the next time.

The formula for successful street vendor negotiation is 50 percent determination, 50 percent willingness to walk. There's often some pantomime involved as well. Imagine a beautiful navy blue scarf calling to you from some vendor's cart.

"Hello there, Cutie," the scarf beckons like a throaty siren. "Won't you please, *please* buy me?"

Or try rubbing the rough-hewn rag against your cheek (if you can bear it) and look miffed. Then, spin on your heels and walk away.

More often than not, before you've taken two or three steps, the vendor will call out a cheaper price (say, $7), which is your cue that you can probably chisel down the price of the scarf to $5.

Out of the corner of your eye, you spot a price tag with an astronomical number on it. Surely, this can't be correct—this is a lowly street scarf, dammit. It has no provenance. Worried that you may be losing your grip on reality, you verify the cost with the vendor.

"Excuse me, is that scarf really $13?" you whisper, incredulous.

He nods his head, as his calculating eyes squint at you, taking you in. Are you a tourist? A native? A sucker? (Supposedly, there's one born every minute.) The vendor stares at you, weighing his options.

Do not despair. Instead, pick up the blue scarf. Pretend to sniff the garment and then look woefully disappointed.

On the flip side, if you hate to negotiate, or find the prospect of walking around with cheap, poorly made accessories in the dead of winter unappealing, you can always opt to play *Scarf Swap* with your scarf-forward friends.

PLAY "SWAP TILL YOU DROP"

Chances are, you've heard of the television reality show *Wife Swap*. Welcome to *Scarf Swap*. It can keep you well scarved in colder climates, and it even helps stave off scarf envy.

Do you have a friend whose taste you admire? Of course you do. The object of the game is to shop together. But start with a money-saving strategy that's guaranteed to save you both at least 50 percent.

Agree in advance to pick out *two* woolen scarves together that you both adore, and then swap them with each other mid-season. The beauty of shared accessorizing is that you can each only sport one scarf at a time, and just when you tire of your own wooly neck warmer, you can move onto hers. Get creative about when you shop to swap. Who wants to buy thick wool scarves in the heat of summer? You do! You do!

Then take the game up a notch by hosting a "Swap till you drop" party. Gather all of your scarf-worthy buddies, and simply start trading clothing. It's not risqué in the slightest because it's not like you're swapping husbands, wives, significant others, or keys like they supposedly do in suburban Connecticut. You're simply exchanging threads—the stuff you've grown to hate (or just can't bear to look at anymore) for the stuff they've grown to hate (or just can't bear to look at anymore). Which makes "Swap till you drop"

perfectly safe in any part of the country.

Tell your friends to scarf it up and bring any clothing they don't wear anymore to your "Swap till you drop" soirée. One person's junk is another's treasure trove.

MOST UMBRELLAS HAVE A SECOND LIFE: IT MAY AS WELL BE WITH YOU

If you are ever asked on an ethics test what you would do if you found a dollar on the street, the correct answer is that you'd return the money to the owner from whose pocket it dropped without delay. But if you happen to be in a taxicab, where the rider just before you inadvertently left his umbrella, you should have no qualms about taking it with you.

Consider the alternative: If you behave like a Good Samaritan and alert the cab driver about the lost rain parasol, chances are excellent that the original owner will never get it back, anyway. But, if you choose to keep the raingear, at least it will have a second life with someone in dire need—yourself.

My recent *Night at the Opera* was a bit different than Groucho Marx's. One rainy night at the Metropolitan Opera, I noticed that a perfectly functional black, wooden-handled umbrella had been orphaned. Forgotten by its owner in the blind rush to escape from the packed opera house, it lay underneath one of the seats in the orchestra section. The auditorium had started to clear out, and I highly doubted that the umbrella's owner would bother to fight his way back through the throng of 3,995 just to retrieve it. Hence, I did what any native New Yorker would. I swiped the handsome umbrella and proceeded to use it for the next several months—until I accidentally left it behind under my seat in a movie theater, where the umbrella no doubt found a third owner and an even better life.

With the way people leave behind their umbrellas all the time, there's never any reason to pay for one. It's raining umbrellas.

THE GREAT AMERICAN WATCH FETISH

As William Gibson wrote in an essay for *Wired* magazine, "mechanical watches are so brilliantly unnecessary."

In fact, all watches, from the lowliest Swatch to a Vacheron

Constantin Tour de l'lle retailing for $1.5 million are, strictly speaking, fossils.

The Vacheron Constantin Tour de l'lle features two time zones, the sunset time, a perpetual calendar, plus an astronomical indicator of the night sky. Certainly the watch provides a plethora of fascinating information, but it's all readily available on the Internet—and for free. But fashion has a way of defying all expectations. Precisely because watches serve no real purpose any longer from a functionality standpoint, they have become the must-have collectible for any man of means.

To look like a millionaire today, you *must* wear a watch. It's a mandatory requirement. But obtain-

ing a fine watch (or a simulation) needn't cost you a CEO's salary. Naturally, it helps to have generous relatives, i.e., the kind who either bequeath you a gold watch upon their passing or who give you one of your own in honor of some milestone that you achieved, such as your christening, Bar Mitzvah, or twenty-first birthday.

But what if you weren't blessed with generous forbears? First, you might try to adopt some. But if you can't seem to finagle that, then you might try asking a living parent for a wristwatch you've spotted on his personage that doesn't come out quite as much as it used to.

There could also be others in your family—a sister or a brother perchance—who suddenly strike it rich and, as a result, upgrade their watches. While you're congratulating your siblings on their newfound prosperity, there's no harm in asking after their old timepieces.

If you have tried some of these tactics to no avail, you can either relent and buy yourself a semi-expensive quartz ticker that looks like something far grander or settle for a super-cheap replica. Hopefully most people in positions of authority will never get close enough to your wrist to know the difference. (To ensure that they won't, wear gloves whenever you're outside.)

If there's little chance that you'll inherit a watch and you've been underwhelmed by the timepiece selection in vintage stores, then, out of necessity, your watch will have to join the ranks of the "visible invisibles" on your body. That's your cue to spend precious little on the timepiece.

Check out Skagen, which makes both replicas plus other modern miracles of Danish engineering starting at around $135. A Skagen watch is the ideal "visible invisible." Its sleek design won't draw too much attention to itself, and yet anyone meeting you for the first time can't fail to take in that your wrist exudes a certain elegance. If Skagen minimalism isn't your style, sometimes you can scoop up watches that resemble Cartier timepieces among Coach's selections, where prices start in the three-figure range, not four.

Luggage That Has Its Own Baggage

Today, that distinctive Louis Vuitton monogrammed taupe-on-brown style has become hackneyed. It's everywhere you don't want to be—in malls, in the Coach section of airplanes, on street corners, and in the back of trucks. (Sigh.)

There are two ways to take advantage of Louis Vuitton's irrepressible popularity. If you're young and broke, you can probably get away with buying a cheap imitation (so that at least you'll look polished on your business trips). Just make sure that your boss, or whomever it is that you're striving to impress, never gets close enough to your luggage to inspect it. Be sure to check it when you first arrive in the airport. Next, quickly stash your knockoff in the trunk of the cab on the way to your hotel. Then have a porter whisk your copycat luggage up to your room upon arrival.

However, by the time you turn thirty, unfortunately, you're too old to play hide-and-seek with knockoffs. By that advanced age, you're expected to have pockets deep enough to afford the generous pouches and sturdy stitching that are synonymous with the Louis Vuitton monogram, or do without. So buck the Louis Vuitton trend, if need be. Invest in a cheaper classic, such as a T. Anthony duffle bag or a tweedy Hartmann herringbone-themed duffel bag at a fraction of the cost.

SWEATWEAR

If ever there was a clothing category to trim back on, it's gymwear. You're just going to perspire your way through it, which will make it smell funky. You're literally losing money through your pores! Instead, collect the screaming logo-strewn T-shirts that you receive at corporate events and model the ugly shirts at the gym. A cheaper alternative to costly yoga clothes: Buy light cotton pajama bottoms and use loose T-shirts as tops.

THERE ARE NO MICROSCOPES IN MARGARITAVILLE, THANK GOODNESS

Lights twinkle; conversation tinkles; liquor flows. In the delicious swirl of a cocktail party, no one stops to examine the cocktail dresses with a microscope—which is why it pays to pick them up for a song. Always anticipate the gala around the corner, and buy off-season. Either shop at H&M or practice a divide-and-conquer strategy at an upscale department store. Buy one black skirt and loosely match it with a black top to form a modern little black dress. Split up the outfit, and reuse as separates later.

If the cost of the item is still stratospheric, it behooves you to befriend the salesperson, who may well empathize with your inability to afford the clothes on display.

"This dress is out of my league but I love it. Let me know when it goes on sale," will often elicit a phone call from the salesperson within a fortnight.

THE NO-SOCK DRESS CODE

Guys, a strict adherence to the no-sock dress code can keep you in tasseled loafers for years to come. True, it entails forgoing socks on weekends and at parties, even when it's freezing outside. In fact, as temperatures drop, it becomes even more important to show off your bare ankles. Doing so proves that you understand that looking like a millionaire-in-the-making entails some sacrifice, but you're willing to do your part.

Every time you opt for no socks, your accessories are truly invisible, and hence, cost nothing at all.

HOW TO MAKE A MANICURE LAST THREE WEEKS

The landed gentry have beautifully manicured lawns and nails. If you don't live in a house, you can probably be forgiven for not trimming your lawn. But sporting unkempt nails will condemn you to project housing in the minds of the power elite even if you live in a perfectly nice middle-class neighborhood!

Are you tempted to take a do-it-yourselfer's approach to a mani-

cure? Don't—instead, try your hand at recycling. Spring for a real manicure; but instead of getting shellacked once a week, opt for once every three weeks. Then extend the life of your manicure by investing in one bottle of clear nail polish and applying daily.

WHY SKIMPING ON THE ITEMS NO ONE NOTICES WORKS LIKE GANGBUSTERS

Imagine for a moment that you are richer than God. (It shouldn't be too hard. Admit it, you fantasize about it daily.)

Pretend that you *could* afford a Vacheron Constantin watch, David Yurman bangles, Cartier diamond love bracelets, and enough Louis Vuitton luggage to line a steamship. You could never model them all at the same time. For if you did, then you'd be an unpaid walking advertisement for all luxury brands, which would make you look like nothing more than—*gasp!*—a mall victim.

The reason that skimping on the items no one notices works so well is because even if you *were* richer than God, you'd need to make choices. Some accessories would have to take a backseat to others.

By paying next to nothing for the items to which no one pays any attention, you'll direct people's eyes to the one or two spiffiest articles on your personage on any given day. You will also be practicing strict budgeting, which is mandatory if you ever want to be truly rich. There's no time like the present to start cultivating the mind-set of a very rich person. Remember always: You are what you think.

CHAPTER THREE

COVET THY NEIGHBOR'S CATALOGS

"Space: The final frontier!" an old *Star Trek* episode bleats from a giant flat-screen TV in the otherwise empty den.

Your good buddy, Chris, is giving you the official tour of his brand-new apartment, and so far, you've observed several items yours doesn't have:

1) A den
2) A flat-screen TV
3) A dishwasher that doesn't leak
4) A bathroom without a speck of mildew in the tub
5) Three closets

Envy is a deadly sin, and you hope you won't die from it. Still, you can't help wondering why Chris needs so much storage space, when his idea of dressing up consists of wearing a clean shirt and pulling a comb through his curly brown

locks. The guy owns two pairs of sneakers in total.

The real ego crusher, however, is lurking downstairs in the communal laundry room. It's not the pristine machinery, although that *is* a marvel of card-operated technology.

No. It's just an ordinary item that was probably left behind by one of the residents a few hours earlier. Still, it's something you'd never see in the communal laundry room of your own building in a billion years.

It's an *Armani* catalog.

You pick it up and silently thumb through its pages.

"What are you doing?" Chris asks, extracting two plaid shirts from the dryer and strolling over to you, the better to peek at your reading material.

"Just looking," you murmur.

"Looking to win the lottery?" Chris jokes, staring transfixed at one of the prices in the catalog. "Wow! Do you think that's a typo?" he asks. "Armani makes clothes, not cars, right?"

"You just don't see things like this in my 'hood," you say, flipping the glossy page.

The translucent skin around Chris's aqua eyes crinkles like a sheet in need of ironing.

"Are you talking about the clothes or the catalog?"

"Yes," you say, biting your lip, "especially the catalog."

What if you feel uncomfortable reading someone else's junk? Force yourself to get over it. After all, it's for a very good cause.

Once you have the catalog in your hands, it's a snap to order it (generally, but not always, for free) so it will arrive at your home with delightful regularity. However, make it a habit to study the catalog before you order it—both to save trees and the nuisance of tossing away something that you never really wanted in the first place.

READ A MORE PRIVILEGED CLASS OF JUNK MAIL

One peek at a posh person's junk mail is like a day spent in the inner sanctums of his or her walk-in closet. To get schooled in the style canon, skim your most elegant neighbor's catalogs (but only after she's thrown them out).

YOUR PERSONAL SHOPPER HAS ARRIVED (IN YOUR MAILBOX)

A store catalog should never be confused with your in-store experience. Make no mistake: The catalog is infinitely better.

The in-store experience is (generally speaking) just a bunch of racks with clothes flopping about on plastic hangers. Maybe the clothes are grouped by designer. Or maybe they're bunched together by color. Or maybe—*woo hoo!*—they're lumped together by size. But one thing they're not: They're not put together with the awe-inspiring vision of a catalog!

A catalog has been discussed, debated, picked apart, put back together, and mulled over by a team of exceptionally talented art directors and photographers, plus a creative director who has pored through all of the merchandise in an effort to "tell a story."

The story is the reason you want the promotional piece in the first place. The actual merchandise isn't as important, as once you understand the look you're after, you can often simulate it with far less expensive items. The personal shopping experience you'll enjoy with most upscale catalogs is *far better* than any with a real, live personal shopper you'll ever find in a store.

A real personal shopper probably isn't going to tell you a story, and if she does, then you should sign her up for open mic night at your local comedy club or a poetry slam. She's in the wrong field.

WHAT'S YOUR STORY?

Start with this: Each outfit you piece together in your ensemble is part of a greater narrative that you want to tell about yourself. A sweater is not a sweater—it's a declaration of your values, your lifestyle, and even your politics. An earring is not an earring—it's a signal of your aspirations.

Are you a traditionalist or a rebel? Are you creative, or are you more mathematically inclined? Do you work for "the man," or have you struck out on your own? Your outfit today says it all. And an upscale catalog can teach you how to piece together your

A turtleneck worn under a business jacket hints of Jack Kerouac. This look is better suited for entrepreneurs than for corporate titans.

ensemble in a way that will appeal to those you are meeting for the very first time.

Studies show that interviewers make up their minds about candidates within thirty seconds. Employers would never be able to do this if our clothing didn't tell a story that even a total stranger could read with perfect clarity.

Only you can be the author of the narrative that you wish to relate about yourself. But a catalog is like an excellent ghostwriter, doing most of the editing for you. And every author needs a great editor.

What is your catalog of choice, and what does it convey about you?

Are you an all-American, Ralph Lauren–style? A sophisticated career woman, Donna Karan–style? Do you look backwards to a time when life was more stable, Brooks Brothers–style? Are you a suave European, Zegna–style? Do you espouse conservative politics, Armani–style? Or are you an eclectic mix of all different designers? (If so, you probably need the vision of a catalog even more because someone hasn't handpicked which pieces in each collection belong together for you.)

How Well Do You Know Your Catalogs?

Please take the following quiz. Circle one answer in each section.

You	Your Catalog
1. I am mad for plaid 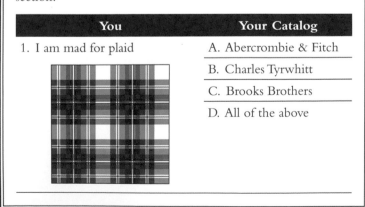	A. Abercrombie & Fitch
	B. Charles Tyrwhitt
	C. Brooks Brothers
	D. All of the above

2. I am a prep-wannabe

A. Urban Outfitters

B. Ralph Lauren

C. Fendi

D. Gucci

3. Diamonds and gems
are my best friends

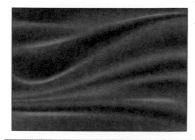

A. Scully & Scully

B. Tiffany & Co.

C. H. Stern

D. All of the above

4. I am a woman on the verge of
massive career success

A. Talbots

B. Neiman Marcus

C. Ann Taylor

D. Chico's

5. I am a modern "Mad Man"	A. Brooks Brothers
	B. Barneys
	C. Macy's
	D. None of the above

6. I am an artsy type	A. Chico's
	B. Anthropologie
	C. Bergdorf Goodman
	D. All of the above

Answers: 1D, 2B, 3D, 4A, 5A, 6D.

WHAT IF YOU DON'T HAVE POSH NEIGHBORS?

What if you're *sixteen* degrees of separation removed from anyone elegant, and your only brush with "Posh" was at a Spice Girls' concert, circa 1996?

What if you live in a working-class neighborhood or in a build-ing with poor, starving artists? Or what if you live on a farm and your nearest neighbor happens to be a cow?

In that case, swipe the catalogs left behind at hairdressers' salons, doctors' offices, and coffee shops. Once you start keeping your eyes peeled for promotional pamphlets, it's amazing how many of them you'll find. They're everywhere.

Do you recycle? Of course you do. There are tons of big glossy catalogs in your communal recycling bin. Laundry rooms are another excellent source for these handy pictorial guides. People skim the pages during the spin cycle and just leave the reading material behind. Your neighbor's carelessness is your windfall.

Don't overlook nail salons. Anywhere where someone is trapped for long periods of time, totally bored, is a fabulous catalog repository. This includes, but is not limited to:

1. Trains
2. Planes
3. Automobiles
4. Taxis
5. Gymboree centers
6. Doctors' waiting rooms
7. Temporary staff offices
8. Gym treadmills
9. The Apple Store
10. Diners
11. Banks (especially ATM vestibules)
12. Real estate offices
13. Ice cream parlors
14. Tanning salons
15. Bowling alleys
16. Airplanes
17. Airports
18. Office break rooms (don't ask permission)
19. Movie theaters
20. Furniture stores
21. Anywhere with receptionists and secretaries

People can be rather cavalier about their fashion brochures, always leaving them behind for others to leaf through. Starbucks is a font of catalogs. Many store circulars are left behind on the tables or unceremoniously stuffed into the magazine racks, where you'll also find certain sections of the *Wall Street Journal,* or if you're incredibly lucky, the Style section of the *New York Times.*

Inspiration: It's everywhere you look.

Ladies' and men's rooms also yield their fair share of catalogs. (If the concept grosses you out, wear gloves when you flip through the ill-gotten pamphlet. Just don't leave it behind. Leave no good catalog behind.)

The world is teeming with scintillating store literature! Make it a habit to study—and learn from—it all.

Of course, if you live in a shopping mecca such as New York, Palm Beach, or Chicago, many times you can make a special pilgrimage to a store and simply *ask* for a catalog. Savvy store marketers actually look for novel ways to advertise, and if there is any merchandising material to be had on the premises, most salespeople will be happy to give it up.

THE ONLINE EXPERIENCE (OR LACK THEREOF)

What about online, you no doubt wonder. The whole world has moved online. And isn't online shopping even better than a Christmas catalog?

After extensive study on this topic, I regretfully conclude, "absolutely not."

As of this writing, online websites are nowhere near their catalog sisters in terms of telling a story. The Neiman Marcus online experience is no Neiman Marcus. And certain companies, such as Bloomingdale's, really do a terrible job with their online presence.

Don't get me wrong. You can buy clothes online from any merchandiser once you already know what you want. But the online

experience deflates fantasy, as the budgets for those websites tend to be as skinny as Tiny Tim Cratchit before the holidays in *A Christmas Carol*. The backgrounds are bland to the brink of blah. As there's not much there to feast the eyes or stir the senses, the online shopper can leave the site feeling rather famished. As a result, the online shopper gets *Scrooged*.

It's kind of a bummer.

IF YOU CAN DREAM IT, YOU CAN OWN IT

Books like *The Secret* claim that if you can see something in your mind's eye, that vision will manifest. Your dominant thoughts turn into *things*. This habit can be particularly helpful if you enjoy fantasizing about expensive items. In a way, your thoughts are magnetic, drawing you to what you think about most often. Visualization helps, and what are giant glossy catalogs if not visualizations of our hopes and dreams?

Athletes use visualization techniques to correct problem areas and make microscopic adjustments. Jack Nicklaus dominated during his heyday partly due to his ability to picture himself exe-

cuting a perfect golf stroke. He'd then return to that image during a real game. By creating a mental blueprint of how the stroke might look and feel in advance, Nicklaus would mentally practice for the next match—a technique that helped him optimize his performance once he was out on the links.

You, too, can harness the power of visualization to ratchet up your performance. If you want to look more successful, make it a habit to surround yourself with the same catalogs as your more prosperous friends and neighbors *regardless* of whether you can afford to buy anything shown in the pages.

Review this promotional material frequently. Doing so will help keep the image you're aiming for front and center in your brain. Pay particular attention to any model

with a demeanor or personal style signature that's similar to your own.

Tear out any inspirational photographs and put them on your desk at home, or scan the pictures and upload them onto your laptop screen. Don't fret about staying on trend. True style trumps trendiness, and you should view catalogs with an eye towards adding one or two classic items a year to your wardrobe, rather than eleven or twelve that you'll never wear again because they're beyond out in the blink of an eye. (Review Chapter One again if you need a refresher course on why.)

If there's any truth to *The Secret* and to the power of proactive visualization, then surrounding yourself with luxe catalogs can only help you achieve your ambitions that much faster.

QUEEN ELIZABETH'S RULES

My friend Elizabeth is a born shopper. A former lawyer, she day-trades from her home computer, but really, she lives to shop. An elegant Korean-American woman who was raised in the suburbs of Boston, Elizabeth is a self-proclaimed lady of leisure.

How does a lady of leisure entertain herself during her copious free time? She shops! She picks up trinkets for her friends (and also advises them on the purchase of any big-ticket items). She snags clothes for members of her extended family—and while she's at it, herself! These days, Elizabeth buys outfits for approximately twenty kids. Some are nephews and nieces; some are the children of her friends. And she does it all for the sheer joy of shopping. When it comes to unearthing a better deal, Elizabeth is like a paleontologist on a dinosaur dig.

Elizabeth says that she only uses physical catalogs for pre-store research. For adult sweaters, she prefers to view the items in person before purchasing them to assess their "tactile appeal."

Elizabeth makes an exception for the *J. Crew* catalog, where she buys polo shirts, traditional crewnecks, and V-neck sweaters directly because the sizing is "forgiving." In pursuit of a deep discount, she also has no problem buying designer

threads online and urged me to sign up for Gilt.com without delay.

When it turned out that Gilt.com wanted too much information about me for my taste including my name, email, zip code, not to mention birthday and grades in high school geometry,[1] Elizabeth gave me one word of advice.

"Lie," she said.

CONFESSIONS OF A SHOPAHOLIC (ACCORDING TO QUEEN ELIZABETH)

Here's where Elizabeth shops, what she buys, and how she saves money every time she swipes her credit card. Remember that it's always helpful to review the inventory before you visit the store in person. The more costly the item, the more it makes sense to spend some quality time with the catalog in advance.

Think of a store catalog as your style Sherpa—guiding you through what would otherwise be a confusing mountain of merchandise.

Jewelry

1. For Diamonds—Have breakfast at Tiffany's but lunch at a wholesale jewelry store. Start your research with the Tiffany & Co. catalog. Follow up with a trip to the legendary boutique to ogle the gems through a magnifying loop. But then, to beat the price, consider paying a visit to Howard Engel at 555 Fifth Avenue. (Don't just pop in. Make an appointment first.)

2. For Pearls—The *Mikimoto* catalog is a joy to behold. However, once you've drooled all over the pages, be like the girl with a pearl earring and canvas the Mikimoto store in person to eye the jewelry.

Hang on to your old clasps. If you have a vintage clasp from a piece of jewelry that you never wear, consider purchasing your pearls from a pearl wholesaler and having them strung with your old clasp.

After brushing up on luster and color, make an appointment to visit with wholesaler American Pearl, where you should be able to secure a substantial discount.

3. For Estate Jewelry—Review auction house catalogs first. Then be sure to check out the state of the art by stopping by the auction house to bid in person.

Adult Clothing & Accessories

1. For Sweaters—Are you feeling fat? With its generous sizing, the *J. Crew* catalog forgives overindulgence, which can be beneficial over the holidays. So don't pass up the pecan pie. Help yourself to seconds or even thirds. (But then make it your New Year's resolution to visit www.bluefly.com for its roomy sizing.)

2. For Work Bags and Luggage—*L.L. Bean* catalog. It's still nifty enough for Muffy and campy enough for Chip after all these years.

3. For Clothes—Bloomingdale's. Check out the catalog, then hop over to the store whenever there's a sale, which is frequently, thank God. Sign up for a store credit card to save your shirt on big purchases like, well, like shirts, for example. Become a Loyalist, and you'll earn points for every dollar

the catalog. Let your fingers do the shopping for your well-clad feet.

THE CATALOG RULE AND THE CATALOG CAVEAT

Caveat emptor—it's Latin for "buyer beware." As Elizabeth says, if you live near the store, you're better off *not* buying from the catalog. Going in person will ensure correct sizing and that the color is everything you've ever dreamed of, and more.

Study the catalog first, but then go in person to assess the craftsmanship of the item.

you spend. Get on the Bloomingdale's email list, and you'll find out about all sorts of fun discounts and friends and family days. Some weeks, I hear from Bloomingdale's even more than my real friends. You've got to love a store that's always trying to save you money.

4. For Shoes—*Saks Fifth Avenue* catalog. If you're not bothered by masses of deal hunters picking through the very shoes that may end up on your feet, do your research in advance and wait for a sale. However, if you despise being around scores of people rummaging through endless racks of shoes, consider purchasing directly from

That noted, tremendous design savvy will come from studying the selections beforehand. You'll know precisely what you're looking for down to the cut, color, style, and designer. And there's even a chance that you'll be able to beat the price on the way to the store (by stopping in a wholesaler like Marshalls or T.J. Maxx first).

However, if your time is not your own and you will not be deterred from shopping via catalog, at least be smart about it. Shun "catalog only" items. Ideally, it's best if the item exists *somewhere* in the real world, not just in the virtual one. (If you're interested in the virtual world, visit Second Life. You can buy all the virtual clothes you want there—but only for your avatar.)

IT'S IN YOUR INTEREST TO MASTER PINTEREST

Today, there's an alternative to both in-store shopping and the traditional catalog. It's called Pinterest, a virtual bulletin board that helps you locate and curate the images you love. It's easy to "repin" a picture from another person's bulletin board onto your own. And, should you find a fellow Pinterest user whose taste resonates with yours, you can follow her (or if you prefer, follow just one of her visual boards). Pinterest is shopper-friendly. Clicking on any picture will allow you to visit the website where the item is sold. (Do be a bit careful, though. Pinterest is so much fun that it can be highly addictive.)

THE TOP TWO LESSONS I LEARNED FROM UPSCALE CATALOGS

1. Aristocrats celebrate different seasons than the rest of us. For nobles, Christmas starts the moment that Thanksgiving ends, and sometimes, even earlier. There is also a "Resortwear" season during early January when American toffs stock up on bikinis, Bermuda shorts, and other must-haves before they pop off for a quick jaunt to Palm Beach.

2. The wealthy shun big logos like swine flu. Yes, there is the occasional Polo logo that's the size of a horse or a bag that's festooned with supersized Louis Vuitton labels or a pair of Chanel glasses encrusted with larger-than-life C logos with bawdy diamond chips. (Sigh.)

But as a general rule, members of this well-heeled tribe consider themselves to be the arbiters of style; you can thank *them* very much. Hence, they will decide which labels suit them, and not the other way around. You'd be wise to follow what these tastemakers do and, for the most part, avoid horsey labels too.

Some Mannequins are Even Starting to Act Like Catalogs

No longer are mannequins faceless, featureless stick figures who happen to model clothes well. Some high-end department stores are showing eerily human mannequins with defined features, facial hair, and even crow's feet. One store in London features mannequins that transmit the prices and other information about what they're wearing directly onto customers' mobile devices. These "mannequin catalogs" could turn shopping into a very Pygmalion-like experience!

The Best Retail Therapy Is Free

Upscale catalogs teach you how to dress for success before you are one. You'll learn how to put together outfits to make a fantastic first impression and tell the story about yourself that you want the world to hear.

Yet, until you actually plunk down money to purchase an item, all of the advice is free. In contrast to the in-store experience, where impatient shop assistants tap their feet at you and say, "Can I help you?" until you feel compelled to help *them* by buying something, reading a catalog is very low pressure.

In the privacy of your living room, with no one peering over your shoulder or tapping her feet, you can come to terms with what you like and what you definitely don't like via the process of elimination. And, by tearing out pages of the things you love, gradually you will teach yourself how to refine your style.

At $0 per hour, this is "retail therapy" in the most productive sense.

CHAPTER FOUR

AMASS A $64 MILLION VOCABULARY

Stick this in your file of embarrassing moments.

You are merely a L.I.P.—the Least Important Person in the room. In spite of your lowly status, you've sunk enough money into your Armani suit to bolster the economy of a small nation.

Out of the corner of your eye, you spot the evening's bigwig, an important personage who holds your fate in his hands. As if on cue, he crisscrosses to your side of the room, ignoring all of the titled muckety-mucks, and swoops in, landing by your side to talk to you, a plebe.

"So tell me," he says, leaning in expectantly, perched on your anticipated brilliance. "What do you think of the situation in Somalia?"

You hem. You haw.

You haw. You hem.

You try to turn the question back on your host. Ahem.

What does *he* think of the situation in Somalia?

Your eyes rove the room like searchlights, looking for someone—anyone—to interrupt this exchange and save you from your ignorance. But alas, there are no white knights (or policy wonks) on either the red or the blue side of the aisle tonight.

You fidget, you chafe, you have the heartbreak of psoriasis. The room feels icy cold and, seconds later, unbearably hot.

At this moment, you realize that you can't contribute *any* gems to the conversation because you have spent all of your time primping for the event instead of prepping for it. And, sad to

Ignorance is not bliss when someone asks you a direct question about current events that you can't answer.

say, you can't pick up an opinion about what's happening in Somalia from a *Bergdorf Goodman* catalog.

You feel like a real empty suit—dapper, but oh-so-shallow.

THE COMMON KNOWLEDGE PARADOX

Years ago, my friend Paul was on his sixth interview at a premier investment bank in New York City when he spotted a colorful American flag painting on the wall.

"That's some painting," Paul said, jaw dropping to the lush Ori-

ental rug hugging the hardwood floor.

"Why thank you," the interviewer said. "Do you recognize the artist?" he asked, skewering Paul with a steely gaze.

"Er . . . ," Paul said, scratching his head.

"It's an original Jasper Johns."

"Who's Jasper Johns again?" Paul asked.

As Paul tells the story, the room became so quiet that he could hear a phone ring . . . across the street! (Or maybe that was just his headhunter calling to yell at him.)

Needless to say, Paul did not land the job in the Private Client Services Group. How could anyone trust him to service high net worth individuals if he couldn't talk to them about their interests?

This sorry tale about Paul failing to land his dream job perfectly illustrates the problem with so-called "common knowledge." You're expected to know it even if you never studied it.

What's more, you're always being tested on it in the strangest places. Like at important job interviews and in unfamiliar conference rooms. In office cubicles, kitchenettes, and elevators. And especially on golf courses.

Depending on where you grew up and where you were schooled, what passes for common knowledge may not be at all commonplace. And yet, the pop quizzes on it keep popping up like evil jack-in-the-boxes that scream, "Gotcha!" Naturally, since the surprise tests are on information that you're supposed to know cold (rather than on anything truly arcane), everyone anticipates that you'll pass with flying colors. And when you don't, the price can be steep. Like Paul, you could lose out on a job. Or you could lose face with someone whom you really care about or want to impress. But just because you didn't study some of the subjects that fall under the common knowledge domain when you were younger doesn't mean that you can't do so now. It's never too late to learn.

THE LEISURE CLASS AND THE PURSUIT OF KNOWLEDGE

Thorstein Veblen was a Norwegian-American economist and sociologist who spent a great deal of time back in the late nine-teenth century thinking about the emerging ruling class and the way its members spent their time off.

Veblen defined "conspicuous leisure" as time devoted to certain pursuits in return for higher status. To be a gentleman, he noted, a man needed to acquaint himself with the fine arts and philosophy, both of which had little economic value.

Whether you consider Veblen an economist who was ahead of his time, a satirist who was appreciated during his time for writing the best seller *The Theory of the Leisure Class* (which was considered a spoof even though Veblen intended it as a serious economic treatise) or a cantankerous crackpot who disdained anyone wealthier than him, it's really hard to argue with his premise about conspicuous leisure.

In short, devoting some effort to studying certain pursuits will lead to a higher status. And these pastimes tend to fall in the liberal arts realm.

Like Veblen, I believe that studying the fine arts can help today's men and women position themselves as genteel. But instead of bothering to learn philosophy, I think most aspirants today would be better served acquainting themselves with current events, business, culture, literature, scandals, and sports.

Review these topics to amass a vocabulary that shows both class and gravitas. It doesn't matter whether you attended a liberal arts college or graduated from the school of hard knocks. When you become a practitioner of lifelong learning, it's easy to master a $64 million vocabulary—along with the priceless conversational

The gentlemen and ladies of tomorrow will spend some time learning about the fine arts today.

rapport that accompanies it—in practically no time.

STAY AU COURANT

Let's briefly return to the unfortunate situation in Somalia. The quickest way to stay up to the minute is via the *New York Times*. Simply go to www.nytimes.com, hit the link that says "World," and if an article about the country you're seeking doesn't pop up immediately, type its name in the Search box.

The online version of the *Times* is your best resource for world news, and the navigation system is even chummier than user-friendly. (Of course, it's probably more productive to brush up on your general knowledge *before* you arrive at a powwow of M.I.M.S.—Most Important Muckety-Mucks.)

If there is a crisis unfolding in a certain country, be sure to read at least three articles about it. If, conversely, world news is slow that day, be happy for small favors, and proceed to catch up on your minimum daily requirement of business news—after reading why it's important to do so in the story that follows.

When there's a world crisis, everyone who's anyone will be talking about it. Sneak a peek at a newspaper so you can chime in too.

Sharpen Your Nose for Business

In certain cities, business is like air. Everyone around you breathes it in night and day and the only way to avoid it is to camp out in a bubble.

A friend of mine—let's call her Barbie—was seated at an upscale bar when a wealthy Texan sidled up to her. Barbie, a poor, starving actress, has a megawatt smile, which she flashed at her new drinking partner with intention. She had several hours to kill, and judging from the thick wad of cash he smacked down on the counter when he ordered her a strawberry margarita, he had several $100 bills that needed to be spent.

It was a match worthy of eHarmony.

"So what do you do?" she purred, sweet as cotton candy. He mentioned that he was a CEO.

"What's a CEO?" she asked.

POOF! Barbie's carriage instantly turned back into a pumpkin.

Because Barbie didn't know the abbreviation for "Chief Executive Officer," she never saw or heard from her Mr. Texan again.

To avoid being treated like a moron from outer space by those who are living and breathing business on this planet, it's necessary to take a passing interest in the business realm.

Still available in paper form as of this writing, the *Wall Street Journal* transports easily to the health club. Browse the first few pages while working out on the treadmill; the

Journal is a fantastic investment in your mental fitness. Skim daily. In a few short weeks, your business acumen will sharpen. Soon, you will be able to hold your own when someone tosses you a business topic as a subject of conversation.

Now that you're a whiz at both current events and business news, it's time to ratchet up your cultural knowledge.

Wow, are you getting smart!

CULTURE FOR NON-CULTURE VULTURES

Compared to sharpening your business brain, goosing up your cultural appreciation is a snap. And few will be able to discern whether the conversational pearls that you drop are the result of years of dedicated study or a couple of minutes a day spent cramming in some of life's cultural wonders.

I highly recommend a little-known reference gem called *The New Dictionary of Cultural Literacy: What Every American Needs to Know* (by E.D. Hirsch Jr., Joseph F. Kett, and James S. Trefil). It contains all of the general knowledge that one should possess (in the shortest of snippets).

Spend just five minutes a day with it, and you'll be able to hold forth on *any* subject of cultural significance for at least a few choice minutes at a cocktail party. Fine art, language, technology, science, history, religion—it's all in here.

Wax prolific on Ruth Benedict versus Benedict Arnold over a breakfast of eggs Benedict. Discuss Ella Fitzgerald and F. Scott Fitzgerald over a nostalgic lunch. Analyze the "protein folding problem" and the "protein structure" over a vegetarian dinner.

In preparation for a convention of bigwigs, you can go even deeper by attending any of 250 online classes offered for free by top schools such as Yale, Stanford, and UC Berkeley. (Go to www.open culture.com/freeonlinecourses.) Master the history of Roman architecture from 753 BC to the present in less than an hour or, if the spirit moves you, the theory of relativity.

Now that you've aced Current Events, Business, and General Culture 101, you're ready for Literature and a reintroduction to the classics. But be forewarned, we are going to move fast. We need to cover twenty-four centuries of classic literature in just a few pages.

LITERATURE: IT'S ALL GREEK TO GORDY

Gordy, a tall, intellectual, bespectacled lender with a background in both investment banking and venture capital, is a Princeton University alum who graduated magna cum laude with a degree in English. He believes that "no one reads fiction" any-more—but that anyone with social aspirations should.

At a minimum, Gordy says, every-one should read five Shakespearean plays and be familiar with all of the Greek myths, which he maintains keep reappearing in movies, TV shows, and works of literature. Master the Greek myths, Gordy stresses, and you'll have the foundation that will make accumulating the rest of your cultural knowledge far easier.

Understanding that not everyone has the time to delve into *The Metamorphoses* by Ovid, Gordy highly recommends *Mythology for Dummies.*

THE DEAD WHITE GUYS' SOCIETY

The literary canon is a collection of works that have earned the seal of approval from academic and cultural establishments. These are the books that are often referred to as "literature," and which everyone is supposed to read and revere.

That said, these days the literary canon has fallen on hard times. There has been a big push against it as some scholars accuse it of being a collection of books by "dead white guys," with few women or anyone of an ethnic persuasion even cited.

Be that as it may, the following are the ten most-taught titles in high school English classes.[2] And Harper Lee of *To Kill a Mockingbird* fame is actually female.

Top Ten Books Read in High School	
1. *Romeo and Juliet*	William Shakespeare
2. *Macbeth*	William Shakespeare
3. *The Adventures of Huckleberry Finn*	Mark Twain
4. *Julius Caesar*	William Shakespeare
5. *To Kill a Mockingbird*	Harper Lee
6. *The Scarlet Letter*	Nathaniel Hawthorne
7. *Of Mice and Men*	John Steinbeck
8. *Hamlet*	William Shakespeare
9. *The Great Gatsby*	F. Scott Fitzgerald
10. *Lord of the Flies*	William Golding

With four plays on the Top Ten list of books read by today's high school students, William Shakespeare is not only a bard but a rock star.

Don't have time to read all ten? You can still purchase them all and crack them open (or at least leave them lying around your living room). Or just look up each online so that you can describe the plot. Follow this immortal mantra: *Veni, Vidi, Wiki.* You came, you saw, you looked it up on *Wikipedia.*

What if you find yourself hungering for a meatier list? If so, there's *The New Lifetime Reading Plan: The Classic Guide to World Literature, Revised and Expanded* by Clifton Fadiman and John S. Major.

The book promises at the outset that it could take "fifty years"

The *Wall Street Journal* is also betting that the rich read voraciously. In a new initiative that dates back only to Rupert Murdoch's takeover of the paper in 2007, the *Journal* has started a column called "Bookshelf" in its Opinion section.

"Bookshelf" recommends a full menu of books—from spy thrillers to autobiographies to histories to science tomes. Sprinkled among these varied suggestions are also the new business books and Wall Street tell-alls you would expect to find.

to finish reading all the books covered. If that sounds like too long a wait to sound über-intelligent, simply devour the essays and pick five books to *actually* read, and you'll conquer the literary canon faster than you can breeze through *Tristram Shandy*.

LISTMANIA FOR A-LISTERS

IS THE GLITTERATI PART OF THE LITERATI?

This is all great advice, you may think, *but are the well heeled truly all that well read?*

As a matter of fact, they are.

According to a piece posted on *Newser*, the online one-stop news source, Apple executive Steve Jobs was a huge fan of the poet William Blake. And disgraced junk bond king Michael Milken collects biographies, plays, and papers on Galileo (who faced arrest but was later redeemed by history).[3]

The literary canon and the *Wall Street Journal* are not the only purveyors of lists.

Every June for the past eleven years, J.P. Morgan Private Bank has sent its clients a summer reading list of ten books specifically chosen for the bank's wealthy clientele. To compile the list, JPM bankers from around the world submitted more than 450 nonfiction recommendations. A committee then chiseled them down to ten, based on "each tome's ability to capture the essence of [their] clients' personal and professional lives."[4]

If you're curious about the J.P. Morgan list (but don't happen to be a client of the bank), you can always venture to look up the list online. And what if you don't have time to read every last suggestion? Take heart. The average review on Amazon is only four sentences. For more intellectually challenging reviews, simply upgrade to the *New York Times Book Review* or, if you're feeling particularly egg-headed, the *New York Review of Books*.

Long story short, you've got a lot of reading *about* reading to do. But you never have to go back to the original source unless you really want to. Bear in mind that anything you ever hear about literature at a party will only be a regurgitation anyway.

The Art of Conversation

The advice in this chapter is designed to help you pick up a few choice sound bites in advance—so that at the very least, you can talk a good game. But note well: Talking doesn't necessarily involve offering an opinion. Truth to tell, it's usually wiser not to.

People who earn seven figures a year generally have *massive* egos to match those big, portly paychecks. Powerful people often consider themselves to be absolute authorities on all sorts of matters unrelated to their business prowess. These folks are used to being kowtowed to by frightened staffs who inevitably always concur with their masters. Spineless sycophants nod their heads yes in total, blind agreement to the wise words uttered by their rich hosts. Under the circumstances, *any* sort of challenge may be received as a narcissistic injury. Your aim should be only to become knowledgeable enough to pose intelligent questions—and from there you can listen hard and pick up more kernels of knowledge. Being a gifted conversationalist takes some finesse and often hinges on knowing when to speak and when to sit quietly and open yourself up to the river of knowledge pooling around you.

America's Enduring Love Affair with Scandals

Poised on a very high pedestal, the rich and powerful sometimes fall mightily; they suffer more than their fair share of scandals. That's why it's mandatory for you to brush up on the major misdeeds of the decade so that you can coo sympathetically when they arise in casual conversation.

However, if someone mentions a story with which you are wholly unfamiliar, do yourself a favor and never ask about it. Nod your head, make gentle clucking noises, and then skedaddle to the washroom where you can Google it from your Smartphone. Charles Ponzi. Ivan Boesky. Michael Milken. The Keating Five. Bill Clinton. Martha Stewart. Bernie Madoff. Eliot Spitzer. Rod Blagojcvich. If you have no idea what each is most famous for, please put down this book and go Google them without delay. (This is by no means intended to be an exhaustive list. It's just a soupçon of what you'll find nestled on the pages of the *Wall Street Journal* once you deign to crack it open.)

Meanwhile, know your audience. If someone at a party raises a scandal as a topic of conversation, bear in mind that he or she may not necessarily agree with the prevailing view and demonization of the perpetrator. Also be forewarned, today's scoundrels rehabilitate themselves rather quickly.

A former disgraced governor takes on a new role as the respected talking head of a serious news show. Redeemed, he runs for public office again. Martha Stewart, now a billionaire, is more beloved than ever. No doubt John McCain will be remembered more for losing to Obama in the 2008 presidential election than for any part he did or didn't play in the savings and loan crisis.

Let's be honest: Our collective memory is short and everyone loves a comeback story. We root for fallen heroes. And we are all willing to forgive, forget, and put the past aside.

That is, unless someone *personally* loses his own money as a result of a scam, in which case feelings may run rather hard against the culprit.

I was at a festive Christmas party in 2009 on tony Park Avenue where I bumped into an acquaintance I hadn't seen in several years. Still blonde, but a bit washed out from wear, she looked as if she had just run a marathon in her red silk crepe-de-chine dress. When I asked her what she had been doing since we had last seen each other, the first words out of her mouth were about Bernie Madoff—her family had lost a fortune and she was livid. I expressed my heartfelt sympathy and moved on. (Sometimes it's best not to spend too much time discussing highly charged, negative topics.)

In any crowd of the great and the near great, feel your way gingerly. Imagine that your mouth is capable of wearing kid gloves and don them—at least until you have navigated your way around the territory a few dozen times.

THE VOCABULARY DIET

Given that it could take fifty years to complete the canon, what's reasonable? How should one cultivate a love for learning if, for whatever reason, it hasn't kicked in yet? Think of it as putting the brain on a diet. There may be some pain, but there will also be much gain.

As crash diets never work, I recommend instead the "one-one-one" diet—one newspaper a day (pick the *Wall Street Journal* or the *New York Times*), one book a week (follow the lists cited here for inspiration), and one museum (or one course video) a weekend.

CONVERSATION STOPPERS

I have deliberately left sports talk for last, as it happens to be my own bugaboo. Thus, I appreciate firsthand how little one may care about the upshot of a particular Super Bowl, World Cup, or tennis or golf tournament. It seems as if all of the sports seasons start earlier and earlier and bleed into each other.

In much of the continental United States, there are only four seasons, but in sports land, there are at least seven: basket-

ball, baseball, tennis, golf, football, hockey, soccer—and that's during a non-Olympics year. As a result, in some homes, the television is rarely off. Whatever is happening in the sports arena is the white noise in the background, and for better or worse, it's foolhardy to completely tune out the noise.

Whenever today's plutocrats aren't waxing prolific about business, art, literature, or scandals, the default topic is always sports. I know several women who have interrupted a passionate male narrative of the deciding game of the NBA finals to ask, "Is that baseball or basketball again?"

I know some men who are almost as ignorant about sports, although the guys are cagier about admitting it. They know that to do so spells social suicide.

If, like me, you are not moved by a particular NBA trade or couldn't care less which teams are in the American versus the National league, please force yourself to glance at the sports section of your local newspaper occasionally, anyway. Skim it just to find out what those sports enthusiasts are yammering on about, the way you might challenge yourself to read a local magazine if you were traveling through a foreign country.

Because make no mistake, you ARE in a foreign country!

You'll be rewarded by *not* asking an insanely dumb question or looking blankly into space when the sports talk transporter descends. As it drops over you, subsuming (some may say "hijacking") the conversation for the next forty minutes, you would be well advised to remember Samuel Johnson's immortal words: "Those who desire to partake of the pleasure of wit must contribute to its production, since the mind stagnates without external ventilation."

Or, in plain speak, if you can't beat the conversation, join it.

CHAPTER FIVE

EVERYTHING YOU NEED TO KNOW TO GET ON THE A-LIST IS ALREADY WRITTEN IN A PROVERB

Today, something bizarre arrives in the mail. It's an ochre-colored envelope with strange, antiquated markings—*calligraphy*, you believe it's called.

Staring at that florid scrawl sets off an instant panic attack. You sweat. Your heart palpitates. You start to catastrophize. What if one of your friends is getting married? That would be a loss. (You have only two.)

Objection! you almost scream. Misery loves company, and clearly, you don't have enough of it. If your friend ties the noose, who will be there for you on New Year's Eve to watch the ball drop? Who

will be around to wish you Happy Birthday, or for that matter, Happy Arbor Day?

As you glide your trembling fingers over the envelope's flowery hand lettering, you flash ahead ten, twenty, forty years. What if you never get married? What if you die and no one bothers to attend your funeral?

Taking a measured breath to steady your thoughts, you tear into the sealed envelope. Calming your shaking hands, you pull out the heavy ochre card nestled inside and review it twice to make sure you read it correctly. To your astonishment, you have received

To Catch a Better Social Life Today, Master Some Folk Wisdom of Yore

Proverbs are short, catchy phrases that contain wisdom, truth, morals, and traditional views in a fixed form that's passed down from generation to generation. The oral tradition favored pithy sayings that were easy on the ears and even easier to remember. Aristotle studied proverbs way back in the BC era, and they have been enchanting and instructing people ever since.

I have collected some of my favorite kernels of folk wisdom, and it's interesting to note how many of them provide golden nuggets of advice to help enhance one's social life. Clearly, people have been seeking guidance in this area since the beginning of time.

While many of these homey phrases date back centuries, today we have modern tools to help implement the time-tested recommendations contained in each proverb—so we should be able to attain results faster than ever before. Following are six gems that have withstood the test of time. May their gentle insights

something even weirder than a wedding invitation.

It's an invitation to a cocktail party. A bona fide in-person socializing opportunity. It seems so . . . pre-Facebook. It's downright analog.

You scratch your temple, trying to recall where you put the damned TiVo manual, because it appears you'll be TiVoing your favorite shows four weeks from this coming Saturday.

Wow, you think, eyes glued to the invitation as if it's a foreign object, *I wonder how I can get some more of these.*

open doors for you and help numerous red carpets unfurl in your direction.

Gather Moss

An ancient proverb, often attributed to Publilius Syrus, states, "A rolling stone gathers no moss." Syrus, a Latin writer, probably penned this maxim all the way back in the first century BC. But, in order to take maximum advantage of this adage today, it really helps to understand it.

If you think of the Rolling Stones simply as a rock band and moss just as some green, spongy stuff, you might just be missing the point (albeit to excellent music).

The moss, in this case, means "a social life." If you travel a lot for business, you may be moving too fast—rolling—to gather a critical mass of moss.

To gather moss, it helps to slow down your schedule and hang out in one place for a while. If that's impractical because relaxing your work rhythm would also halt all paychecks for the foreseeable future, then devise new ways to gather moss while you're stuck at airports or even while you're in flight.

Stop thinking of the airport as a soulless place with greasy food where you fritter away time in between flights. Instead, picture this busy hub as one of the places where your stone "lives" part-time. Because it lives there, it needs to gather moss!

First, sign up for your frequent-flyer program's special deal on airline club membership. Then challenge yourself to stay *off* your mobile device whenever you hang out in the airport club lounge. Instead, engage fellow travelers in conversation.

Where are they traveling? Are they venturing out solo, or do they have colleagues in tow? Don't disturb anyone with one ear glued to his mobile device (or who appears eager to get some work done), but do reach out to the restless and the bored.

You'll likely meet fellow business travelers who may have access to all sorts of thrilling conventions, dinners, and other perks.

Talking to high flyers sometimes has the added benefit of ushering more business deals into your life, and with the added deal flow, the potential for real wealth creation.

My friend Mark likes to tell of a business trip when he went down to a hotel's restaurant and spotted five people sitting alone in a row of tables-for-two. He made an announcement and asked if the lonely eaters would like to share one big table instead. It turned out that they all worked in sales, and the travelers spent a wonderful evening exchanging stories as well as business cards.

Today, the Internet provides new and improved ways to gather moss even before you pack your bags. Check out FlyerTalk (www. flyertalk.com). Whether you're seeking the spiciest buffets in Hong Kong, the secrets of securing better ticket prices, or the inside skinny on frequent flyer status, it's entertaining. Posters converse in a language that teems with airline and airport acronyms designed to spur even the most grounded types to chat about flying.

When the world is your runway, sometimes you have to be more creative to work in a social life.

Another way to gather moss en route is to arrange games on the green even before you land. Golfers can link up with other enthusiasts while up in the air. Members of the Flying Blue Golf Club (www. fbgolfclub.com) can search for fellow golfers by location and handicap and then organize a round at their final destination. Look for more online golf clubs if this one, started by Air France and KLM, takes off.

Or join foursquare, the mobile application that rewards people for frequenting restaurants, bars, and hotels. Once you've checked in to a venue more often than anyone else in the foursquare network, you'll be crowned "Mayor" of that hotspot, which is like being the boss of moss. You'll receive

discounts and coveted "mayor specials" on food, drinks, and tickets. You'll be a dignitary, baby!

Foursquare also gives you the power to pull in all of your Facebook and Twitter followers. Friends in the network will know where you are whenever you check in. So if you find yourself at the same airline club lounge week after week, it could be a golden opportunity for you to meet with someone else in the network face-to-face and turn the deadly downtime into productive uptime.

Action One: Gather moss in today's airports. Make in-person connections, not just flight connections.

EARLY TO BED

A great proverb has many fathers.

Benjamin Franklin (1706–1790), the consummate diplomat, politician, inventor, author, and coiner of snappy sentiments, is often credited with, "Early to bed and early to rise makes a man healthy, wealthy and wise," although this phrase appears in other forms as early as 1496. The "early to bed" epigram was published in two of Franklin's works: *Poor Richard's Almanack* and *The Way to Wealth,* a collection of adages and advice based on work ethic and frugality.

Franklin, a noted polymath, had numerous careers, and to keep up with them all, he probably noticed that good sleeping habits made him feel better and think more clearly. If you are similarly ambitious, you'd do well to follow Franklin's motto. However, for today's Renaissance men and women, sleep does not always come when beckoned. If you suffer from insomnia, specific cures are cited in Chapter Twelve. But if you work an oddball shift, slaving away during the wee hours, catnapping during the day, and struggling to catch up on your semblance of a life in between, then your social life has two potential pitfalls. The first is that you have to work during the times when most shindigs take place so you'll never be able to get to them. The second problem is psychological: You might be more prone to dark, cantankerous moods.

The graveyard shift could be disrupting the way your body releases melatonin, which is a hormone produced by the pineal gland that controls your sleep-wake cycle. Located at the back of your brain, the gland releases melatonin when you are in a dark room. (During the ordinary course of things, this occurs at night.)

Do you feel like you always have your grouch on? Do not self-diagnose. Instead, make an appointment to consult a sleep specialist who can recommend solutions. You might consider eternal moodiness as a cue to investigate if there is any way to change your shift to the daytime. The graveyard shift is only appropriate for someone with a robust constitution. If your job makes you feel as grim as the Grim Reaper, your body may be trying to tell you that the graveyard shift isn't right for you.

Action Two: Make sleep a priority so you'll function at your best. If you can't get your work hours changed, see a sleep specialist.

FLOCK TO BIRDS OF A FEATHER

"Birds of a feather flock together" is another proverb with numerous authors, including, but probably not limited to, William Turner in *The Rescuing of Romish Fox* (1545) and Benjamin Jowett's 1856 translation of *Plato's Republic.*

This colorful truism is particularly instructive if you happen to enjoy spending time alone. Think of ways of adding a social element to a pastime that might ordinarily be considered solitary. For example, if you enjoy running, consider using a site such as Craigslist as a bulletin board and advertise for a running buddy. Or explore a site such as Meetup.com to locate people who are passion-

ate about the same activities as you. You could organize a morning jog in your city or find a group that already runs together on the weekends. If you're a writer, you might consider putting together a writer's group that meets semi-monthly.

If part of the reason that you're a loner is because you hate being bossed around by officious organizing types, then take the initiative to start your own club. Be realistic. Chances are, you won't ingratiate yourself with everyone you meet, but as the group leader it's also easier to pick and choose which members of the club will become regulars.

Action Three: Find your flock. Turn solitary activities into social opportunities by doing them in groups.

Build Bridges

A very wise person named Anonymous once wrote, "Build bridges instead of walls and you will have a friend." But how do you erect those proverbial bridges if you live in a place where it's impossible to meet new people?

Not every locale bustles with electrifying openings, posh premieres, and scintillating soirées, but every city, town, or suburb is home to groups of people. Your charge is to ferret out the "connector" in the crowd and befriend that person.

A connector is someone who knows exponentially more people than the rest of us combined; therefore, he's easy to spot. It's the guy who is always bumping into friends and acquaintances on the street, the fellow who's sometimes jokingly referred to as the "Mayor of the parking lot." Chances are he's right in front of you, if you only know where to direct your attention.

First, walk to the periphery of the room. Now, from the sidelines, closely observe the inhabitants. Do you see that paragon of amiability in the middle of the

Connectors know large numbers of people and are in the habit of making introductions.

room, in the midst of a large crowd? Notice how everyone around him seems to be subtly jostling each other in an attempt to command his attention? *He's* the connector.

Connectors can also be female, of course. (Connectivity is gender neutral.) It's the woman that's hosting the biggest luncheon of the year, the lively networker who has kept in touch with every boss she's ever had even though she now lives 1,000 miles away from them. It's the person in the center of the room, in the center of the crowd, and at the hub of society in *this* little universe. Reach out to this one person, and you've built a bridge to the whole community.

Connectors may seem super confident and unapproachable, but they're not. That's because at their core, they're people attractors who thrive on adding new members to their circle—people just like you. Now that you've identified the central force that holds the human

nucleus together in this town, you really have no choice.

Approach the person, flash a megawatt smile, and be sure to say, "Hi."

Connectors *live* to connect. So keep your connector wired by tapping into his or her very essence—the ability to bond with other people.

What if you don't happen to have any friends in common? In that case, talk about your true love for your shared city or town.

Connectors are like human phone books of potential friends and acquaintances. With deep links to the social and civic leaders of the community, these connected kingpins can plug you in to everyone who's anyone in an instant. The number of acquaintances in your contact base will multiply exponentially, as will the number of invitations you receive. Your social calendar will teem with A-list events and happenings, causing you to wonder how you ever became so popular. Yes, this is your life—or it can be, anyway—once you befriend a connector.

Action Four: Build a bridge to a "connector," and you will be connected to the entire community.

PUT YOUR EGGS IN MANY BASKETS

"'Tis the part of a wise man to keep himself today for tomorrow, and not venture all his eggs in one basket," Cervantes (1547–1616) wrote in his novel *Don Quixote*. While the expression has been used (sometimes to death!) in the financial field to convey the benefits of diversifying one's investments (in order to build a "nest egg"), the maxim has particular relevance to today's social networking options.

There are numerous strategies you can employ to make new online friends, and one of the pleasanter side effects of social networking is often an energized social life. Start with LinkedIn, Facebook, and Twitter. Create your electronic profile, and import it across all three platforms. Fill out the "Experience" portion of LinkedIn's Profile section (being sure to include all past positions). Take advantage

of LinkedIn's "Recommend this person" feature, and ask former colleagues to praise your work. Position yourself as an expert by answering questions from others in your field. Spend an hour a day burnishing your online presence until it glows.

Not seeing the results you want fast enough? Then don't put all your eggs in the new media basket. Instead, escape from behind your screen and engage in some off-line schmoozing.

You eat three meals a day. Why allow your newspaper to be your sole dining companion? Newspapers, while clever, are rather dry. While they've perfected the written monologue, they don't have mouths and ears, which makes conversing with them difficult!

Shake things up by inviting real, live human beings to join you at the table instead. Urge your contacts to meet you for breakfast, lunch, and dinner. You'll ignite your social life and, in so doing, may even uncover some new business opportunities. And having some money flow into your coffers attracts more of the same.

Action Five: Keep your options open by putting your proverbial eggs in various baskets. Explore the brave

*new world of social networking. Then
continue your networking off-line.*

CATCH FLIES WITH HONEY

The colorful proverb, "You can
catch more flies with honey than
with vinegar," can be traced back
to Giovanni Torriano's *Common
Place of Italian Proverbs* (1666). The
saying also appeared in Benjamin
Franklin's *Poor Richard's Alamanack*
in 1744, and illustrates one of the
techniques that diplomats like
Franklin use in order to persuade
people to their way of thinking.
To wit: Polite arguments and flattery are more convincing than
confrontational tactics.

Avoid vinegar. Always think
before shooting someone a caus-
tic email. It's fine to *draft* scath-
ing emails, of course, just never
ever send them. Instead, keep
them under cloak of dark-
ness by filing them
in your "Drafts"
folder. Then, take

*With new media
connecting us all
through Twitter
feeds, Facebook, and
LinkedIn, it's a small,
social world after all.*

twenty-four hours to cool down,
and rewrite your communiqués to
express your viewpoint with elo-
quence and grace.

The "catch flies" nugget
acknowledges that getting along
with people who have different
opinions is not always easy. But
by remembering to add a "smile"
to your communications, you can
sometimes persuade the receiver;
and even if you don't, he'll continue to respect you.

In sum, if forming friendships
is new to you, think about what it
means to "catch flies with honey."
Don't be too judgmental in the
beginning. Just stick to your task,
knowing that as long as you commit to energizing your social life,
it will improve little by little.

Hang out with whomever
will have you as a friend—at first.
Potential interactions with crimi-
nals and psychopaths
notwithstanding, the
benefits that accrue
by being with
new people will
outweigh most
of the draw-
backs. At a mini-
mum, it's easier to
make new friends
once you already have

a few acting as "people magnets" to help pull new recruits into your circle.

Anticipate that you won't like everyone and that everyone certainly won't like you back. But if you make it your mission to gather moss in spite of a hectic lifestyle, go to bed and rise early in spite of the various activities that are all competing for your time and attention, and find your flock even if you're painfully shy by nature, your social life will gradually become more multidimensional. Build bridges to enough people, and eventually you will bump into a connector.

Connectors are to friendship formation what the "Daily Double" is to TV's *Jeopardy*. Connectors ratchet up your game to a whole new level. Because these kings and queens of society live to connect, they will put you in touch with many new people, and chances are your personal life will improve dramatically thereafter. To find these connectors, try various approaches, both online and off. Don't forget to keep those metaphorical eggs evenly distributed.

Above all, when you find yourself on opposite sides of an issue with a brand new friend, remember to catch flies with honey instead of vinegar. Longstanding friendships can tolerate more vinegar than most brand new attachments will bear.

You Become Who You Hang out With

"You are who you meet."

I believe it is a powerful notion. And when you roll it around in your mind a few times, you'll recognize that it has the ring of truth to it. So make it a point to meet some influential people. Then, figure out new ways to stay in touch with them.

Successful people surround themselves with successful people, so never begrudge another's advancement. Instead, make those who are achieving their goals part of your entourage. Stay close to those who are achieving great things in their lives, and you will move that much faster to your ultimate goal.

CHAPTER SIX

THE BODY OF A MILLIONAIRE

You don't remember feeling this pinched before—and for a change, you are not referring to your dire financial situation.

No, you are referring to the way your black pleated pants feel now that they've come back from the dry cleaner's.

Tight! Like the zipper might burst at any moment. Constricted! Like some mammoth force is pushing against your stomach and hips and melding them together into a giant squishy pretzel.

You're certain that the uncomfortable tug along the waistline is entirely due to the mysterious dry cleaning fluid used and not to any massive weight gain on your part.

You've always been thin, and you still are. It's not as if you've been wining and dining clients or even going out at night.

In point of fact, in order to get out from under your credit card debt and start paying your landlord on time, you recently put yourself on the austerity diet. You've been eating home-microwaved macaroni and cheese for—*OMG!* you think, suddenly catching the reflection of your physique in a department store window. You look like one big . . . hippopotamus. Jowly in the cheek area. Rotund in the butt area. And with your college reunion just around the corner.

Now you can't go. Not when you're feeling broke and looking fat. Not when everyone else who shows up will look like a model and be as rich as a king.

Staring at the immense figure reflected back at you in the

glass makes the next decision a snap. Determined to liberate the thin person trapped inside the fat one just in the nick of time for your reunion, you stop off at the local bodega and buy seven quarts of grapefruit juice—one quart for each day of the week. While you're in a fasting frame of mind, you also stock up on pink grapefruit (it's the grapefruit-on-grapefruit diet) and bottled water.

You will look amazing for your reunion even if it kills you! And you will look like a million bucks even if you are flat broke.

HOW TO ARRIVE AT YOUR IDEAL WEIGHT BASED ON YOUR LOCATION

Before you worry about going on a diet, figure out where you'll be spending the majority of your time. You may not have to lose quite as many pounds as you fear. In certain parts of the country, achieving your ideal weight requires ample deprivation; in other parts of the country—not so much!

When you look like a million bucks, you are at your "millionaire weight," regardless of the number showing on the scale. Let's take a quick trip across the country to assess what that number should be, depending on where you are.

TO LIVE AND DIET IN L.A.

I love L.A. But I'm happy that I live on the other coast. Doing so gives me more wiggle room. I can weigh fifteen pounds more in Manhattan than I would have to if I lived in L.A.

In L.A., one needs to be five pounds past anorexic just to be considered skinny. There is a reason for this. In the Hollywood culture of the West Coast, everyone is either in the movie business or has an uncle who is.

All the waiters trying to break into the business are serving the agents who are pitching the studio heads on tomorrow's next big star. But make no mistake, film is an unflattering medium.

On screen, the actors and actresses appear heavier than they do off-camera. Film automatically adds fifteen pounds to the stars' faces and bodies. Even with modern technology, there's no getting around it. As a result, in real life all of the film stars are fifteen pounds thinner than they ought to be. And those toothpicks of the silver screen are the role models for the rest of the West Coast population.

Consequently, many in L.A. obsess about calorie, carb, and fat counts all day long and spend every spare second at the health club, trying to drop one or two clothing sizes.

THE BIG APPLE DIET

L.A. is nothing like Manhattan, where years can go by without any cool celebrity sightings. Celebrities come to New York City to be ignored. Manhattan has just as many famous actor and actress residents as Los Angeles, but you never see them because they're always hiding behind their polarized sunglasses or dashing out of high-end restaurants before the paparazzi arrive.

Manhattan is a financial capital, not a movie capital. As a result, the only "celebrities" you ever bump into in Manhattan are inordinately wealthy business people or politicians. These second-tier celebrities are less concerned about the fifteen extra pounds that TV might add to their physiques, and most of these B-listers have never even seen themselves on film.

However, Manhattan is the world's best walking city, a lifestyle choice that keeps off the poundage. Most natives eat three square meals a day but walk it off quickly. Manhattanites are five pounds thinner than they ought to be.

THE MOTOR CITY DIET

In Detroit, where I have also logged some time, one rarely sees an A-list celebrity, a politician, or a wealthy businessperson just hanging out. Yet similar to L.A., the Detroit culture revolves around cars. With few super skinny role models to emulate and a lifestyle that's a bit sedentary due to its car centricity, some folks are fifteen pounds heavier than they ought to be.

DIETING, DENVER-STYLE

In Denver, conversely, everyone is busy skiing their asses off—

literally. This may be the reason why Colorado is the least obese state in the nation. Washington D.C. has a trim population too—perhaps driven by politicians running away from the paparazzi sniffing around for scandals.

When it comes to weight, there is a sliding scale. Before you worry about going on a diet, figure out where you'll be spending the lion's share of your time, and adjust your weight goals accordingly. And remember that a few pounds either way can make a big difference, depending on whether you wish to define yourself as *East Coast Elite*, *West Coast Wealth*, or *Midwest Money*.

Now that you've mastered the geography of dieting, it's time for a quickie course on how gender influences perception. When it comes to looking like a million dollars, there are significant differences between how men and women wear their weight.

THE TEN POUNDS RULE: FOR WOMEN, LOSE. FOR MEN, GAIN

"Honey, do I look fat?" If you're a guy who's asking, rest assured, a little extra padding might not be such a bad thing.

One of the side effects that comes with wealth acquisition—either real or imagined—is cushioning. This is one situation in which it's easier to look rich than poor in the developed world. The rich are fêted nightly. They have fabulous banquets and black-tie dinners they must attend, and even their expensive personal trainers can't work fast enough to take it all off.

For women, however, fat hasn't been in fashion since the early 1600s when Peter Paul Rubens painted zaftig maidens. "Living large"—or even pretending to—often necessitates slimming down. As the old adage says, "You can never be too rich or too thin." This may require becoming a diet diva. You may have to learn to live without carbs indefinitely. Or fat. Or chocolate-covered pretzels, God forbid. But while you're busy looking like a millionaire, make sure you stay healthy enough to stick around and enjoy it.

There are also some tricks you can practice that will make you seem more svelte without requiring an ounce of sacrifice. Complete the exercise opposite and discover how to be your own mistress of illusion.

EXERCISE FOR WOMEN:

How to appear twenty-five pounds thinner without lifting a barbell

Your real weight: _____ lbs

Action	Visual Poundage Lost
1. Wear high heels	1. For every inch of heel height, subtract three pounds
2. Wear contour on cheeks	2. Subtract three pounds
3. Wear an underwire bra	3. Lift, separate, and subtract three pounds
4. Wear monochromatic clothing	4. Minimize curves and subtract eight pounds
5. Stand tall, shoulders back	5. Subtract two pounds
6. Wear control-top pantyhose	6. Suck it in, then subtract two pounds
7. Wear a hair volumizing plastic insert, such as a "Bumpit" on the crown of your head and comb your hair over it.	7. Subtract four pounds

Your wardrobe-adjusted weight: ____lbs

Bumpits™ elongate the face.

WHY CAN'T A WOMAN BE MORE LIKE A MAN (WHEN IT COMES TO WEIGHT)?

Life's unfair for the fairer sex. Basically, if we want to look like a million dollars, we have no choice but to look malnourished. And that can't be good for our health (or our collective sense of self-esteem). But, as the exercise on pg. 75 demonstrates, there are simple ways to deceive the eye to make everyone think we're considerably thinner than we really are.

Women who are whizzes at algebra can lose even more weight—visually, if not in reality—if they always keep in mind this simple equation. *Search for clothes and accessories that lengthen the body's* y-*axis and reduce its* x-*axis.*

Anything that adds height and subtracts width is visually thinning. You can argue that shoulder pads went out with Nancy Reagan, and you'd be right. But those pads were sky-high. Wearing today's smallish shoulder pads will appear to reduce your waist size by broadening your shoulders. Similarly, big hair—that is, hair that's slightly teased—will add height and visually reduce the width of your face for a slenderizing effect that's most fetching. Hair extensions also subtract visual poundage and can be clipped on when your scale won't cooperate.

SHRINKAGE WITHOUT SHRINKS

There are also some simple ways to tweak the way you view your body image. First, vow to ignore Bruce Springsteen's lyrical advice and put your "Glory Days" behind you. No doubt you remember your welterweight from college fondly—who doesn't?—but it's time to let the memory go, just like the frat parties of yesteryear.

All weight is relative. What's considered skinny in one city may be considered obese in another. Observe local customs before starting any diet.

Aim for your ideal weight, not an idealized number. To arrive at yours, simply take the lightest number that you hit back in college and add ten pounds to it plus one-quarter of a pound for every year over the age of twenty-five (up to ten pounds).

There is no such thing as a magic number; there is only your correct number adjusted for your real age and imaginary income.

What if you saw your adjusted ideal weight—and passed it—a long time ago? In that case, go slow. See how many pounds you can drop simply by making certain lifestyle adjustments, such as drinking less alcohol and substituting brown and green foods for

Try substituting green foods for white before going on a diet.

white foods, before embarking on an all-out diet campaign.

Losing too much heft too quickly can make you look drawn, tired, and more wrinkled than a raisin in the sun. Studies show that most poundage lost through dieting has a way of creeping back over time anyway. But a changed lifestyle can last a lifetime.

IF IT'S ALL WHITE, IT'S ALL WRONG

Bread, bagels, cookies, crackers, pretzels, ice cream, potatoes, pasta, white rice, and pie all have something in common: They are all-white. They're made with white flour, sugar, salt, and depending on the item, milk.

They're also teeming with carbohydrates, which are hard to shed unless you're Michael Phelps. (Most of us aren't.)

White foods make your body feel lazy and move like a tortoise. Implicated in diabetes, all-white foods pack a double whammy: A daily intake of them stimulates your body to crave these foods even more. Where possible, make smart substitutions.

THE BANISH WHITE DIET

Instead Of:	Try:
White Potatoes/White Rice	Brown Rice
White Pasta	Whole Wheat Pasta
White Bread	Full Grain Breads
White Beans	Yams
Bananas	Fruit in Vibrant Colors
Anything Made with White Flour	Green Leafy Vegetables
Butter	Olive Oil

Some all-white foods are all right. Cauliflower, parsnips, and pearl onions are on the okay-to-eat list.

THE CHEESECAKE FACTORY

Someday, when you're not famished, toddle over to The Cheesecake Factory. Observe the supersized portions. While many restaurants serve more food than a person should consume in a meal, this eatery serves more food than a person should consume in a day. While most restaurant-made omelets might contain three eggs, these generous omelets might have seven. While most slices of carrot cake might contain 700 calories, a slice in these quarters might have 1,549 plus 24 grams of fat.

Next, check out the patrons as well as the servers, and see if you don't find them to be somewhat

Size matters: Smaller portions lead to smaller waists.

Boteroesque, or rotund. While the food at The Cheesecake Factory is scrumptious, the chain is an excellent advertisement for why it's imperative to limit your portion size.

The average dinner plate has a 12" diameter. If you want to get thin faster, start serving your food on 9" diameter plates. You'll feel fuller just looking at a smaller plate that's overflowing with food. And, in time, the three inches you lose in diameter will come straight off of your waistline.

WHEN THE BEST BOOB JOB MONEY CAN BUY IS A BRAND-NEW BRA

As we age, certain body parts that used to point up start to droop. Gravity exerts its vicious toll, and suddenly everything we once prided our sexuality on—our lips, breasts, and butts—all seem to be heading in the wrong direction. (South.) You don't have to be a Google map to know you're lost. Your charge is to reverse the direction, and one place to start is with your twin peaks.

If you pick up one suggestion from this chapter (and you're a woman), it's buy a better bra. This is one item on which you don't want to pinch pennies.

Bra sizing is an antiquated art, on par with ivory painting, calligraphy, harpsichord playing, and certain dark arts. You must go get fitted in person. While it's not quite as torturous as a visit to the dentist, no one would confuse brassiere buying with a pleasurable pastime.

You may have to try on many different sizes and brands before you find the perfect fit. You may have to model your purchase in front of a saleswoman you've never met before so she can view your lingerie-clad torso from all angles to make sure that no body fat spills out from the sides. You may have to endure a strange woman's hands pulling on the straps as she demonstrates how you should correctly wiggle your boobs into the cups. But don't let any of that dissuade you. Do not try to shimmy out of the experience. Never buy a bra from a catalog, because if you do the undergarment probably won't fit.

Unless you are a bra saleswoman by trade, you are likely to get your own bra size incorrect. Chances are, you are not the same size you were in high school or

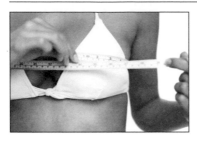

Most breasts are hard to measure. See a professional bra saleswoman.

college. (Honey, you may not even be the same size you were last month.) Various brands size their cups a bit differently than others. Do not try to guess your size. Eighty percent of women guess wrong. That's not just a blooper—it's a drooper!

Instead, take an hour and force yourself to visit a very upscale brassiere store. Have the saleswoman measure your chest so you'll know your correct size. One perfectly fitting bra will make every item of clothing lie on you the way the designer intended.

MEN ARE THE LUCKIER SEX BECAUSE . . .

A Little Extra Padding Never Hurt a Man's Prospects

If a woman is a little overweight, she's considered fat. If a man is a little overweight, he's considered distinguished.

His extra padding is equated with business lunches and client dinners, where presumably he's building good, strong, working relationships that will make him financially comfortable.

Golf, the businessman's pastime of choice for schmoozing clients, burns only 721 calories per round and has never helped a guy get thin. And this is a good thing because if a man is too skinny, everyone will automatically assume that his financial prospects have popped faster than a dot com bubble (or, even worse, that he never had great expectations).

So if you're a guy who has developed a gut recently due to your hard-driving, master-of-the-universe lifestyle, think of the extra poundage as a rounding error in your favor.

Do not automatically attempt to go on a stringent diet unless your clothes don't fit, you feel sluggish, or your doctor tells you to (in which case, review "If It's All White, It's All Wrong" and "The Cheesecake Factory" sections of this chapter. The suggestions will work just as well for men as for women.) Instead, think of ways you can convert that fat to muscle for a manlier build.

And if you happen to be cursed with a quick metabolism, fear not. There are numerous ways to slow it down (or at least appear to).

FOR MEN ONLY: HOW TO LOOK MORE SOLID THAN YOU REALLY ARE

Are you naturally trim and athletic? Do you hit the tennis court with regularity? Have you miraculously maintained the star athlete body you had during college? Adding a couple of pounds (or more muscle mass) to your lean physique may help colleagues and potential clients take you more seriously.

You don't have to accumulate three chins to add gravitas, but having a sturdier build will help you seem like a more solid businessperson. (If you need a role model, think of Jack Welch. He's tall, handsome, muscular, and definitely a guy's guy.)

Hit the gym. Your body burns approximately fifty calories per pound of muscle each day but just a few calories per pound of fat. If

you build muscle, you'll bulk up nicely. To turn a slightly rounded, effeminate chest into a masculine one, follow a regimen of weight lifting and resistance training. Of course it also helps if you know how to use the machines at the gym correctly.

HOW TO TRAIN YOUR PERSONAL TRAINER

Call it bravado. Or freakish overconfidence. But the plain fact is, most guys hate to ask for directions—either in the car or at the gym.

Personal trainers know this. (And some of them don't really care to train you all that well because then, guess what? You'll no longer require their services.) But any strength-building routine will no doubt involve working out on some of the machines, and you should ask as many questions as necessary to learn how to use these instruments of muscle tone and torture.

Join a gym that offers a free personal training session as part of the package. Be specific about your needs. Are you trying to change your body type? Develop six-pack abs? Strengthen your core? Build muscle mass? Tone your muscles for a sleeker appearance? Sculpt your butt?

Never expect a personal trainer to guess your goals. (Trainers aren't psychics and neither are psychics most of the time.)

Come with a list of your objectives so you'll stay on track.

The Other Way to Achieve "Mass Appeal"

It bears repeating: Super skinny guys don't look like millionaires. Scrawniness of any kind conjures up visions of poor, starving artists and malnourished cats.

To look as if you have some financial backing (even if you don't), it helps to have a little honest-to-goodness padding. Are you cursed with a quick metabolism? Don't be afraid to bulk up, or appear to anyway, by following some of the guidelines below.

1. Layer up. An undershirt under a button-down shirt under a sweater under a jacket adds visual poundage. For extra padding, wear a down vest.

2. Break the visual line. Pair a navy suit with a brown belt

The Ugly Truth: Going for a pretty boy body may work against your quest to look like a millionaire. Many male millionaires are a bit heavyset—a result of consuming too much foie gras and champagne.

instead of a black one. The brown color won't disappear into the background and will, thus, interrupt the monochromatic visual line of the suit. This will make you appear heavier than you really are.

3. Wear a fat tie. One with a crazy pattern is best.

4. Channel your inner professor and wear bulky eye-

glasses. Frameless spectacles may be in these days, but tortoiseshell frames add heft around the cheekbone area.

5. Lighten your palate. Beige jackets add more dimension than their navy counterparts. White shirts fill you out more than their darker cousins.

6. Sport tiny sunglasses. Your face will look fleshed out by comparison.

7. Go wide. Don wide wale corduroy pants and a belt with a motif that declares your attachment to millionaire values. Motifs to consider: anything that hints of a sprawling country estate, such as whales (think Nantucket), ducks (think East Hampton), or candy stripes (think Martha's Vineyard).

FOR MEN AND WOMEN

Get a Leg Up by Standing Tall

CEOs of Fortune 500 companies are human skyscrapers. Sub-consciously, we seek leaders who are tall because we associate height with authority. According to Malcolm Gladwell's *Blink*, over 14.5 percent of men in the United States are six feet or over, but among CEOs of Fortune 500 companies, the number jumps to 58 percent.

Everyone, it seems, is biased in favor of tallness.

Another telling tidbit: Of forty-three American presidents, eighteen have been six feet or taller. That's 42 percent. Even scarier, the taller candidate (of the final two) almost always wins.[5]

A paper in the *Utah Law Review* called "Height Discrimination in Employment" states that we have not elected a shorter-than-average president since 1896 (President William McKinley, 5'7", who apparently was teased for being shorter than average). Taller equates to winner.[6]

The long and the short of it? Being tall turns out to be a big advantage. Taller people are also happier according to a paper from the National Bureau of Economic Research, which found that both men and women who were above average in height (5'10" for men; 5'4" for women), reported higher levels of happiness than shorter people. The study found that taller people tended to have more education and higher income levels than their shorter counterparts.[7]

And those who are short keep getting short-changed. Some data suggests that every additional inch of height is associated with a 1.8 to 2.2 percent increase in wages—or roughly $789 a year.

Do you wish to look like a portrait of success? It stands to reason that you should stand up straight and add some heel height if need be.

For men, adding stature can be a bit trickier than for women where the only thing required is a higher heel. Men may prefer to hide the added height with elevator shoes that look like they have a one-inch heel (while covertly adding three to four extra inches of height).

Boots for men are also an option, although not at the office.

In conclusion, if you want to be a ruler, start shopping with one. Buy shoes that add height, and wear clothing that projects the illusion of added stature through shoulder pads and other accessories that draw the eye up and out.

The Tall Club: U.S. Presidents by Height Order

The average man is five foot ten. The average president of the United States has been considerably taller.

1. Abraham Lincoln	6 ft. 4 in.
2. Lyndon Johnson	6 ft. 4 in.
3. Thomas Jefferson	6 ft. 2½ in.

4. Franklin Roosevelt	6 ft. 2 in.
5. George H. W. Bush	6 ft. 2 in.
6. Bill Clinton	6 ft. 2 in.
7. George Washington	6 ft. 1½ in.
8. Andrew Jackson	6 ft. 1 in.
9. Ronald Reagan	6 ft. 1 in.
10. Barack Obama	6 ft. 1 in.
11. James Monroe	6 ft. 0 in.
12. John Tyler	6 ft. 0 in.
13. James Buchanan	6 ft. 0 in.
14. James Garfield	6 ft. 0 in.
15. Chester Arthur	6 ft. 0 in.
16. Warren Harding	6 ft. 0 in.
17. John F. Kennedy	6 ft. 0 in.
18. Gerald Ford	6 ft. 0 in.
19. William Taft	5 ft. 11½ in.
20. Herbert Hoover	5 ft. 11½ in.
21. Richard Nixon	5 ft. 11½ in.
22. George W. Bush	5 ft. 11½ in.
23. Grover Cleveland	5 ft. 11 in.
24. Woodrow Wilson	5 ft. 11 in.
25. Dwight Eisenhower	5 ft. 10½ in.
26. Franklin Pierce	5 ft. 10 in.
27. Andrew Johnson	5 ft. 10 in.

28. Theodore Roosevelt	5 ft. 10 in.
29. Calvin Coolidge	5 ft. 10 in.
30. Jimmy Carter	5 ft. 9½ in.
31. Millard Fillmore	5 ft. 9 in.
32. Harry Truman	5 ft. 9 in.
33. Rutherford Hayes	5 ft. 8½ in.
34. William Henry Harrison	5 ft. 8 in.
35. James Polk	5 ft. 8 in.
36. Zachary Taylor	5 ft. 8 in.
37. Ulysses Grant	5 ft. 8 in.
38. John Quincy Adams	5 ft. 7½ in.
39. John Adams	5 ft. 7 in.
40. William McKinley	5 ft. 7 in.
41. Martin Van Buren	5 ft. 6 in.
42. Benjamin Harrison	5 ft. 6 in.
43. James Madison	5 ft. 4 in.

The average man is 5 foot, 10 inches tall.

TO HAVE THE BODY OF A MILLIONAIRE

In order to be successful at anything, it helps to start with a plan. This is just as true for arriving at your millionaire weight as for any other goal.

1. Figure out where you want to live and what the ideal body type is for that region. Denver, L.A., Manhattan, and Washington D.C. trend considerably thinner than other cities in the United States. Certain states are hotbeds of activity; other states are couches of obesity.

2. Adjust your ideal weight for your gender. For men, gaining weight sometimes adds a patina of respectability. For women, it's hard to be too rich or too thin. That said, there are more ways for women to dress skinny than for guys. Start taking advantage of these sartorial secrets to lop off the weight visually that won't come off in actuality.

3. Give up the quest for the magic number of yesteryear. Adding a couple of pounds to your welterweight from college is age-appropriate.

4. Wear heels. The taller you are, the wealthier you look. Remember that stalky basketball players earn seven figures a year and tall CEOs are today's giants of green—then reach for the stars.

CHAPTER SEVEN

HAIROGRAPHY FOR HEIR- AND HEIRESS-WANNABES

If women's hair is from Venus and men's hair is from Mars, then your hair must be from Pluto. It's really alien.

Sometimes it springs up in a terrible fright, giving you that I've-just-been-electrocuted look—very Albert Einstein. Sometimes it lays down flat, plastering itself to your head in lifeless despair.

And the battle wages on—the straight hair fighting the frizz for hair-wide supremacy.

Uniform texture is not really your hair's strong point, you think, examining an undecided strand in your cracked bathroom mirror. Such pilary wishy-washiness hasn't benefitted you in either your career or your personal life.

At work, your boss no doubt considers you disorganized—not a huge plus when it comes to getting promoted. And, frankly, your personal life is sort of a mess too. You have a grand total of two great

friends, which is the very reason that you decided to attend your college reunion in the first place. You had high hopes of reconnecting with some of your old friends in an effort to broaden your social life.

It's a pity your hair refuses to cooperate with this worthy ambition. Today, your hair could double as a string mop.

You call your friend Hadley, your style guru on speed dial.

"Be honest," you say. "Do you think I need a haircut?

"Absolutely," Hadley says, "but you know, it's not a good idea to

do it the day of a big event. Hair needs at least three days to recuperate from a cut."

"Now you tell me!"

"No worries," she says brightly. "Do you have an egg?"

"For my old classmates to hurl at me when they don't get my jokes?"

"Don't be daft," she laughs. "Did you know that with just one egg, you can give your hair a quick protein bath? You hair will look brand, new."

Easy for Hadley to say, you think. She has long, shiny, tawny hair that's one texture and one length. In Hadley's last life, she was probably a thoroughbred horse.

In your last life, you were probably a mutt, and some of that mixed-breed hair still graces your head.

"Oh please. Just try it!" Hadley whinnies. "How can you be so sure you won't like something until you try it?"

That Hadley. She's irrepressible.

Reluctantly, you acquiesce, agreeing to let Hadley stop by with a half-dozen eggs and some hair recipe that she pulled from a magazine. Her hair resuscitation scheme sounds pretty harebrained.

Some people were born with rich hair. Try not to envy them.

Then again, what do you have to lose?

HAIR-O-NOMICS

Was your hair "to the manor born"? Or does it look like it

Rich hair should have movement.
(CREDIT: BEN SMITH/
SHUTTERSTOCK.COM)

rolled out of bed in a single-room-occupancy hotel?

Feel free to be candid. It's only your hair that you're diagnosing, the same mop at the top of your head that you've become accustomed to by now. To help with your assessment, kindly stroll to the nearest bathroom mirror with this book in hand. Study your hair closely. Peer at it. Good. Now, it's time to play Hairography.

If your hair were a car, would it be a sleek Ferrari, an elegant Mercedes, or a clunky Buick?

Excellent. No judgments. Stay where you are; don't move; now look again.

If your hair were an animal, would it be a sexy panther, a mighty lion, or a prickly porcupine?

Rich hair is plush.

Now you've got the hang of it.

Is your hair abundant and free flowing, radiating health and luster? Or is it skimpy and impoverished, flaky, broken, and brittle? Does your hair look well groomed or completely burned out from too much living (or dying)?

In sum, when it comes to your personal and career aspirations, is your hair an asset, a debit, or a full-blown bankruptcy case?

Last but not least, amid any other hair issues, how do you feel about the color?

Rich hair is plentiful.

Rich hair cascades.

Rich hair is unforgettable.

IN PURSUIT OF RICH HAIR

Rich hair is healthy, strong, and plentiful. It comes in a vast array of different textures and colors, but there should be enough to frame the face, enhance a great feature (such as the eyes), or counterbalance an imperfection (such as a weak chin). How you arrive at your best texture is a balance among your will, your hair's muscle, and your budget. Beyond texture, there are the two *C*'s—cut and color, which are also counterbalanced by another critical *C*—cash.

Here's how to find your most luxuriant look for the least outlay.

SURRENDER TO YOUR HAIR'S REAL TEXTURE

Lay down your chemical straighteners, your curling agents, and your blow dryers. The good fight can't be won. Surrender is your only option.

Forcing your hair to fight against itself is time- and cash-consuming. You're paying a team of experts to change what Mother Nature wrought, and your hair has the bad manners to grow back exactly the way it was.

The conservative strategy—both in terms of cash and natural resource preservation—is to inflict breakage on your hair only once, by changing the texture or color, never both. Whether you have naturally curly locks that you wish were straighter or bone-straight wisps that you wish were curlier, make peace with imperfection.

If you can live with your hair's essential texture, there are numerous cheap home remedies that will make it look considerably healthier. And the beauty is most of the ingredients are already in your fridge.

A Day at the Home Spa (Otherwise Known as Your Bathtub)

Does your fringe look frazzled? That's not a savvy look for either social or career advancement. Treat your hair to a day of pampering worthy of a magnate-in-the-making. These do-it-yourself remedies cost just pennies per treatment as all of the ingredients hail from a grocery store.

Don't Hold the Mayo Conditioner: Take a half-cup of mayonnaise and comb it all the way through damp locks. Let sit for fifteen minutes. For best results, cover hair with a shower cap. Then wash out the mayo (thoroughly!) with your regular shampoo.

Yolko Ono Shine: Take one egg yolk, whisk it with a fork, and add one teaspoon of water to the mixture. Apply to damp hair. Gently massage into your scalp. Be sure to wash out mixture with plenty of cool water.

Some head turners also swear by whole eggs. Take three, add one tablespoon of lemon juice, and mix in a blender. Comb eggy medley through clean damp hair and let sit for fifteen minutes in a towel. Rinse thoroughly. This will leave hair at its gossamer glossiest.

However, best not to use both eggs and mayonnaise on your hair at the same time lest you end up smelling like an egg salad sandwich.

Holy Moly Guacamole Deep Rx Repair: Expose damaged, chemically-treated strands to the wondrous properties of nutrient-rich avocado oil. It supplies

vitamins A, B, D, and E, and leaves hair feeling well loved. Rub two tablespoons of avocado oil in a circular motion into the scalp. Let oil seep in for five minutes. Then wash out and follow your normal hair cleansing routine.

Oktoberfest High Octane Volume: Combine beer and apple cider vinegar in equal parts. Apply to clean, damp tresses. Then rinse with water to expunge the beer scent. Soon you'll sport a nice thick head of hair.

With any home remedy, be ultra conservative about the proportions until you have found the ideal balance for your hair. Always remember that humans have five senses, and be sure you're not doing anything to enhance your look that will make everyone around you

An innocent pair of scissors turns into an instrument of hair torture in the wrong hands—yours. See a professional stylist.

faint at the smell of you. Beauty may be only skin deep, but oddball smells sometimes dig in considerably deeper.

Once your hair is in the richest condition of its life, it's time to give it a good cut.

THE FIRST CUT IS THE DEEPEST

Radical haircuts are for the depressed and those seeking a big change in their personal lives. But even if you're quitting your job,

Bald is a thousand times sexier than a comb-over that fools no one.

getting divorced, and moving to Timbuktu, never take matters into your own hands. Even professional stylists usually don't trim their own locks, and for good reason.

To get a great cut, first find a Hair Guru. Worship him. And then (*sigh*) dump him.

How do you find your very own Hair Guru? Simple. Ask friends with great coifs who they use. Supplement with Internet research. Then arrange a consultation before he lays a blade anywhere near your head.

Don't be afraid to sink a fortune into the project the first time. But once the Hair Guru has snipped your fringe in a manner befitting an artiste, ask if there might be a junior assistant on staff who could follow the Guru's lines for considerably less lucre. Always remember, imitation is the sincerest form of flattery (and the cheapest).

Or follow your lifelong ambition to become a hair model. What? You never aspired to this status? No worries. Your hair needn't look like Beyoncé's or Brad Pitt's to audition.

Research beauty and hair institutes in your area. Some need hair models (a.k.a. hair guinea pigs) on which their students can

experiment and will provide salon services ultra cheaply (or even for free).

But beware, agreeing to a cut means you are willing to give the stylist full *shear control*, and while hair always grows back, sometimes that doesn't happen quite as fast as we might like.

TO COLOR OR NOT: THAT IS THE QUESTION

MEN

Every week, there's another article about how more men are dying their hair. The prevailing wisdom

suggests that these gents are doing it to compete with younger guys in a tough job market.

Personally, I advocate against men trying to fight Mother Nature on this one. I believe that most men color their hair so poorly that they are likely to stand out at job interviews—but not in the way that the guys intend.

Even top-notch hairdressers at premiere salons haven't mastered the art of making dyed hair on women look completely natural. Most color specialists have fewer male customers than female, and thus lack expertise in the art of male camouflage. While the population as a whole has acclimated to seeing women of all ages sporting dyed locks, men with dyed plumage are sometimes still viewed as strange birds.

Done poorly, the dyed effect can be strangely off-putting, making a healthy man in his early fifties look like he's sickly, old beyond his years, vain, and wearing a bad toupee. These attributes are unlikely to help older gentlemen trounce their younger competitors in any sort of job-hunting joust.

If you're a man who insists on tinting your own hair (or having it dyed at a salon), at least have the self-knowledge to keep your temples gray. The effect will look more natural (and draw less pejorative commentary).

WOMEN

Most women over a certain age color their hair, and the habit is starting earlier than ever. Girls of ten or eleven now routinely dye their hair to express themselves; the youngest age of entry used to be sixteen or seventeen. But at the other end of the age spectrum, some intrepid ladies are choosing to kick the habit.

Stroll down the streets of New York, Chicago, Boston, San Francisco, or Seattle, and you can't help but notice that, these days, more and more women are embracing the power of pewter. There's a silver fox on every corner.[8]

It's a trend supported by a seismic shift at the workplace where women are no longer in the

minority. Add to that an economy that has made everyone question her discretionary spending, and suddenly, gray is looking rather fetching—at least on some.

More magazine claims that gray matters dominate its blogs and reader discussion sites. GQ magazine trumpets "Gray is the new black." *Oprah* magazine dedicated a whole issue to the movement that's only grown stronger with Lady Gaga's appearance on the September 2010 cover of *Vanity Fair* sporting gunmetal locks. People went gaga over her new look.

You can gray gracefully or, in the words of the old Oil of Olay commercial, "fight it every step of the way." But if you opt for gray, alas, it won't save you much green—at least not in the short term. Contrary to urban legend, going gray does not mean "zero maintenance."

THE PROBLEM WITH GRAY

"You're only 30 percent gray," your colorist chirps like a bird forecasting the coming of a new season (winter), "You've got absolutely nothing to worry about."

But each time you pay her a visit, you're grayer than the time before—necessitating, at first, highlights, followed by single process color—then it's both—at greater and greater frequency. Help!

Eventually, unless money is no object, you are bound to ask yourself:

"What would happen if I went over to the gray side? Wouldn't I be free of this monthly drain on my finances, free of my hairdresser and her sing-songy voice, free, free, free at last?"

The answer is "sort of." But probably not for a long spell.

Women who let their hair go into neutral face five challenges. The first is blending: how the new steely hair integrates with the older original hair. Gray hair tends to grow in either very rough or super fine. Gray also sometimes sprouts in patches, lending a streaky or skunk-like appearance to otherwise lustrous locks.

The second challenge is the yellowing of gray hair, and not in a blonde way! Gray hair has considerably less natural oil than pigmented strands and doesn't always hold its gray hue.

The third challenge is coping with the surreal lack of self-recognition. Suppose that you've always thought of yourself as a blonde bombshell, a dark-haired diva, or a ravishing redhead. Once you take your face out of a yellow, brown, or red frame, and substitute a silver- or ice-colored one, the whole equation changes. You peer into the mirror: A stranger stares back at you. Your eyes may appear considerably lighter or darker against the shock of gray hair. Your facial skin may look ruddier or conversely more washed out with a halo of slate around it, necessitating a full color reevaluation.

The fourth challenge is clothing. While many silver seniors say they feel happy and more authentic about themselves, most also admit that going gray instantly adds ten years. Ouch. Surely this requires a massive clothing trans-

Putting a gray frame around your face means you may have to use more makeup products than before to add back some color.

fusion. One's go-to wardrobe colors may look positively dowdy with the new "power gray" hair.

Last but not least is the psychological challenge. Today's silver foxes often feel as if they are part of a countercultural cult, in rebellion against a society that uniformly embraces a youth culture.

"Look young forever," television, print, and Internet ads bleat. Women who buck the trend may experience feelings of inferiority as others of their gender spurn them for not trying to look the youngest they can or feelings of invisibility if men ignore them for their younger-looking sisters.

THE GRAY SOLUTION

If going gray causes you to temporarily misplace your self-confidence, sometimes the only solution is to hit the bottle—the color bottle. You may need to dye your gray hair an intermediate shade to blend in better with your old hair while you're waiting for your whole head to catch up. Don't gloss over the importance of hair gloss. Adding it can help maintain a healthy color as gray hair some-

Consider adding a spot of color to gray hair with an accessory, such as a jazzy hair clip.

times looks like a gray cloud *without* a silver lining.

If some of your gray hair has faded to yellow, your colorist can add violet tones to your lowlights, which will neutralize the sickly pallor. You may also need to use a shampoo with a bluish-purplish tint especially formulated for ashen hair.

Many women who get "gray makeovers" use the change in hair color as a built-in excuse to radically alter their makeup. Don't shy away from change.

This is the moment to recalibrate your lipstick, eyeliner, eyebrow color, and blush. You may find that you need a greater variety of products. Finally, run a critical eye down the rest of you. This time, go find a full-length mirror. Assess your physique quadrant by quadrant. This may be just the impetus you need to treat yourself to a full body makeover.

Bribe your most elegant friend (or make an appointment with a personal shopper at a department store) and explain that—newsflash—you've just let your hair turn gray. You may need to dress in a hipper, more sophisticated, or more fashion-forward manner to coordinate with your brand-new hair color.

A silver fox.

Of all the challenges associated with graying, the psychological one is the hairiest. For, unfortunately, the stuff going on inside your head is even scarier than the mess going on outside of it.

Perhaps you always hated the construction workers' catcalls, but now find that *not* receiving them is even worse. Even other women look at you askance, wondering how you get away with modeling your real hair color while they're still dependent on their stylists' pigmented potions. To compensate for feelings of low self-esteem, some silver foxes use the transition to hit the health club to get in the best shape of their lives.

The Silver Lining

Once your hair is 100 percent gray, of course, you will save a fortune on maintenance. Unlike your dyed sisters, you won't need to have your roots touched up every four to eight weeks and your highlights relit every two to three months. You won't feel like a hostage to your colorist's sudden price hikes. You won't toss hundreds of dollars down your hairdresser's drain. You're free, free, free at last.

You might also feel more authentic about your age, which may benefit you in certain circles and hold you back in others. For example, if you're competing for a job against others who are roughly your age, going gray could make you look older. If having gray hair in your field translates into "wise and experienced," that could be a plus. If, conversely, you're competing against people who are half your age, going gray could be perceived as a negative.

In sum, letting your hair go au naturel is a personal decision, but more and more women are experimenting with it. Whatever you decide, you are not alone.

However, if reading about the travails of graying not-so-graycefully sends you flying to your colorist faster than you can scream, "Gray, gray, go away!" you'll need to find an ideal color for your skin tone. Complete the exercise below. Good luck.

Exercise: How to Arrive at Your Richest Hair Color

Studies show that men and women tend to see their own hair as several shades darker than it really is and their skin as several shades lighter than it really is. As a consequence, people's barometers for choosing their correct hair colors are way off.

Add to that the fact that at most salons the indoor lights bear no relation to natural light, and you might easily wonder why everyone is paying hundreds of dollars a pop to look worse, not better.

To recalibrate your hair color, first figure out whether your complexion is warm or cool. (This has nothing to do with your scintillating personality.)

Your skin has a "warm tone" if: you have golden, olive, or dark skin, and brown or dark eyes. Many persons of Latin, Asian, or African descent fall into this category.

Your skin has a "cool tone" if: you have fair skin and blue or green eyes, you burn before tanning, and the veins in your wrists run blue rather than green.

Warm skin tones look lovely with golden shades, such as caramel and bronze in a darker shade than your skin. Don't go too light, or your hair will turn orange. Avoid black, which will wash you out.

Cool skin tones look comely with ash blondes and cool browns.

Avoid colors such as gold, auburn, and copper, which will bring out your natural ruddiness.

If you were blonde as a kid, you can turn back the clock and be blonde again. (If you weren't, you still can but you'll need to consult with a stylist about which shade, and then most likely plan to experiment a bit until you arrive at "your perfect blonde.")

DO BLONDES REALLY HAVE MORE FUN?

A survey by Clairol in 2007 found that 32 percent of respondents thought that the first female president would be blonde while 31 percent thought she would be brunette. (However, it's possible that Hillary Clinton's disappointing election bid in 2008 may forever skew the results going forward.)

In the same survey, 76 percent of women said brunette was best for making a good impression on a job interview. Blonde came in a distant second (12 percent) and red, absolute last (3 percent).[9]

Of course, it all depends on the job for which one is applying.

My friend Kathy, a stunningly groomed brunette and a beauty copywriter by day, says, "The majority of successful men and male celebrities marry blondes or women who dye their hair blonde."

She attributes it to the fact that "men are easily fooled, due to their visual natures. Fake breasts, fake blonde hair . . . doesn't matter."

Kathy attended the pre-game parade of the 2010 MLB All-Star Game where she noticed that "something like 98 percent of the players had blonde wives." Considering that only 2 percent of the population is actually born with blonde hair, that's one staggering baseball statistic.

"I just think blondes attract more attention," she hypothesizes.

While Kathy never experimented with a Marilyn Monroe mane, she did perm her hair once, which apparently led to "disastrous results."

"My husband left me and moved to Colorado," she says, "maybe not as a direct result of the hair, but it didn't help!"

These days, Kathy is happily married to someone more hair-worthy: a military man who adores her sleek Katharine Hepburn looks. However, even *he* got excited when Kathy, trying out a new hair color on the job, allowed the test salon at her company to add golden streaks to her chocolate locks.

"Men like different looks, and my husband liked the differentness of it," she admits with a laugh. "He thought it made me look younger, but he was wrong."

WHY EVEN JENNIFER ANISTON DOESN'T HAVE JENNIFER ANISTON HAIR

Friends don't let friends ask for Jennifer Aniston–colored hair. Any study of *InStyle* over the years reveals that Jennifer Aniston has experimented with numerous shades of honey, brunette, and strawberry blonde. Hence, asking for "Jennifer Aniston hair" doesn't mean anything. Your hair stylist knows this because five hundred other clients have asked her for

Jennifer Aniston hair. Your hair-stylist just isn't going to tell you.

When it's time to camouflage your gray locks, force yourself to kick the magazine habit. Instead, ask your stylist to show you sample hair strands dyed in the color of your choice. The problem with magazine shots is that every model in them has a battalion of retouchers. The models' hair, skin, and eye color have all been digitally corrected, adjusted, and enhanced. As a consequence, you haven't the slightest clue what the person's real coloring looks like, so it's impossible to compare it to your own.

Queen Nefertiti. (CREDIT: VLADIMIR WRANGEL/SHUTTERSTOCK.COM)

THE WORLD'S FIRST HAIR DYE (PROBABLY BRUNETTE) CAN BE TRACED BACK TO ROYALTY IN ANCIENT EGYPT

Hair tincture has been part of looking aristocratic for the past thirty-three centuries.

Egyptian queen Nefertiti (ca. 1370 BC.–ca. 1330 BC), renowned for her outstanding beauty, was a trendsetter. To this day, she is still considered by some to be "the most beautiful woman in the world." Pretty high praise if you can get it.

Nevertheless, the stunning Nefertiti had some serious competition, as hubby Amenhotep IV also had two other wives. No doubt Nefertiti experimented with henna when her long dark locks first started turning gray.

Back in the day, the Egyptians had hand mirrors, much like the ones we have today. Being wealthy, Nefertiti also had plenty of hand maidens to hold up the hand mirrors to her scalp while she was bathing. She probably spotted a few gray hairs, panicked that she'd fall out of favor as wife number one, and asked her maidens to apply henna to her hair.

Tragically, Nefertiti later *did* fall out of favor as wife number one and went missing for several years while Amenhotep had a child with wife number two!

Don't let that sorry fact stop you from experimenting with henna if you have naturally brown or auburn hair.

ON HAIR LUXE WITHOUT THE BUCKS

In conclusion, to find your most luxuriant hair look without going into bankruptcy, follow these tips:

1. Never force your hair to fight against itself. Learn to live with your hair's natural texture and simply resolve to put it in the best condition possible through cheap but proven home remedies.

2. Spend a lot of money on the first cut. Don't scrimp. Invest in a Hair Guru, but later have his masterwork copied by his junior assistant or a hair student.

3. Men, never say "dye." If you choose to ignore this advice, at least let your temples gray naturally.

4. Women, you can't go gray cold turkey. Don't expect big savings to accrue by going au naturel. For the first few years, the money you save on touchups will be reabsorbed on other costly items such as makeup, clothing, and possibly, psychotherapy.

5. To find your ideal hair shade, take a good, close look at your skin color. Don't follow magazine shots. Instead, ask to look at dyed hair strands.

6. Hair coloring has been part of female beautification for over 3,000 years. With these tips, hopefully it won't take quite that long to find the perfect condition, cut, and color for your hair.

CHAPTER EIGHT

DEVELOP AN OBSCURE HOBBY

Your friend Hadley says that it's "as easy to fall in love with a rich person as a poor person." You wonder if this is just another one of those myths that sounds vaguely promising but is patently false.

Today, at a get-together with one thousand former classmates—most of them exceedingly well turned out—you find little to chat about with any of them. Forget love. There's not even a basis for friendship here.

To be fair, you could have done some homework before trek-king all the way up to the wilds of New Hampshire. You could have reviewed the Pig Book to refresh your memory on people's names after all of this time. You could have dug even deeper by looking up some of your old friends on Facebook or LinkedIn or Instagram.

Coulda. Woulda. Shoulda. But didn't, didn't, didn't. Stupid. Stupid. Stupid!

Now you find yourself paddling through a sea of barely recognizable faces at your college reunion, struggling to recall whether someone used to be a dorm mate, a study mate from Political Theory 101, or one of your former roommate's numerous conquests.

Each time someone shouts out a jovial "Hello!" you have a panic attack. First, you squint at the name on the white badge dangling from a fifteen-inch long,

skinny, green silk cord around his neck. Then, quickly (and hopefully before the person registers that you've forgotten his name), you jerk up your head to eye level, and try to manage a semi-sincere smile, as if to say, "There you are! And boy, have I wondered about you all of these years!"

Adding to the awkwardness is the fact that everyone who showed up today seems to remember who you are perfectly. Perhaps your harrowing job, recent grapefruit juice fast, and studious avoidance of your building's landlord these many months hasn't beaten quite as much life out of you as you had feared.

"Have you been skiing lately?" a former classmate asks.

"I haven't been doing anything lately," you say, furtively eyeing his name badge. Aha! His name is "Claude." Your eyes quickly race up to his face. You don't know Claude from Adam.

"Because," he says, a distant look swimming into his gray eyes, "I remember how you used to love cross-country."

"I'm afraid my life's been all downhill ever since," you joke.

"So what *do* you do for fun?" he asks, cracking a wan smile at your lame attempt at humor.

"Well, I work a lot."

"Been working hard too."

Silence. Silence. More silence. Thunderous silence. Whoever coined the phrase "Silence is golden" never suffered a college reunion. Finally, just to break the silence, you say:

"Oh, and I recently tossed a boomerang."

"Wow! I tried that once," Claude says, "and it conked me in the head by accident."

"The same thing almost happened to me," you say.

"Did I hear you two talking about boomerang throwing?" a reunion chair named Rich interjects. "It's deceptively hard."

"You need a strong arm," class president Sally says, coming over to join the conversation.

"And the ability to duck," adds class vice president Steve.

And quite suddenly, just like that, you are surrounded by a large crowd of class leaders, all chatting about the joys and catastrophes of boomerang throwing!

"Have you met anyone yet?" your friend Hadley texts.

"No," you text back, "but when I get home, I'm going to take up boomerang throwing for real, this time."

Who knew that boomerang throwing would be such a crowd pleaser?

Where the rich unwind from life's stresses: Provence.

HOW TO WIN INFLUENTIAL FRIENDS: DEVELOP A HOBBY

F. Scott Fitzgerald once observed, "The rich are different than you and I." One way they are is that no matter how busy they get, they always have more than enough time to pursue a hobby.

An interest in horseback riding inevitably leads to owning a stable. A passion for French wine ultimately results in a country house in Provence with a world-class wine cellar. A passing fancy for natural wildlife can't be nurtured without the once-in-a-lifetime safari through Africa.

You can't afford to indulge in those pastimes, but with some pluck, you can develop one that will generate grudging respect among the elite, anyway.

Make time in your life for an avocation, and pursue it with zeal.

Cultivating a hobby is a superb way to mingle with the great and the near great, whether your interest in the smart set is primarily professional or recreational.

THE COURT CONNECTION

Many of today's most popular hobbies started thousands of years ago in ancient courts where aristocrats had nothing but time on their hands. No one had to work for a living so nobles could idle away their days, perfecting their pastimes. The great news is that with a couple of notable exceptions, many of the recreations that stretch back the longest are the cheapest to pursue right now. And if you join a club to enhance your playing level, you'll schmooze with the very people who you aspire to befriend.

The Game of Bridge: Your Bridge to a Lustrous Past and Some Valuable New Contacts

According to an ancient Chinese dictionary, the first playing cards appeared in AD 1120 during the reign of Seun-Ho.[10] Royalty, the first devotees of these cards, used them to gamble and divine the future. But even professional card readers couldn't have foreseen how beloved the game of bridge would become.

Fast-forward six hundred years. A game called whist, the pre-cursor of today's contract bridge, became trendy among the upper classes, and a lawyer named Edmond Hoyle became a whist tutor to members of high society.

By the 1920s, bridge surpassed whist as the darling of privileged intellects. Because it's a game of skill that relies on the powers of deductive reasoning, it's some-times called a "mind-sport."

Take up this passion and you'll be in heady company. Warren Buffet and Bill Gates both play. Malcolm Forbes, Dwight Eisenhower, and Winston Churchill were also avid bridge players.

"Bridge is a great way to learn from inferences," famously claims the Oracle of Omaha (who turned some of his inferences into billions of dollars). "A lot of decisions in life are made from inferring from what you know."[11]

Furthermore, belying bridge's snooty reputation, older blue bloods will be ecstatic to have you as their fourth, especially as bridge is beyond "out" these days. Take advantage of the game's recent dip in popularity and learn how to play by joining a local bridge club before young blue bloods rush in to supplant you at the table.

People have gathered over lively games of mahjong for centuries.

Membership in the American Contract Bridge League costs less than $40 a year and can help you make a bridge to all sorts of worthwhile connections.

The negatives? Pick up the bidding conventions too slowly, and everyone seated at the table will consider you a dummy (and not the kind that sits silently as the declarer masterfully plays both hands). No one, repeat, *no one* will let you be their fourth.

LOOKING FOR LOVE? MASTER THE ART OF WAR

Anyone who has ever fallen in love is no stranger to the games that often precede the state of bliss. But finding a suitable catch when you're not of the class also takes strategy. If you're female and smart as a whip, consider learning how to play chess. It has a noble heritage and it takes eons to master the game—two important considerations for any hobby worth pursuing.

Chess originated from the two-player Indian war game known as *Chatarung*, which dates back to 600 BC. Four centuries later, Persian traders introduced the game to Western civilization. Originally, the piece next to the King was called the *ferz* in Persian, defined as a "male counselor to the King."

But the ferz went to Europe for a sex-change operation and was transformed into a Queen. Yet, intriguingly, she had no power. She was the weakest piece on the board. The Bishop also had limited mobility. With the King, Queen, and Bishop all doddering, the pace of the game crawled, and even checkmate could feel anticlimactic.

By the late 1600s, the rules had changed dramatically, and the Queen morphed into the strongest piece on the board while the Bishop became a long-range piece that moved with alacrity and force.

In spite of the Queen's rise to power, chess today is still an all-male game. The U.S. Chess Federation claims that 95–97 percent of its members are male. For females interested in this sport of kings, this could provide a real opportunity to break into a club where the boys are not protected by their minions, locate a prince who doesn't yet have a queen, and get invited to his castle. (In chess, it's always a good idea to plot a few moves ahead.) Joining the U.S. Chess Federation costs less than $50 a year, or less than two speed dating events.[12]

But full disclosure here: In addition to the mega time commitment (aficionados sometimes say that it takes *several lifetimes* to master the game), it really helps if you're a genius.

That's right, women, being egg-headed is a plus. Having an IQ on par with Einstein's or Kasparov's is a Darwinian advantage when it comes to (check) mating.

GAMES MILLIONAIRES PLAY

Contract bridge and chess both share an aristocratic bloodline. However, they're both sedentary, and eventually you will need to stretch your muscles.

When you do, you may want to reconsider some of the seemingly obvious ways of befriending today's business barons, such as mastering a gentlemanly game of country club tennis or learning how to ride a horse. Today's aristocrats are less likely to hang out at the same courts and stables as you since many of them have their *own* courts and stables. You could squander a fortune on court and riding fees and never talk to anyone well off. Life is so unfair!

Instead, look for sports that either cost no money or, if they do, at least lure

Among the landed gentry, familiarity with horseback riding starts young.

your target to the same spot where you'll be. Skiing is pricey, but even the rich aren't rich enough to have a ski slope in their own backyard.

However, when it comes to mingling with taut titans, skiing can be a slippery slope. Assuming that you can afford the extravagant ski trip and the exorbitant equipment, not to mention the costly lift tickets, you always have to steer clear of the family side of skiing. Stick to the singles lines at the lift and try to engage with someone during the ride. Don't wait to connect at the teeming après-ski bars, which can be noisy and distracting. (Warning: Never try to tutor a snow slider of lesser proficiency, lest you put your friendship on a downhill slope

before it's had a proper chance to lift off.)

OBSCURE SPORTS

Boomerang throwing dates back to King Tut. Apparently, he was an avid collector, and numerous boomerangs were found in his tomb.

Before you say, "Tut, tut," to this ancient pastime, consider its pluses.

You don't need to understand why the boomerang returns to be a phenomenal thrower (although once you begin tossing around a boomerang, your interest in physics will increase exponentially). Just know that for such a well-balanced object, the numbers are gorgeously lopsided if you're a woman. Like chess, boomerang throwing today gears almost exclusively male. Go for it, ladies. According to the U.S. Boomerang

Long before the Australians started tossing a boomerang, King Tut did. What a trendsetter!

Association, today there are hundreds of thousands of boomerang throwers, including competitive athletes, recreational throwers, master woodcarvers, casual woodworkers, aeronautical engineers, high school science teachers, artists, and anthropologists. It's a heady, artsy, sciencey, athletically fit group to hang out with, and it's so easy to be embraced by this community.

The cost of entry is nominal: one boomerang, plus a couple of lessons in boomerang throwing. Yet you can find scores of new friends (plus some previously undiscovered arm muscles) with this outdoorsy hobby that's fun to talk about. Of course with boomerang throwing, you would expect the return to be excellent.

The downside? Ample open space is a requirement, so the sport may not acclimate to the culture of certain cities. Plus it's easy to conk yourself in the head by mistake.[13]

COLLECTIONS AND OTHER ARMCHAIR HOBBIES

What if you were the type of person who finagled out of gym class in grade school? What if you never had an athletic bone in your body and still don't? What if you come down with a cold just thinking about tossing a boomerang outdoors? Is there any hope for you?

Oh, be still. There's another easy entrée into the club: You can become a collector.

Collecting has all of the positives of other hobbies and none of the negatives. You don't have to be a genius on par with Kasparov to understand it. You don't have to be a master communicator the way that you need to be with bridge. You don't have to own a horse or keep your skiing prowess bottled up for fear of leaving a few fragile egos behind in the powder.

Best of all, you'd have to be the world's most incredible klutz to conk yourself in the head with a collectible. Most collectibles are ultra safe.

To get started, simply choose the object of your affection. Pez dispensers. Perfume bottles. Cowboy boots. Stamps. Dr. Who paraphernalia. Coca-Cola memorabilia. Antiquities. Autographs. Hats. Hammers. Harley-Davidson motorcycle jackets. Coins.

Quilts. Depression glass. Fourteenth-century looms. The beauty of being a collector is that it auto-

matically makes you an expert—a curator of the curiosities that pique your interest. The learning curve is smooth and natural. It's almost impossible to fail at it. Every collector is a genius when it comes to his or her own collection.

Take those Pez dispensers. Did you know that Bullwinkle Pez Dispensers from the early sixties are worth between $250 and $399 and that one with a brown stem is harder to find than one with a yellow stem? That buttons on clothing used to be jewels made in sets that were attached and removed each time the garment was worn? That Depression glass, which is now a hot collectible, used to be given away for free at movie theaters and at gasoline stations? You'd know all

of these tantalizing tidbits and more if you were a collector.

Collecting automatically brings you into contact with other like-minded individuals so you can bond over your interest. You don't have to join an association, so all of the money that you've set aside for the hobby goes directly towards your collection. Yet make no mistake, you are part of an exclusive club. You can mingle with enthusiasts at fairs, yard sales, stores, shows, auctions, and even virtually, via Facebook groups and fan pages, Twitter, LinkedIn, and the trading pages of eBay. You can post pictures of your collection on Pinterest so enthusiasts can find you.

Most collectors are passionate about their subject and are keen to trade stories about it along with actual items. Your common bond is like a well from which you can always go back and drink. Conversation will never run dry.

Start first by amassing what you love. Should you ever need to sell, chances are strong that someone will shell out a lot of money to relieve you of your prized possessions. But in the interim, while you're busy selecting your chosen pieces, you'll find plenty of devotees of the very items you love to collect.

★★★

A shared hobby is a great democratizing force. All of your prospect's advantages—his or her superior station, upbringing, estate, glorified title, major stockholder status, numerous board positions, and independent wealth—will simply vanish before the successful completion of the task at hand.

Will you bid and make your bridge contract while your prospect and his partner watch (and squirm) helplessly? Will you succeed in forcing checkmate upon your opponent's unguarded King?

Will you trounce him in a competitive game of tennis? Or reach the bottom of that icy ski slope faster than she?

Do your boomerangs actually come back? Does your collection of George Washington memorabilia leave hers in the dust?

Or will it be the other way around?

When you compete, bond, and enjoy each other's companionship in a place where you both start out as equals, the divisions of class disappear, and real friendship has a chance to take root.

SOME POPULAR HOBBIES AND WHETHER OR NOT TO PURSUE THEM

Like dogs and spouses, hobbies keep people alive. Pursue a hobby with vigor and you might inadvertently stumble on a second career, or even a third or a fourth one. There are thousands of recreations. I have taken merely eleven and ranked them on one criterion alone: their ability to draw you into chichi circles. The lower the activity's ranking, the more likely you are to meet toffs while doing it.

1 means likely;

3 means try it and see;

5 means unlikely;

8 means, "Honey, you can do better."

I recognize that each person's experience will be unique, and that sometimes, it may take only one new friend to usher you into a whole new social set, which could seriously skew the ratings below. The following represents only my own opinion, and honest men and women can differ.

Hobby—Athletic	Ranking	Comments
Health Club	8	Unless you join a ritzy club located in a desirable zip code, the chances of making new friends while wiping sweat off the treadmill is remote.
Sailing	3	Country club fees are sky-high, docking charges can be prohibitive, and it costs a bundle to buy a boat, which will "pay you back" by requiring constant repairs. But if you can manage the fees, you will likely meet some well-to-do sailors.
Skiing	1	Pricey, if you view it as a way to spend a vacation but beyond reasonable if you look at it as an investment in meeting new friends on swanky slopes.
Tennis	8	Unless you're taking lessons because you're already friends with wealthy lobbers with their own courts. If so, the ranking catapults to 1.

Hobby—Outdoor Games	Ranking	Comments
Croquet	3	The U.S. Croquet Association has been trying to elevate this backyard game to a real sport, complete with heavier equipment, new rules, and beautifully manicured courses opening all across the country.
Hampton Classic (as a spectator sport)	2	Lift a Mint Julep with well-heeled white shoe WASPS in Southampton.

Hobby— Outdoor Games	Ranking	Comments
Skeet Shooting	3	Started in 1920 in Andover, Massachusetts, a small group of upland hunters began shooting clay targets as a way of practicing their wing shooting. The social quality of this sport makes it superb for holding charity fund-raisers around it.

Hobby— Classes & Random	Ranking	Comments
Cooking classes	5	Those who bake bread together will invite each other to their respective dinner parties. But is there anyone whose dough has already risen to great heights who's taking the class?
Writing classes	8	Writers are notoriously poor. Trust me on this.
Collecting	1	Ranking depends on which items you collect. George Washington memorabilia brings together an up-and-coming group intrigued by the Founding Fathers and scholarly research. Cowboy boot collectors are extraverted and tend to travel great distances in pursuit of artistically arresting boots.
Dogs (Owning one or more)	3	A beloved topic among the titled classes. Should you choose to breed or show dogs, the ranking rises to 1.

CHAPTER NINE

BLEND IN TO STAND OUT

You can tell by the subject line of the email that it's going to be horrific news and, sadly, your suspicions are confirmed. A former officemate's life has been abruptly cut short—a tragedy. The office will be closed tomorrow, and everyone on the team has been asked to attend the service as well as the family reception afterwards.

Your supervisor Mr. Bucks, who could double as a mannequin in a high-end clothing store, will be in attendance along with several of the company's most important clients. You know it would behoove you to dress the part.

With a heavy heart, a light wallet, and an impending feeling of dread, you head home during your lunch break in order to riffle through your closet and conduct a quick inventory check. Your mix 'n' match options are even worse than you had feared.

To be precise, you own:

1) Eighteen cotton plaid shirts in every color of the rainbow

2) One Armani suit (unfortunately not in a conservative color)

3) Six pairs of brand-new sweatpants (Odd, since you never work out.)

You know that black is the funereal color of choice but wonder if anyone at the church will notice that the only all-black item you own is a ski parka.

On the way back to the office, you loiter outside a ritzy department store and gaze longingly at the windows.

The mannequins just inside are dressed, head to toe, in black. Blame it on your wacky starvation diet or your stress level (high), but you swear that you can hear one of the mannequins calling out to you.

"Come inside! Come inside! We won't bite!"

Knowing that your landlord would not only murder you but brag about it if he ever saw you set foot inside this store, you lower your head to avoid detection. You shuffle through the revolving door into the fiery hell of clothing temptation.

The overly lit first floor smells like a mixture of potpourri, costly French perfume with hints of jasmine, plus a musky cologne that goes straight to your head like a shot of vodka.

Boy, you think, breathing in that heady aroma, *you could easily sink your life savings here.* It's a pity you don't have any.

One blissful hour later (after a silent prayer that your credit card won't be rejected) you plunk down half a month's salary on an elegant black suit. After all, if you don't dress up for other people's funerals, they won't dress up for yours.

Why Black Is the New Black

Considering that the only two sure things in life are death and taxes, you'd think we'd all be better equipped for events hosted by the Grim Reaper. Tragically, most of us aren't.

Here's one area where the wealthy few really are our best role models. Since so many of them started life with giant inheritances, it may be that familiarity with funereal rites starts in the crib. All the more reason to monitor these trust fund titans closely, and then do our best to emulate them.

When the power elite attends a funeral, the women wear black and the men wear charcoal or navy.

Nobody wears indigo or maroon, even though doing so carries the Emily Post stamp of approval.

Nobody strolls around a funeral swathed in *eggplant, chocolate*, or *olive*—or any other food-inspired color—even if technically, they could get away with it.

On these sad occasions, it's not considered good form to simply slide through in mourning attire that can barely pass inspection. Try to do right by the person whose life you are commemorating. Stick with the basic funereal palette.

What if you've "had your colors done" and know for a fact that you look positively ghastly in black? Can you get away with wearing a more skin-flattering shade, such as dark goldenrod? No, you can't.

But console yourself: Funerals are not like other events. You are *supposed* to look absolutely dreadful, so wearing black is eerily appropriate.

Think of yourself as a member of the chorus in a Greek tragedy because that's precisely how you're

Worn by members of the chorus, Greek masks created a sense of unity and conformity.

expected to look. And just like a member of a Greek chorus, you are supposed to quietly fade into the background, not stand out.

SITUATIONS WHERE YOU WANT TO BLEND IN

Consider it one of life's ironies: Many of the times when you most want to stand out are actually situations where a cleverer strategy is to blend in. And the way to do that is through your clothing, demeanor, and general concern for others.

Here are six situations where it's smarter to blend in than to draw attention to yourself:

1. Funerals
2. Weddings
3. Black-Tie events
4. Mondays through Fridays at the office
5. Country Clubs
6. Church or Temple

FUNERALS

Funeral-Appropriate Etiquette

The world's wealthiest folks trundle out the color black at the drop of a—well—of a person.

Black is the de rigueur color of choice for funerals. If you're a guy who wouldn't be caught dead in a black suit, so to speak, then wear charcoal, but keep the sartorial mood appropriately somber by accessorizing with a dark gray tie.

If you look like Death warmed over in dark colors and happen to be Jewish, take solace. At least you won't have to worry about seeing yourself during the mourning period. During shiva, the week-long period of grieving for closest of kin, all mirrors in the bereaved's home stay covered. One reason is so the mourners can avoid vanity during the period of bereavement and focus on their loved one rather than themselves.

Another way to fade into the background at a funeral is to not allow your cell phone, pager, iPhone, or iPad to ring, ping, click, tick, tock, vibrate, or otherwise make a nuisance of itself, thus demanding your instant attention like a small needy child.

Follow these simple guidelines, and funerals can sometimes present some interesting bonding opportunities and *Big Chill* moments—after the services are over, of course.

But don't be a networking ninja. Your business and personal life both need to take a backseat to the person whose life it is you are memorializing.

While you're busy trying to recede into the background, remember *not* to hand out business cards or write any big checks (unless you happen to be the chief mourner). Attempting to close business deals on the tabletop of someone's coffin is the height of tackiness.

Keep your decibel level dialed down to a low murmur. Act appropriately. Offer gentle condolences to the family members of the departed and a promise to any potential new business contacts you meet that you'll circle back to them a few days *after* the service. Then, simply make it a point to follow through.

One Get-Together I Was Happy I Missed

My good buddy Joanne called me a few months back to invite me to a "birthday party" for the mother of a mutual friend. It was eleven thirty on a Friday morning, and the party was to start in an hour.

"I know it's kind of last minute, but it's at the University Club," Joanne urged, in that persuasive way she has.

I feel great affection for my friend Joanne and generally welcome opportunities to spend time with her. Still, I demurred. If our mutual friend had really wanted me to attend his mother's party, I reasoned, he might have invited me. It's not as if he didn't have my address, phone number, email address, and Facebook address.

"He won't mind," Joanne pressed. "We'll have a great time. Oh, c'mon. Won't you please come with me?"

"I don't think so, Jo. Sorry."

"But we can hang out . . ." she wheedled plaintively.

As fate would have it, Joanne had completely misread the announcement.

In fact, the "party" was a memorial service commemorating our friend's mother's long and celebrated life, which was now, sadly, over.

But all was not lost. Joanne confessed her gaffe to everyone at the service, and apparently they found it endearing as, by coincidence, our friend's mom was blessed with buckets of joie de vivre. She would have *wanted* her last rites to feel more like a party than a funeral, they reasoned.

But just imagine how things *could* have turned out with a less understanding crowd.

As a general rule, you want to try to blend in at a somber event, not stand out. And wearing muted colors and not showing up behaving in a ludicrously ebullient manner is often the key.

THREE SHOPWORN CLICHÉS AND HOW TO AVOID THEM

1. "Is there anything I can do to help?"

Unless you're willing to foot the bill for the funeral service or the coffin, there's no way to follow through on this open-ended offer. Instead, make a specific suggestion such as, "Can I help you write the obituary?"

2. "It's all for the best."

It may or may not be, but saying that it *is* definitely positions you as unsympathetic. Instead, show that your heart is in the right place, by saying something thoughtful such as, "I'm so sorry for your loss."

3. "I know exactly how you feel."

Do you? Really? Are you an empath or a gifted psychic? Chances are, you have *no idea* how the mourner feels. With death often comes an element of shock, and even key mourners may be out of touch with their feelings. Instead, tell the bereaved that your "thoughts are with them" during this sad time.

WEDDINGS

The Good Guest

Weddings and funerals have something in common: You are *not* the focus of attention that day.

Large weddings bring together a giant cross section of humanity. An added benefit for singletons on the prowl: Most of the guests on both sides of the aisle are in a blissful, nuptial state of mind.

But to be a successful wedding networker, you have to behave yourself, which generally means having the good grace to blend into the background.

The bride is the center of attention for the whole day, and no one must be allowed to detract from her radiance. If she mandates that you wear a hideous bridesmaid gown, then her wish is your command.

If her husband-to-be has determined that puce is the theme color

for the groomsmen and you're one of the chosen ones, then you are honor-bound to wear the putrid shade—even if the color puce makes you puke.

And what if you aren't part of the wedding party but are just a lowly wedding guest?

In that case, your sartorial plumage needs to help you fit in without forcing all eyes to rivet upon you. As a wedding guest, your only job is to witness the nuptials and blend into the festive scenery.

In the spirit of receding into the background, try not to eat, drink, dance, flirt, or talk too much either.

Be polite and circulate. Be gracious to bores. (There are bound to be a few.) Don't be a pain in the butt about where you're seated, or spend one second worrying about why your host stranded you in Outer Siberia when all of your old buddies from college are at Table One. Table the catty talk about where you've been tabled. You're in the world's best place for meeting some new people no matter which table you're at because your charge is to get up after the meal and mingle.

BLACK-TIE EVENTS

How to Look Like a Million at a Cotillion

The story of *Cinderella* is a timeless classic, but if you're over the age of six, it's time to let it go—hopefully before the stroke of midnight tonight. After all, you don't want

"The little black dress will become a sort of uniform for all women of taste."
—Vogue prediction, 1926

to be mistaken for a bumpkin in a pumpkin.

At most black-tie events, being the belle of the ball in the way that Cinderella was, is actually a poor networking strategy. You don't want to make any flamboyant entrances or exits, such as leaving the venue via a grand carriage (or in a humongous stretch limo).

While on the premises, you simply want to look like you belong. And how do you accomplish that, you may wonder? By observing what the Inner Circle wears and how it behaves, and following suit.

What does the aristocracy wear to a black-tie event? Black, of course, even though *everyone* in the room, from themselves to their spouses to the service staff, is bedecked in black.

There is a beauty to black that transcends all class levels.

As Coco Chanel once said, "Women think about all colors except the absence of color. I have said that black has it all."

Men have no choice. They must wear black tie, which means a black tuxedo with ribbed silk facings (usually grosgrain) on a shawled collar or peaked lapel, trousers with a single silk or satin

Pea green is a fitting color for an exotic tropical drink, not for tuxedo wear.

braid covering the outer seams, a low-cut waistcoat or cummerbund, a white dress shirt with a turn-down or detachable wing collar, a black ribbed silk bow tie, shirt studs, cufflinks, black dress socks (made of silk or fine wool), black patent leather court shoes or patent leather oxfords.

Guys, *please* don't try to get too creative with your tuxedo attire. Light blue, orange, green, pink, or coral jackets are unacceptable under any circumstances, even in Floridian climates. Instead, confine the pastel colors to the tropical drinks you imbibe. And forgo any tuxedo garb that bears an uncanny resemblance to army fatigues. Here again, your only charge is to blend in seamlessly.

THE OFFICE

What We Can Learn from *Rhinoceros* about the Dress Code

In Eugène Ionesco's brilliant play *Rhinoceros*, the inhabitants of a small provincial French town turn into rhinoceroses, with just one fellow named Bérenger as the lone holdout against the mass metamorphosis. Purportedly a play about the response to the sudden upsurge of communism, I think it works almost as well as a simple fable about peer pressure. When the pressure is on to look buttoned-up, it's usually easier to follow the herd. Consider: Corporate America didn't get to where it is by looking funky.

To wit, every company has a uniform. If you want to get ahead, you really have no choice but to wear the outfit. It's one of the cardinal rules of playing the game (and excelling at it).

The dress code varies widely from company to company. At some business establishments, the wardrobe is a two- or three-piece suit; at others, it's a jacket and tie; at still others, it's khakis and plaid shirts. At some companies, the full regalia might be relaxed on Fridays. But whatever the requirement is, you are duty-bound to follow or risk censure. For if you pull a Bérenger move and try to buck the trend, your boss will either resent you ("Why does she get to express herself? She's just a peon."); sabotage you ("I'm not sure if I can trust him to entertain our clients."); envy you ("How come her plaid shirt looks so much more expensive than mine?"); or secretly worry that maybe you ARE a rhinoceros! Helpful career tip: These are not the emotions that you want to rouse in your boss.

If you don't adhere to the dress code, you'll never blend in. You won't be considered a team player and you'll never get ahead. You'll just be a rebel *with* a cause—unemployment.

In today's modern workplace, blending in is a much smarter strategy than standing out.

Wear the most expensive and most conservatively cut suit that

you can afford. For men, the crucial items are the jacket and pants. For added stature, you might try sporting a vest once in a while but only if the fabric is an exact match.

In the for-profit world, clothes should look like they cost money. Don't try to affect a professorial image by wearing a suede vest or by showing up in a vintage suit. Other statements to avoid: the slumming-in-Beverly-Hills look, as expressed through hoodies; the-family-lost-all-of-its-money look, as illustrated by tattered cuffs; the spent-some-time-in-prison look, as demonstrated by wearing low-riders or any pants that expose a "crack" in your polished veneer.

Are you calling on a client today? Give yourself the once-over. Pretend that you are Sherlock Holmes and inspect your clothing for any clues that you appear downtrodden. Take out a magnifying glass and check to make sure there are no frays around the hems and cuffs, no beginnings of holes in the elbows, no shine on the fabric that wasn't there to begin with, and no stray pet hairs anywhere.

Women, in lieu of a suit, you can sometimes get away with wearing a jacket and skirt or pants in coordinating fabrics, but your outfits must be put together with flair. Find a personal shopper at a department store whose judgment you trust and follow her advice to the button.

If money is an issue (and when isn't it?), then follow the 80/20 rule. That is, spend 80 percent of your money on any item you wear above your waist and 20 percent of your money on any item you wear below it. Most people's eyes are drawn to clothing that's worn at eye level or higher. Jackets and tops stand out more than skirts or pants.

If you are strapped for cash, invest all of the money you have in one perfectly tailored jacket, and you can probably get away with wearing the same pair of pants with it every single day for weeks on end (as long as the slacks are dark enough).

And what if you own a nice suit but can't swing the hefty dry cleaning bills? In that case, experiment with the "poor man's dry cleaner's," otherwise known as your shower.

Hang your jacket on one hanger, taking care to fasten all buttons. Then drape your trousers upside down on a pants hanger. Place both garments *as far away* from your shower nozzle as possible, as you don't want to get them thoroughly soaked, just steamed. (Hopefully, there's a towel rack conveniently located in your bathroom.)

Turn on the hot water to "scalding" to create steam heat, pulling the shower curtain tight to prevent any water from spraying on your clothes. Then close the door for approximately ten minutes. Once the wrinkles have disappeared, let your clothes breathe for a few minutes until they no longer feel damp to the touch.

Voila! Steamed and dry-cleaned, you're now ready to take on the client machine.

COUNTRY CLUBS

Tennis Whites

The tennis court is not the place to express your sartorial individuality. Not when there are entire committees at country clubs devoted to momentous decisions, such as the "percentage of white" clothing allowed on the tennis courts.

At some clubs, the percentage is 80 percent white. At others, it may be more or it may be less. Why risk an infraction? Just wear 100 percent white—or better yet, ask your host in advance about any clothing requirements on the tennis court, golf links, or poolside. If you're still unsure, call the club in advance to double-check their rules and regulations.

Never trust Google when it comes to scouting out a club's

dress code. Call the club directly and ask to speak to someone in the manager's office. The rules can be very specific and the staff won't think twice about enforcing them. (On the scale of 1–10, the embarrassment factor is at least a 15, if *you're* the one who's in violation.)

Take the innocent baseball cap, for example. At some clubs, the "cap must be worn with the bill facing forward." Other clubs have strict rules about where hats can and can't be worn.

You might be allowed to wear a hat on the patio for lunch but have to remove it in the dining area. (Hint: It's good idea to have the chat about the hat *before* you're being dragged out of the dining room by your ear for disrespecting the dress code.)

If there is a chance that your day will extend into night, don't forget to investigate the dining room dress rules. Ask if the dress code is "jacket and tie" (if you're a man) and what attire is specifically not permitted (if you're a woman).

Getting invited back to someone else's country club (or ultimately being allowed to join it) is really an exercise that's all about blending in.

What color tennis whites are you going to buy, again? Oh that's right—white!

CHURCH AND TEMPLE

Church Chic

Believe it or not, not everyone is in love with Match.com and the other Internet dating services. I know several people who attend church or temple as part of their dating strategy. Don't get me wrong: I have no doubt that they are there first and foremost to commune with the big guy upstairs. But while they're at it, they're thinking that their particular house of worship also draws a very nice crowd of attractive, affluent people.

Whether you're attending service to pray, or to eat, pray, and love, the best and only strategy is to blend in through both your clothing and demeanor, so you can "be one with" the rest of the congregation. However, due to certain recent changes in the dress code, it's not quite as easy as it once was to vanish into the whole.

In the old days, understanding the dress requirement was a snap—jacket and tie for men and a suit or nice dress for women.

But today, in an effort to tap into younger churchgoers' more casual lifestyles, some churches have relaxed their dress codes enough to make even Zen Buddhist sticklers say, "Oy vey!"

In some evangelical churches, for example, the traditional service has been supplanted by a rousing get-together in which the beloved hymns and organs have been replaced by loud Christian pop music, PowerPoint projections on immense screens, electric guitars, and a festive rock 'n' roll ambience. In these modern mega churches, where the pastor is likely wearing jeans and a shirt, there's no reason to dress more formally. You're strongly encouraged to come as you are, and if that includes sneakers, so be it.

However, in many Christian churches today—Protestant, Catholic, Orthodox—members still trundle out their "Sunday

"Sunday best" is no longer synonymous with "wear a ginormous hat." (CREDIT: CHIPPIX/ Shutterstock. COM.)

best," although what one wears on Sunday may not be all that discernible from outfits worn on Saturday or on any given Thursday.

Men have a choice: You can wear jackets and ties or shirts and slacks. Women have never enjoyed so much clothing freedom. Today, you can wear suits, dresses, skirts, or slacks. The possibilities are endless. Just make sure that you show the proper deference.

Don't flash the flesh. Tank tops of every stripe are frowned on as is any clothing that reveals too much cleavage. Skirts should be long enough to cover the subject matter. Err on the side of "matronly" rather than "sexy mama" even if it cramps your fashion sensibility. And unless your congregation is located in warm climate and specifically encourages them, never wear shorts.

TEMPLE THREADS

Whether you are deeply observant or attend services only intermittently always show respect in temple by your choice of clothing and general behavior. The *bodywear bylaws* are streamlined. Rule One: Jackets and ties for men; dresses or skirts for women. Rule Two: (for women only) Don't pull a Hillary—as in Clinton. Pantsuits for women are generally not worn to Conservative or Orthodox services, although a two-piece suit consisting of a jacket and skirt is always welcome.

Here, coverage is key. Items such as *yarmulkes* or *kippahs* (skullcaps) and *talliths* (prayer shawls) for men are usually available for visitors outside the door of the main sanctuary.

WE ARE FAMILY

Religious observance is a team effort. As Mahatma Gandhi said, "All humanity is one undivided and indivisible family." Nowhere is this more apparent or important than in a religious service. Blending in, through the collective singing of hymns and reading of prayers and adherence to the dress code, is always preferable to standing out.

Whatever the faith, the congregation acts as one during a service. For this reason, it's important to blend in. If you can join in a hymn, it's a pleasant way to participate. If you are in a temple and can follow the Hebrew (or the transliteration), then feel free to read it aloud with the rest of the participants.

Always follow the congregants' lead if you are unsure about the elements of a service; rise when they rise; sit when they sit. If you get lost during a service, ask a fellow worshipper to help you out. Better that than loudly flipping through the pages of the prayer book in a desperate attempt to catch up. As Garry Shandling once commanded, "No flipping!"

Don't leave the service for any reason (unless you feel violently ill or are coughing or sneezing so loudly that people in the front are turning around to glare at you). Try not to fidget or talk, lest you disrupt the prayers and meditations of the other worshippers.

After the service is the time to hobnob with other congregants. You may discover many leaders of your community attend your house of worship: political honchos, business tycoons, and other notables. There may be some promising study groups and other worthwhile affiliations you can find through your church or temple, not to mention singles groups, if dating is your intention.

Services are just the first step, so be sure that your decorum during them allows you to get to step two.

THE MORE CASH, THE LESS FLASH

When it comes to today's platinum plutocrats, the instinct to blend in runs deep. Think if it as a form of camouflage.

In the United States, most billionaires walk around freely, unencumbered by bodyguards or armored limousines. Most billionaires in this country never worry about being kidnapped for heavy-duty ransom money, as they might if they ambled around unprotected in other parts of the world.

Part of their freedom derives from the fact that America is one giant melting pot, with a substantial group of people who consider themselves middle class.

And part of their freedom derives from the fact that today's wealthiest individuals are experts at not drawing too much attention to themselves.

A member of the nouveau riche might don a humongous logo as a way of signaling her intention to break into the upper crust, but the tendency among those who have been part of the landed gentry for centuries is to eschew huge logos, baubles, and other flashy items. At a black-tie event, everyone dresses in black. At a religious service, everyone wears what all of the other congregants are wearing. And at a picnic on the beach, billionaires sport blue jeans, just like the rest of us. In this country, we are all equal, even when we aren't.

In conclusion, before you ever worry about standing out, strive to fit in. It's a great piece of wisdom to follow, not just for your wardrobe requirements but also for your conduct in general. Paris Hilton supposedly said, "Life is too short to blend in." Be sure to ignore her advice, and do the exact opposite.

CHAPTER TEN

SHAKE THE ACCENT, AND OTHER ELOCUTION TIPS

It accompanies you everywhere you go, yet you can never hear it. By now, you're so used to it that you're only dimly aware of its presence. And yet you suspect that your accent has cast a dark shadow on your prospects—both at the office and socially.

There must be something funny about the way you talk, but you have no idea what it is. And you're not expecting enlightenment anytime soon.

Take tonight for example. There you were at a posh charity party benefitting some V.I.C. (Very Important Cause). You did not spill anything on the one and only V.I.C. outfit you own. You did not slip on the polished hardwood floor of the V.I.C. ballroom en route to the spicy shrimp cocktail. You did not get any spinach dip stuck in your teeth.

(There was no spinach dip.) This time, you were fluent in your current events (although no one specifically asked you about them, go figure).

But as you doubled back to the bar to snag a martini, someone introduced you to a very prominent tax attorney—someone you wouldn't mind taking out to lunch sometime—especially if the meal could be written off as a business expense.

"Where did you grow up?" the lawyer asked, green eyes glinting at you through sexy tortoiseshell spectacles.

"Right here," you said.

"Really? In this ballroom?"

"Yes. I mean no," you corrected, sober as a judge. "I grew up in this town."

"Because you just don't sound like you come from around here."

Then your business-expense-to-be shuffled off in a most uninterested manner!

Thinking back on it later, you realize two salient points: (1) Everyone on the planet always asks you where you grew up, and (2) They never seem to believe you. Even though you grew up just around the corner.

What's up with that?

IS IT TIME FOR A VOICE MAKEOVER?

You can attend all the right schools. You can live in the toniest of neighborhoods. You can look preppier than a Brooks Brothers' mannequin. But your quest for status will fall flat on its face if no one can understand a word you're saying.

You want to blend in with the Inner Circle, and that's pretty hard to do when every muckety-muck in the universe is always asking you to repeat yourself because he didn't understand what you said the first time, or questioning where you grew up, or staring at you as if you'd dropped down from another planet, such as Texas.

The plain fact is if you want to hang out with the millionaire set, then you also need to *sound* like you belong. The ability to understand and be understood is key.

When it comes to communication, only you know how big a language barrier you face. Here's a quick self-diagnostic to help you decide if you should try to conquer the problem once and for all or if it's small enough to let it be. Simply answer "Yes" or "No" to the following questions:

1. Do your friends ever laugh at you when you're *not* trying to be funny?
2. Do coworkers ever imitate the way you speak when you're supposedly out of earshot?
3. Does everyone ask what country you're from, even though you grew up in the United States of America?
4. Do you use filler words, such as "like" and "you know"—you know, like all the time?
5. Do you secretly believe that George W. Bush's pronunciation of the word "nuclear" was correct?

If you answered "Yes" to at least two of these questions, you may be in need of a voice makeover. But the good news is you don't have to be a Trust Funder to afford it.

You can make a huge amount of progress on your own, and then only if need be, pay a voice coach at the end to polish off any pesky rough spots.

WHAT'S YOUR VOCAL TICK?

There are four main vocal issues that could prevent others from understanding what you are saying:

1. A foreign accent that makes you sound markedly different from those around you.
2. A regional dialect that makes you pronounce certain English words and phrases differently.
3. A region-specific vocabulary for certain go-to items and popular phrases.
4. A tendency to use a lot of filler words, imported from the San Fernando Valley or elsewhere.

CAN YOUR ACCENT PASS A POLYGRAPH TEST?

If you do have a foreign accent, you should be aware that a recent study conducted at the University of Chicago showed that many people perceive statements as "less truthful" when they are uttered by non-native speakers.

This is grotesquely unfair, especially since the difficulty that the listeners encounter is really a processing fluency issue on their part. But instead of deciding that the problem statements are simply harder to understand, they perceive them as less honest. Ouch.

As an unjust consequence, non-native speakers with an accent are considered less credible. Unfortunately, the credibility problem only worsens with the thickness of the accent.

The study concludes that "accent might reduce the credibility of non-native job seekers, eyewitnesses, reporters or news anchors."[14]

In short, if you have a heavy accent, it could hold you back in both your social life and your career. Fortunately, there are some relatively painless ways to shake the accent, that is, to minimize it if you are so inclined. You will probably not be able to erase it completely, but you can make it a lot milder.

The following suggestions will work whether you have an accent that's as thick as cream soda or if you have just a hint of an accent or a drawl.

Foreign Accent Reduction 101

The United States has often been described as "one big melting pot." Depending on where you grew up, your English could be spiced with an accent from the Old Country. If your family has moved from one region of the United States to another, you may even have a spoonful of a regional dialect on top of the original accent, and people may have difficulty comprehending you.

But it's easy to practice sounding neutral, and doing so needn't cost you a penny. That's because what's known as "non-accented American English" is also "Newscasters' English." Your TV is your tutor, and lessons are being given nightly on the national news.

Make it a habit to listen to your TV announcers. With few exceptions, newscasters have been trained to speak with what's sometimes referred to as a "neutral accent."

Repeat the news anchors' key phrases and practice the way they are spoken. Pay attention to pacing, but go slow. The slower you talk, the easier it will be to control your accent and adopt that of your news announcers. Once you train your tongue, so to speak, you will be able to utter the same phrases as these respected on-air personalities, considerably faster than before.

A side benefit: In addition to gradually lessening your dialect, you will gain credibility. Newscasters are reliable sources of information. The former anchor of the *CBS Evening News* Walter Cronkite was once called "the most trusted man in America."

In the United States, professional football isn't just a game. It's a special language.

Make it your mission to watch a lot of nightly news, but only mimic the news announcers, never the sports announcers. (Sorry, guys.) In the United States, professional sport is practically its *own* language, and you definitely don't need to shriek about tackles, blocks, and false starts; or layups, offensive fouls, and three-second violations; or corner kicks, yellow cards, and headers—not until you've mastered the more sober lexicon (and mellower pacing) of plain, old news stories. But stay optimistic. Once you've conquered the news, you can graduate to professional sports. And then you'll sound more American than ever.

MIMICRY

If you find it dull to imitate your TV newscaster, you can always rent or purchase movies instead and replay your favorite parts to imprint a particular actor's speech pattern in your mind. Just make sure that the star you're mimicking doesn't have an accent.

Australian-born actor Anthony LaPaglia supposedly lost his accent by taping the movie *Dog Day Afternoon* and watching it numerous times. He also recorded himself reading little pieces of it. According to an interview he gave on NPR, he'd repeat certain phrases over and over again each day—something he felt he needed to do in order to lessen his native pronunciation so he could secure American roles.[15]

When you study a performance in order to mimic the actor's speech, first notice what he's doing with his mouth, lips, and tongue. Also listen for pauses and phrasing along with which syllables are stressed. But after you've closely observed his actions numerous times, just relax and try to do your best impersonation of him.

One reason that mimicry often helps with accent reduction is because if you allow yourself to get into the "character" of the actor, your mouth, lips, and tongue may all slide into the correct positions, more or less automatically.

Experiment with mimicry and see if you can get it to work for you.

HOW TO ERASE A DRAWL

Do you have a drawl that sounds like it strolled straight out of a Tennessee Williams play? If you have longer vowel sounds, slower enunciation, and a tendency to drop some of your *r*'s and *t*'s, you might. Within the Southern States of America, there are many different dialects. And linguists, those friendly folks whose job it is to pay attention to such things as diphthongs, coronal stops, and postvocalic *r*'s, can trace some Southern dialects all the way back to Elizabethan English.

Your dialect has a proud lineage, so if you live in the South, it may be smart to hang on to your accent because those around you may respond better to hearing messages in their regional tongue.

But if you've moved up North or elsewhere in the United States, you may want to minimize your drawl so you'll blend in seamlessly with those around you.

Southern accents sound gracious and hospitable, but they may not advance your cause as well in the brisk, get-down-to-business northern part of the country.

To lessen a drawl, start by listening to as much accent-free speech as possible. If you grew up south of the Mason-Dixon line, tune in to radio stations from the Pacific Northwest and deliberately imitate the sound of the words. You can find these stations via the Internet if not on a local radio station.

Next, download recording software to your computer (or use an old-fashioned tape recorder) and record yourself reading a newspaper story or pages from a novel aloud. Be sure to take notes on your observations. There may be some things you hear that warrant

century, and it's high time to make peace with "how the other half" talks!

If you possibly can, videotape yourself having a conversation with some Northerners and play it back a few times (once your friends have left the room, of course). Do they talk faster than you? Do they clip their vowels? What other differences can you detect? Take notes on any discrepancies you hear between their speech patterns and yours so that

correction. Note: The way that you sound in a recording is the way your voice actually sounds to other people. Hearing *yourself* talk when you're in a conversation with others can be deceptive because your inner ear amplifies the soundtrack, which makes your voice sound more resonant than it really is.

As a next step, experiment with immersion. Surround yourself with friends from the North. Admit that "the war against Northern aggression" ended way back in the nineteenth

you can work on those areas.

Lastly, don't hesitate to croon about your struggle. Pick an artist you like whose lyrics are easy to understand and sing. Frank Sinatra is one performer whose catchy musical numbers are easy on the ears and tongue.

It's almost impossible to belt out "New York, New York" with a dialect, so be sure to sing the anthem as often as you can. In the shower. On street corners. In New York taxicabs. Get into the spirit.

Don't get discouraged. Partying with Northerners, crooning Sinatra, and watching plenty of American flicks will practically guarantee that you'll enjoy a rich, engaging social life while you work on minimizing that accent. And have no fear. With practice, most of the suggestions above will help lessen most accented speech in the continental United States— including Midwestern twangs, Midland dialects, Western drawls, and New York accents. The trick is to surround yourself with the very people whose speech you are trying to emulate.

REGION-SPECIFIC VOCABULARY

If you get teased about the way you articulate certain words and phrases, you can train yourself to alter your pronunciation. You may have to remind yourself to say "wash" instead of "warsh," "talk" instead of "tawk," and "car" instead of "caah," but change can happen. It's only a matter of dedication.

twang, noun. 1: a harsh ringing sound like that of a plucked banjo string; 2a: nasal speech or resonance; 2b: the characteristic speech of a region, locality, or group of people.

Keep a diary of the expressions that cause you the most trouble. Read them aloud five times a day. When you stumble on a figure of speech that makes you slip back into the old pattern, for example, the way the phrase "park your car" might for a Bostonian, slow down as you read aloud and consciously pronounce the more difficult sounds, such as *r*'s. Over-enunciate the problem sounds until saying them begins to feel more natural.

There are also certain words and idioms that are common to particular regions in the United States and which don't translate readily in other parts of the country. For example, in the South, the residents speak of "billfolds," "fixings," and "supper," whereas in the East, these items are more commonly referred to as "wallets," "ingredients," and "dinner." So when asking a mogul back East out to dinner, remember to actually use the word "dinner" so that he or she at least knows to which meal you are referring! And if that mogul is about to make you wildly wealthy by becoming your first big client, it's your "wallet" that's getting fat in the East, and a "billfold" if it's in the South.

VALLEY GIRLISMS

Unfortunately, Valley Girl–speak isn't confined to California's San Fernando Valley. And the affliction doesn't just strike young girls. Valley Girlisms have been heard thousands of miles away from California, and sadly, men and women of all ages are highly susceptible.

While this bizarre form of communication may have originated in the Valley, the language is highly contagious and should be viewed as a cross between a regional dialect, a foreign language, and a lethal virus. Like a foreign language, it can be incomprehensible to American ears when spoken at a high pitch and frequency. But like a virus, it sneaks into the system, spreads rapidly, and is difficult to kill. Once Valley Girl–speak has invaded your vocabulary, it proceeds to hijack certain words and phrases, and before you know it, you're saying "like"—like all the time—and even the outmoded "awesome" semi-occasionally.

Many Valley Girl victims attest that "the language went out of circulation in the late 1980s," but, like, that's totally impossible because these folks are still using it today. Like totally. They really are.

How can you tell if you've caught the Valley Girl bug? Do you think, "I'm like freaking out totally," is a sentence? If so, that could be a clue. Do you say, "Oh! My! God!" as both a positive exclamation and a negative one? That could be a sign. Adding the word "right?" at the end of each sentence is another giveaway. The rising popularity of one-word questions that ask the speaker to authenticate what he just said is proof that Valley Girl talk has not been stamped out. Really? Honestly? Seriously? Fer sure.

In the musical *My Fair Lady*, Professor Henry Higgins teaches a flower seller how to speak like an English noblewoman. Follow Eliza Dolittle's example and shed your linguistic tics. It's "like" and "you know" and other Valley Girl-isms that keep you in your place, not your wretched parents or profile on MySpace.

Here, the best and only cure is to ask an extremely forgiving friend to keep a meticulous log for you. Implore your buddy to jot down every single time you utter the word "like" or "um" or "er" in conversation (or what masquerades as such once Valley Girl–speak enters the picture). Recording yourself speaking can also work wonders, but only if you can bear to listen to yourself

as you play back the recording. Do not run out of the room!

Speaking in Valley Girlisms subtracts valuable IQ points. It just makes you sound dumb. Most American-born tycoons are smart enough to have shed it years ago. And if you desire to hang out with them, you should too.

The One Exceptional Accent that Disproves the Rule: British

Accent reduction can reap big rewards unless you're British. For some inexplicable reason, several centuries after America declared its independence from the Brits, most Americans still think English accents are beyond posh.

If you are British born and bred, you are probably better off *keeping* your native lilt and vocabulary—even if you think no one in America can possibly understand a word you are saying. It will only add to your allure. So by all means, continue to call elevators, "lifts," potato chips, "crisps," and the Atlantic Ocean, "the Pond." Don't fret if your British intonation doesn't sound terribly upscale. On American shores, no one will be able to tell the difference. (How-

ever, unless your name is Gwyneth Paltrow, never try to fake a British accent. Few Americans can get that cut-glass upper-class accent to sound legitimate, and botching it will make you sound like a fraud.)

NEWSCASTERS' ENGLISH

In the course of my research on this topic, I stumbled onto an accent-reduction website that claims that while the standard American English accent is considered the profes-

English lessons are given for free on your local TV station.

sional accent, it "does not exist naturally in the United States." I beg to differ. The "New York accent" has started to disappear from Manhattan, and it's being replaced by the non-accented Newscasters' English at every turn.

Some may think it's because so many out-of-towners have moved here, bringing their own accents with them, and demographically, there is some truth to that theory. But personally, I believe it's because Manhattan is by far the most expensive place to live in the United States. By and large, the working class has fled from Manhattan en masse. It can no longer afford to live here. And the New York accent departed with the mass exodus.

But the accent didn't travel far. It migrated to nearby territories, such as Staten Island, leaving Manhattan as a true island unto itself, where one hears Newscasters' English all day long.

At a recent networking event I attended, a passing acquaintance of mine felt that I would benefit enormously from meeting a good friend of his, a speech therapist. The woman claimed that she "could tell where anyone had grown up, just by the way they spoke." Yet, after a boast like that, she was unable to figure out that I had grown up in New York City. (It was perhaps the first and only time in my life that I considered that to be a major compliment.)

If I could teach myself how to sound like a newscaster, you probably can too if you're a native. And you don't even have to be best friends with Dan Rather.

However, if you want to accelerate the process, you can always call your local university for recommendations of a licensed speech therapist or an English as a second language (ESL) program.

Make a commitment to work on your accent, and put the promise in writing. Your vow can be just one simple sentence, such as "I will lose my accent by _____ (pick a date)." Then, let your friends know of your plan. Studies show that writing down goals helps people achieve their dreams faster.

Easing your accent will help others treat you with the gravitas you deserve. Instead of struggling to figure out what you are saying, they will be able to sit back and actually listen to your ideas. For when it comes to prospecting, good, clear communication skills never hurt anyone's prospects.

SOME STUMBLING BLOCKS

1. Vowels. The English language has many subtle vowel sounds, and the way they blend with consonants can vary from region to region. If you are a non-native speaker, buy a couple of English-as-a-second-language guides and study what's known as "minimal pairs." These are pairs of sounds that non-natives often confuse, such as "bad" and "bed" or "sheep" and "ship." Exaggerate the sounds until you can hear the difference.

2. Blended speech. Certain words in English always seem to run together. A good example of this is the phrase "Won't you," which may sound something like "Wonchoo." Other words may be blended in one region of the United States but not in another, such as the phrase "Y'all." Commonly believed to have originated in the Southern United States, the blended pronoun is also associated with African American Vernacular English and some dialects of the Western and Midwestern United States.

3. Beginnings and endings. Certain languages don't have an equivalent sound that correlates to one in English. In Spanish, there is no "y" sound that directly corresponds to the one found at the beginning of the word "yellow." Native French speakers may insert an "h" sound where there shouldn't be one, by saying, for example, "He's hat home," instead of "He's at home."

4. Change doesn't happen overnight. By most counts, the older you are, the harder it is to cast off your accent or dialect. But the same thing can be said about picking up any new skill, such as learning how to drive. Force yourself to depart from the familiar and surround yourself with friends who are native speakers. Making mistakes is part of the learning process, and only with tons of practice can you shake your accent or regional dialect for good.

CHAPTER ELEVEN

YOUR PERSONAL BRAND

*T*hank God it's not Friday. Thank God it's only Tuesday, you think, head bent to the ground, chin nestled into your wooly scarf, while you carve a steady beeline through all of the other workers marching to their offices on this wind-bitten morning. It's just shy of 9 AM.

If it *were* Friday, and you were facing another weekend without a plan in sight, you'd have to admit that, while you have mastered the twelve laws of material success, have amassed a $64 million dollar vocabulary in record time, and have learned to skimp on the items no one will notice, you are not "there" yet.

You have seven close friends now—admittedly that's a 250 percent improvement—all due to your huge social networking push, but you are still waiting with bated breath for the lavish invitations to red carpet affairs, openings, and galas.

A splash of Dunkin' Donuts coffee topples from the telltale white, pink, and orange cup onto your right hand, the slight burn reminding you that you have precisely two minutes and forty-seven seconds to negotiate the final stretch to your office—if there's a chance of sliding your butt into the black leatherette chair before your supervisor arrives.

You sprint the final eighth of a mile in your generic power sneakers, which you plan to change out of once you arrive in your cube. They're looking a bit ragtag around the edges, and you know that the slightest hint of sartorial seediness troubles your supervisor deeply.

But, unfortunately, Fate has other plans for you this morning,

and you bump headlong into Mr. Bucks as you both enter the building.

Dressed so immaculately that it wouldn't surprise you if he had personally commissioned Giorgio Armani himself to hand-tailor his suit, Mr. Bucks juggles a Starbucks grande latte and the *Wall Street Journal* in one hand and a Dunhill leather briefcase in the other. He wears soft black Gucci loafers, even though there are three feet of snow on the ground on this harsh, wintry morning.

You suppose that, at his exalted level, even costly Italian shoes might be considered disposable. He glances at your sneakers and purses his lips, as if to comment, but then shakes his head, thinking better of it.

You both nod your heads "Good morning," and scramble into the elevator, silently. He heads towards the "power control center"—the panel of buttons at the front of the cabin—while you slink towards the back. Mr. Bucks emerges at floor 14, the executive floor, while you continue onto floor 17, the final stop for back office types and nobodies with forgettable titles.

You and Mr. Bucks are so close, and yet so far.

WHAT'S IN A BRAND?

If you have dutifully followed some of the suggestions in the previous chapters and still feel like you're not cozying up to the great and the near great, it may be time to take a big step backwards and think about your personal brand.

For, just like Dunkin' Donuts and Starbucks, each of us has a "brand" that we broadcast to the outer world. And just like the big boys, our success (or lack thereof) often stems from the way we package ourselves, the consistency

of our "brand personality," and the number of opportunities we have to display it.

A chance encounter with a boss *is* one of those opportunities, even if no words are exchanged. (And if there aren't any, it might be wise to ask yourself why there aren't.)

A brand is a snapshot of the way other people see you. I like to think of it as two or three core adjectives that describe the image you portray.

Perhaps your brand is "spunky" and "hardworking," while your boss's brand is "smooth" and "eminently promotable."

But make no mistake, your personal brand needs to support your aspirations or you will never be entrusted to handle important clients or secure those large paychecks that come with enhanced responsibility. As previously noted, it's absolutely essential to dress for success even before you become one. Beyond that, there are other ways to brand yourself that will either help (or hurt) you in your quest for stature.

Fortunately, there are spectacular examples of intelligent branding everywhere you turn, and you don't have to be an advertising legend on the order of David Ogilvy to master the secrets of image management and use some of the same tricks as the big brands to make a more positive impression on everyone you meet.

THE GREAT AMERICAN COFFEE TREATY

If you pay attention to television advertising as I do, it sometimes seems as if Dunkin' Donuts and Starbucks are at war with each other over the identical market share, but in fact, the opposite is true. Each chain is reaching out to an entirely different audience. There is no coffee war; only huge profits.

Dunkin' Donuts targets the working man. "America runs on Dunkin'" the current tag line asserts. This is code for "the real people of this nation, the people who get up and go to work every morning and make this country great" drink Dunkin' Donuts coffee.

It's the Budweiser crowd, the men and women who drive Ford pickups and who work their tails off each day, every day, for eight hours a day. Meanwhile, Starbucks has set its sights on a richer demographic with more disposable income and a lot more time on its hands. Starbucks seeks to capture those who won't blink about spending $4 on a latte and have just enough freedom from the nine-to-five grind to enjoy that overpriced coffee concoction in the store.

The advertising for these two brands heavily influences people's perceptions. So much so that if you carry a cup of Dunkin' Donuts coffee to work every day, you may be inadvertently branding yourself as "working class" by association.

There is nothing wrong with identifying with this class, being of this class, or being damned proud of it. But if you're broadcasting that you're a working-class Joe or Jane, you're not positioning yourself as part of the management class.

But what if you like the taste of Dunkin' Donuts' coffee? After all, it doesn't have a bitter, toasted flavor. And it's not pretentious. Beyond that, you don't have to memorize bizarre foreign names for sizes. Mostly, you're not standing in line with a bunch of posers every morning. You're simply procuring some coffee to help keep you awake at your mundane job, so what exactly is the big deal?

"The big deal" is that, in the last ten years or so, branding has become so sophisticated that there is no such thing as "just coffee" anymore.

The brand of coffee that you choose has become a style statement, and those who work and socialize with you are just as likely to pick up cues about your aspirations by your coffee selection as all of the other brands that you carry on your personage. Particularly if your coffee brand happens to be one that is heavily advertised. If you carry it, then its brand becomes part of yours—by association.

Branding has little to do with the actual taste of the coffee. One person's sour ink is another person's toothsome brew, and tastes differ widely.

Branding is all about the trappings that come with the coffee.

Is the logo a sophisticated forest green or a peppy pink and orange? Are the cups in foreign-sounding sizes like *grande* and *venti,* or in American easy-to-understand sizes like small, medium, and large?

Do people mill about in the store all day long, lounging on couches while they strum their laptops, or do they dash in and out because they have real jobs they need to get to by a certain time with real clocks they need to punch?

As of this writing, Dunkin' Donuts is actually the coffee that most American palates prefer, plus it's a heck of a lot cheaper than the other brand. So if you wish to broadcast that you're moving up in the world but you still prefer the taste of Dunkin' Donuts, why not buy your coffee from Dunkin' Donuts, but transfer it to a Starbucks mug or cup?

Hey, I'll never tell.

IDENTIFY YOUR BRAND

Please take the following quiz. It should help you pinpoint the message you're advertising about yourself to the world at large. Don't overthink your answers. Just pick the first one that comes to mind.

1. If you were a coffee, your name would be:
   A. Dunkin' Donuts
   B. Starbucks
   C. Folgers
2. If you were a shoe, you would be called:
   A. Keds
   B. Gucci
   C. Kenneth Cole flip-flops
3. You buy:
   A. One pair of sneakers a year
   B. Three pairs of sneakers a year or more
   C. Zero pairs of sneakers a year
4. If you were a handbag, your shape would be:
   A. A messenger canvas bag
   B. A structured leather briefcase

A cup of coffee is not just a cup of coffee. It's a signal of your aspirations and part of your "personal brand."

C. A slouchy hippie, boho bag
5. Your mobile device is:
   A. A 2G LG with a full keyboard
   B. An iPhone
   C. An old Motorola cell, circa 2006 or earlier
6. If you were a newspaper, people would call you:
   A. *New York Post*
   B. The *Wall Street Journal*
   C. The *New York Times*

QUIZ ANSWERS

Mostly As—Through your preference for certain accessories, you may be inadvertently labeling yourself as "working class." There may be slight adjustments you need to make if your goal is to hang out with a more refined group. But don't panic. With just a few tweaks, we'll have you looking oh-mi-gosh posh in no time.

Mostly Bs—You are a mover, inching up the corporate and social ladder, step by step. By your dress and general demeanor, you show the world that you've got leadership skills galore. Just take care that your attempts to tag yourself as an up-and-comer don't require extravagant financial outlays that will eventually land you in the poorhouse. It's hard to look like a million bucks in debtor's prison.

Mostly Cs—You are frugal to a fault, which either means you have no money whatsoever or a great stash stuffed inside a mattress somewhere that you amassed by hoarding pennies and nickels.

If you typically brew your coffee at home to save money, always ride the subway to avoid ever paying cab fare, and rarely invest a penny in footwear or new and improved technology, you may appear penurious to your target market—a potential turnoff.

Think of ways to prove that you're not miserly, either through your good works or generous bequests.

YOU, INC.

For their comparatively miniscule size, most accessories cost an arm, a leg, and a waist. But at least the money isn't wasted because accessories get noticed. Accessories signal your aspirations, so it makes sense to spend as much as you can possibly afford on each clothing accent, and get more mileage out of fewer of them.

If you are just starting out in the workforce, seek innovative ways to stretch your accessory "belt for the buck." Some belts, such as the ones you find at if-you-have-to-ask-you-can't-afford-it Hermès, are reversible, so you can snag *two* sumptuous waist-cinchers for the price of one.

We have already covered the accessory known as coffee. Now let's review some of the other embellishments that can help or hurt in your quest for status. From the most to least important, these adornments include shoes (including sneakers), handbags, mobile devices, and your daily newspaper.

As the architect Ludwig Mies van der Rohe once remarked, "God is in the details."

Why You Need Two Pairs of Great Shoes and Three Pairs of Great Sneakers

If you were a sentence, the punctuation at the end of it would be the pair of shoes on your feet. Is your punctuation a solid period, a wishy-washy ellipsis that keeps everyone hanging, or an exclamation mark that makes people perk up and take notice? If you have aspirations to lift yourself up, you have no choice but to punctuate yourself with a bang.

Great shoes are non-negotiable. The well-dressed finish their look with a beautifully appointed, polished, elegant shoe. "Court" shoes are classic work or job-interview shoes. For men, these are traditional loafers, wingtips,

or lace-ups. For women, these are pumps or T-straps.

Wearing courts conveys confidence and helps higher-ups identify you as someone who can be trusted to step up to bigger assignments.

For business, your heel height should never stretch to more than three inches (if you're female), or one inch (if you're male), even if you were short-changed in the height department.

Court shoes step out nicely to parties, events, and outings. For courting the smart set, you'll advance further with courts than with flats, sandals, or platform shoes. Start with two pairs of court shoes (one in black, one in brown), and expand your collection as appropriate. If you're female and can afford a third pair of court shoes, choose an eccentric but plush color, such as emerald green.

When you traipse about in emerald green pumps, everyone will automatically assume that you must be Imelda Marcos's young, affluent cousin. (For surely, if you're modeling green high-heeled shoes, you must be closeting a pair

of white, red, navy, gold, and silver back home.) However, no matter how many pairs of shoes you amass, never follow in the footsteps of Helena Bonham Carter at the 2011 Golden Globes by wearing one shoe in one color and another shoe in a contrasting color. One would have to be color-blind to appreciate that look!

Flats, while comfortable, may convey that you're flat-footed, plodding, and frumpy. One study found that men, on just seeing flats detached from the woman wearing them, automatically assumed that she must be a fifty-plus, divorced accountant.[16] For the record, there is nothing wrong with being fifty-plus, being divorced, or being an accountant! But if you're in the habit of trampling the tarmac in flats, you need to be aware of the "brand" they communicate. Wearing comfortable shoes may paint you as a bit older or less fashion-forward than their high-heeled counterparts.

For better or worse, the office is not a basketball court. And while one study showed that people who buy three pairs of sneakers or more per year tend to be "leaders,"[17] those leaders still need to *remove* their sneakers at the office in order to be considered for management positions.

There is a high correlation between athleticism and leadership, but do try to keep the athletic shoes confined to places where they will be appreciated, such as gyms, locker rooms, and tennis courts.

If you wear sneakers to the office to spare the heels of your court shoes, simply make sure that no one ever sees you entering your office building or leaving it. You can do that, can't you?

YOUR HANDBAG (OR MANBAG), YOUR SIGNATURE

I have had two careers in my life so far—the first was in advertising where I started as a receptionist and eventually rose to creative director. As a cub copywriter, an assignment floated across my desk one day to write a print campaign for Cole Haan handbags. The New York ad agency where I worked was pitching the account, and because I was one of the few women on staff, it was practically a given that I would be included in the brainstorming process. I was especially proud of one of the headlines I crafted for the pitch campaign: "Your handbag isn't your signature. Your signature is your signature." But, now, several years after the failed pitch and with the wisdom that 20/20 hindsight brings, I confess that I have radically changed my point of view.

Your signature *is* your signature; there is no dispute about that. But so is your handbag.

To date, the reason women love their pocketbooks has eluded journalists, bloggers, and psychologists of both sexes. On the surface, a handbag is an encumbrance, and it can become rather burdensome once it's laden with keys, credit cards, sunglasses, reading glasses, pens, odd notes, ancient receipts, dry cleaning stubs, pens, random lipstick, and other makeup products.

But the fact that one's daily luggage sometimes expands into baggage doesn't stop most women from hauling their contents around in larger and larger bags. Some view handbags as status symbols on the level of cars, and in certain parts of the country the handbags are becoming almost as large as cars (and almost as expensive).

Due to skyrocketing inflation, both in handbag size and cost, I believe it's more practical to think of these accessories in terms of their *shapes* (rather than their brands per se) and to consider what the *shape* of your purse may be saying about you.

Lug a messenger bag, and a messenger you will always be—a mere go-between, rather than someone to whom one delivers important communiqués. Please don't shoot the messenger for saying so. Instead, send a message by trading up to a more structured bag at the earliest opportunity. Messenger bags are rectangular, hang by large, wide straps, and can't seem to escape from their courier heritage.

If you're a guy sporting a messenger bag, it could be because "manbags," those European pouches that hang from smallish straps, just never quite caught on in America. If you're disinclined to start the trend on these shores, it's imperative to remember that there are other options. Carry an old-fashioned rectangular briefcase, and look like a man of stature rather than a bike messenger.

If you're a woman accessorizing with a messenger bag, it may be because they tend to weigh less than other compartments of their size, and no doubt you feel like all of the stuff inside *yours* is essential. Take my word on it: Precious few of the items you are porting are mandatory. Weed through them. Throw out. Lessen your load. Then transfer your loot to a small, structured handbag that's less than eight inches wide. Shapes that brand you as an up-and-comer include square, rectangular, or if you want to make heads spin with bag-envy, circular.

Chanel understands that smaller is more elegant, and if you can afford one of their quilted bags, it's well worth the price, because the item will last forever. Coach is the working woman's alternative.

After unpacking your numerous items (and relentlessly throwing out 90 percent of them), you should be able squeeze them all into a traditional handbag. But if your packrat instinct still won't quit, pack all of your belongings in a Longchamp classic Le Pliage canvas bag. While it looks like the younger, more stylish sister of an old-fashioned tote-bag, at least it will make you resemble a prepster rather than a messenger. This bag carries a special perk: all of the other Le Pliage-toting ladies will admire your taste, a confidence booster. For an exponentially larger wad of

cash, you can invest in a Mulberry, which is almost the size of a man's briefcase, but softer and less bulky.

If your back strains easily or you feel like you must keep your hands free for easy access to your mobile device, it's perfectly acceptable to purchase a bag with a shoulder strap. But make sure that the bag dangling from the strap has structure.

Do not, under any circumstances, squander your money on anything with fringe or on any item that resembles a floppy, boho bag. (Boho rhymes with no-no, probably not a coincidence.)

Handbags are supposed to provide structure and order, the way a medicine cabinet does. You don't want everything inside your pouch peeking out and flopping about all over the place or you'll look like a bag lady.

Never feel compelled to get too creative or funky with your handbag, shoes, and belt color combination. It's hard to go astray when their colors match, safe as that choice may be.

The Clash was a great English punk

If you can fit inside your handbag, it's too large for you.

rock band in its heyday. But if your handbag, shoes, and belt all clash, you'll look disorganized, disheveled, and discombobulated.

GOING MOBILE

There is a keeping-up-with-the-Joneses aspect to buying a mobile device these days, as the six biggest brands vie with each other over all sorts of gadgetry designed to lure the youth market. What was once just a phone is now a Bluetooth-, WiFi-, and USB-enabled commando communications station capable of delivering detailed navigation instructions and mapping through a GPS device, weather reports custom-tailored to your zip code, a high-resolution camera, a video camera and player, a slide show for photos, music player, FM radio, calculator, stop watch, memo pad complete with stylus, games, applications, office tools, data transfer capability, data storage, Internet, email access, and mobile web access to Facebook, LinkedIn, Twitter, and foursquare.

Ironically, the more features that are added to the mix, the shorter the lifespan of the mobile. Young, rich consumers now update their devices every six months. Clearly, consumer loyalty today is almost as short as its attention span.

In case the combination of office-ware, entertainment, and infotainment isn't enough to keep you merrily competing with your friends about whose toy is cooler, the gadgets now come in a rainbow of fashion colors, including some that are rarely seen in clothing, such as bright magenta, bubblegum, and a pinkish color called "candy heart." Black is still chic as well.

When purchasing a mobile, consider first the way you intend to use it. For example, sometimes amid all of the fun features, the phone won't work all that well. Voices may sound fuzzy or distended. If you've given up your landline and need to make important calls to your boss, clearly you require an appliance that is, first and foremost, a phone.

It pays to comparison shop. Some ritzy mobiles that shall remain nameless might retail for hundreds of dollars but be found at Costco for under $50.

To locate the best deals, read phone reviews and ask around. Be sure to play with the models displayed in phone kiosks a few times before committing. Become proficient with the gadgetry so that your opinion will be informed.

Finally, consider where you will store your mobile (when it's not attached to your hand, that is). If you wish to model the mechanism on a Batman-like utility belt for easy access, perhaps the phone and belt should match in black.

By contrast, if you plan to house your wireless in a car-sized handbag, you might prefer your device in a fashion-forward color, such as blossom or pale peach, so you can locate it among all of the other items stashed in your purse. Pay close attention to the advertising messages paid for by the mobile's manufacturer because the personality of the master brand *will* rub off on your own personal brand.

THE SMARTEST ACCESSORY $2 CAN BUY

Spotted on the runways of the Fortune 500, the season's must-have accessory is enjoying a moment. It's black and white, tucks neatly under your arm, requires no wait list, and complements absolutely everything. Is it a handbag? Of course not, silly. It's the *Wall Street Journal.*

Get into the habit of reading it, and you may actually learn a thing or two about investing your money while trying to behave as if you've had it all along. While you're at it, why not swipe a copy of *Barron's* from your doctor's office and the *Financial Times* from your neighbor's recycling bin?

A Brand-New You

Some branding distinctions barely matter. Are you a Mac or a PC? Who cares? They're both amazing.

If you're artsy, you may identify more with a Mac, but being a PC conveys some very positive characteristics as well, and may indicate that you're a heady, financial type. And unless you're lugging your laptop around with you (which you don't have to do any more because your mobile device has so many of the same functions), your choice of Mac versus PC isn't truly being broadcast to the outside world.

Do you wear boxer shorts or briefs? Here again, who's looking? (Um, that was a rhetorical question.)

Boxer shorts may symbolize that you have more of a preppy orientation than someone who wears briefs, but in that few people will ever know which type of underwear you wear (or see you in it), it hardly matters for the purposes of identifying yourself as a baron-to-be.

But the brands you wear that are seen by the outside world *will* influence people's perceptions of you. No one is exempt from the forces of branding. So you may as well marshal those forces to promote "the brand new you" that will signal your dreams and aspirations and help you achieve them faster.

Always remember, you are a luxury brand in the making: You are the richest coffee, the softest Italian leather court shoe, the most structured handbag, and the coolest mobile device of all time.

Today, you are reading about tomorrow's tycoons and robber barons in the *Wall Street Journal*. But tomorrow with persistence, pluck, and wise accessorizing, your name could be memorialized in those pages too.

CHAPTER TWELVE

MILLIONAIRE SKIN

It's ten o'clock on the night of your BIG BIRTHDAY—the one you've been dreading. You've consumed three glasses of wine on an empty stomach, and the room is spinning like a kaleidoscope.

Your best friends, Hadley and Chris, are seated on either side of you at a long, skinny bar with a humongous gold-leaf mirror behind it. Seeing your tired, demoralized face staring back at you in the mirror, you feel like you can't possibly be this old with so little to show for it.

"Happy birthday to you!" Hadley croons off-key, as the bartender pours another round for her and Chris.

"No thanks," you say to the bartender, waving away the offer of a free birthday merlot. "With my advancing decrepitude, I'm afraid I can't handle it."

"Wimp!" Chris barks, downing his fourth beer.

Hadley and Chris each throw an arm around your back and together attempt a spirited "Happy Birthday" duet in your honor. Their voices, drunken and off-key, sound discordant. Nevertheless, you're deeply touched by your friends' enthusiasm.

"I used to be able to drink you under the table," you say to Chris. "Now look at me. Three glasses, and I have to tootle off to sleep." He rolls his aqua eyes heavenwards, as if he's heard this line once or twice before.

"Age is a mindset, not a number!" Hadley spouts, all energy, bonhomie, and shining, tawny hair.

"Easy for you to say," you respond. Your voice sounds thin and distended with a slight echo, as if you are hearing it through a long tunnel. "You guys are both far better preserved than me."

"Nah!" Hadley and Chris say in unison, then laugh at the coincidence of their spoken exchange.

"Jinx!" they scream at each other.

You're delighted that *some people* are having fun at your big birthday celebration, even if *you* don't happen to be one of the lucky ones.

Brusquely, you remove Hadley's arm from your back and pivot her stool, forcing her to turn towards you and stare right into your face. You move a lock of hair away from your forehead. With your right index finger, you trace a sloppy horizontal line across the top of your forehead.

"Look at this," you say, glowering at her.

"Look at what?" she says, her features stamped with worry. She is three centimeters away from your face, studying it, as if you might have a rash that's contagious.

"I'm sorry," she says, "but I just don't see anything."

"It's my first wrinkle," you moan.

"Shows character," belts out Chris in a husky baritone.

"Well the good news is," Hadley says, peering closely at your forehead, "that you're being utterly paranoid. It's not really a wrinkle. It's just a tiny line. Clearly, you've been working way too hard. Tell your boss to ease up."

"Yeah," Chris chimes in, "tell that Mr. Bucks to cut you some slack."

They both toast Bucks, your supervisor, in his absence.

They still feel like they're immortal, you think. *Wait till they turn my age.*

Then it hits you like a ton of bricks. Both of your friends already celebrated their big birthdays months ago.

As you study the reflection of the three faces in the barroom mirror, you can't help but notice that you look ten years older than both Hadley and Chris, even though you're all the same age.

MILLIONAIRE SKIN VERSUS YOUR SKIN

Some people have no lines or wrinkles on their faces, even

into their forties, fifties, sixties, and beyond. One reason may be because these people are millionaires: richlings who employ an army of dermatologists to zap every beauty buster, the moment it appears, with a magic injection or a laser. Money may not buy happiness, but it can certainly purchase the patina of eternal youth. For the rich—as a friend who must remain nameless once boasted— "A week without Botox is like a week without sunshine."

Another reason that rich skin sometimes preserves its youth longer is because having money in one's coffers has a way of easing stress. And a life free of stress can do wonders for the complexion.

But have no worries. Even if you don't have car trunks of cash to fritter away on a dermatologist's lotions, potions, and lasers, there are three strategies you can follow that will make your skin look younger and less stressed at any age. And the real beauty is these procedures cost practically nothing.

1. You can find your ideal sleep quotient.
2. You can go on a skin diet.
3. You can consider sun protection a religion and yourself a true believer.

Pursuing these tactics will make your skin appear fresher, firmer, and more resilient. I call that "millionaire skin."

ANTI-AGING PART I: ON FINDING YOUR IDEAL SLEEP QUOTIENT

The Myth of 8 Versus the Superhero Insomniac Myth

From time immemorial, we've heard that we need eight hours of sleep per night. But in our fast-paced, hard-driving, 24/7 world, actually *getting* eight hours of sleep every night seems ludicrously luxurious.

We are multitaskers. We have demanding jobs. We have our Facebook, LinkedIn, and Twitter accounts to catch up on, after all. We have our online profiles to polish, websites to tweak, and multiple mobile devices to check.

Add to that rigorous workload a relationship with a significant other, and possibly kids (or parents) who require our undivided attention—so when precisely are we supposed to find these eight hours of uninterrupted shuteye?

Yet, even assuming that we could find the time to nod off for eight straight hours, there's a second myth that's equally potent, and in some ways, it's much more appealing. And that's the myth of the "superhero insomniac."

Legend has it that Abraham Lincoln managed beautifully on just three hours of sleep a night. Bill Clinton famously claimed that he slept only five hours a night. Margaret Thatcher slept but four hours a night and said, "Sleep is for wimps."

If these masters and mistresses of the universe could do it, why can't we?

For starters, it's not necessarily true that these high-powered politicos *thrived* on a lack of sleep. Since Bill Clinton's heart attack, which he blames partly on fatigue, he claims that he's been trying to sleep more. And while Lincoln may have slept only a few hours per night, the sleep deprivation probably did little to lift his clinical depression or help his skin, which was grizzled and pockmarked.

John F. Kennedy and Marilyn Monroe—both famous insomniacs and, perhaps not coincidentally, romantically linked to each other—unfortunately died too young for us to draw any conclusions about whether they *thrived* on the absence of sleep.

In fact, it's eminently possible that all of these larger-than-life people would have been even more productive, and even fresher looking, with a little more sleep. Sadly, we'll never know.

Scientists say that the need for sleep is highly individualized. While some people have a gene that allows them to survive on a great deal less than eight hours a night, most of us need more sleep than we get. By most accounts, eight hours of peaceful slumber is the average daily minimum requirement. And it's not just the quantity of sleep; it's the quality.

Repose restores, rejuvenates, and revives the body. Eight hours a night can help replenish energy and keep weight off. Ample rest also keeps the brain in good working order and makes the complexion look radiant. Get enough sleep, and you'll produce more human growth hormone (HGH), which helps skin stay thick and elastic, and guards against

Millionaire skin holds up to close scrutiny in any light.

the wrinkles of time. If that's not reason enough to "get your beauty sleep," then do it to preserve your sanity. Sleep is essential for survival, optimal performance, concentration, and short-term memory. Frequent visits to the Land of Nod will also boost your mood and energy levels.

Before you invest a whole lot of money in anti-aging injections and other treatments that supposedly "turn back the clock," try setting your *actual* alarm clock so you get at least eight full hours of sleep tonight. In the morning, witness how much younger you look and how much better you feel. Then be sure to do it all over again tomorrow night.

HOW TO CALCULATE YOUR IDEAL SLEEP QUOTIENT

According to the National Sleep Foundation, the average adult needs between seven and nine hours of shuteye each night, but only you can assess how you react to different amounts. Start a snooze diary.

Pay special attention to your mood, energy, and health after varying amounts of rest. Also, take note of any and all compliments. For example, if you start sleeping one hour more a night and friends start asking if you've "lost weight," or what you've been doing to look so fresh, it could be a clue that you've found your optimum sleep amount.

Once you determine your ideal number of sleep hours, try to get the *same amount* consistently, even on the weekends. Force yourself to go to bed and wake up at roughly the same time each day.

PERCHANCE TO DREAM

Think of it as "revival of the fittest." Catch the right amount of sleep and your skin will look luminous. You can have millionaire skin at a fraction of what most millionaires actually spend to maintain their youthful looks because retiring an hour or two earlier each night costs you nothing. Even if you later opt for Botox or a laser treatment at a dermatologist's office, you will be starting the process on a younger-looking, firmer canvas, and it's likely that your skin will react to the treatments more favorably.

But what if you are one of the 40 million Americans who suffer from insomnia? First, for laughs, study the chart below to learn what some famous insomniacs tried in order to combat the condition. But when you're ready to actually catch forty winks, follow the suggestions in "The Nonmedical Cure for Insomnia" sidebar directly following.

Famous Insomniacs	Their Cure for Insomnia Was . . .
Abraham Lincoln	Took long walks in the middle of the night.
Charles Dickens	Could only sleep on a bed that was aligned on a north-south axis, with the head of the bed pointing north, and then had to position himself in the exact center of the bed.
Franz Kafka	Kept a diary detailing the condition.
Groucho Marx	Called total strangers on the phone in order to insult them.
Margaret Thatcher	What cure? Said, "Sleep is for wimps."

Famous Insomniacs	Their Cure for Insomnia Was . . .
Marilyn Monroe	Took sleeping pills (but died of an overdose).
Napoleon Bonaparte	Reviewed military strategies while tossing and turning at night; took catnaps during the day.
Robert Burns	Wrote poetry about the condition.
Tallulah Bankhead	Hired young, gay caddies to hold her hand till she drifted off to sleep.
Theodore Roosevelt	Drank a shot of cognac in a glass of milk.
Thomas Edison	Once the lights went out, the man who invented the lightbulb couldn't sleep. To make up for it, he catnapped during the day.
Winston Churchill	Owned twin beds. When he couldn't fall asleep in one bed, he'd switch to the other.

The Nonmedical Cure for Insomnia

It's hard to have millionaire skin when you're sleep-deprived. That's because skin that doesn't get enough rest loses its elasticity and starts to sag. Yet while catching your Zs is the inexpensive way to improve your skin's tone and texture, sometimes your body simply refuses to cooperate.

According to the National Institutes of Health, over 70 million Americans find sleep to be an elusive bed partner several nights a week. Do you have trouble falling asleep at night? Or do you tend to wake up in the middle of the night and then have difficulty getting back to sleep? Here are some methods to try before resorting to meds.

1. Turn your bedroom into a media-free zone. Don't watch TV, plug in to your computer, check your iPhone, or even work out in your bedroom—none of these—for at least three hours before you hit the mattress. Computer monitors and TVs emit blue light, which causes the brain to stay awake. You want to train your body to relax in your bedroom, not be hyper-alert.

2. Feng-shui your space. Bright yellows and oranges are less conducive to relaxation than more muted colors, such as pale blue or lilac. If you live in an urban area with screeching traffic, sirens, or loud, cavorting pedestrians that never quit, invest in heavy drapes and double-paned windows. Conversely, if you just moved to the country and it sounds eerily quiet at night, try dozing off to a soundtrack of waves or chirping birds.

3. Never mull through the items on your to-do list while horizontally inclined. "To do" is the opposite of "to sleep, perchance, to dream." Write your to-do list for the following day at least four hours before you settle in between the sheets. Do you have a big day ahead? You may want to lay out your clothes in advance (so that you won't have to mentally comb through your wardrobe while you're trying to drowse). Multitasking and sleeping don't mix.

4. Master the mystifying mumbo jumbo of marketing lingo. "Decaffeinated" means the beverage has less caffeine in it, not zero caffeine, and even green tea has 1/3 as much caffeine as black tea. Don't drink any coffee or tea after 6 PM. Alcohol, too, can be a real sleep killer. Fall asleep to a liquor buzz, and you'll usually be wide awake a few hours later. Pity.

5. If you still can't sleep, experiment with melatonin (0.5 to 3 mg), calcium (1200 mg divided between two doses a day), or magnesium (400 mg). Try one of these remedies at a time to assess its impact, never all three at once. Unless there's a real reason for your sleep disruption, such as jet lag, stay far away from over-the-counter sleep inducers until you consult a doctor or a sleep specialist. The side effects are sometimes worse than not sleeping at all.

6. Practice stellar sleep hygiene. Brush your teeth well and take care of other grooming requirements before your head hits the pillow so you won't need to wake up later to attend to them. Keep your bedroom approximately seven degrees cooler than the rest of your house, and if you feel chilly, wrap yourself up in a blanket like a human pita.

7. If nothing seems to work, get up and read. There's no point in tossing and turning about *why* you're tossing and turning.

8. As a final step, consult a nutritionist. You'll discover all sorts of dietary changes you can try to improve your slumber. Better to alter your diet than drink hot milk, count sheep, or "imagine yourself on a beach somewhere"—unless all of that works for you, of course.

To Avoid Lines and Creases

Let's be honest, lines are rarely welcome. This includes lines at the supermarket, lines at the gas station, and especially, lines on the face. True, some facial lines may give us character, but most of us would prefer to look more superficial and have the character lines (if any) etched on the inside. And the unfortunate fact is, we may be inadvertently drawing those lines on our faces during our sleep. According to the American Academy of Dermatology (AAD), resting on one's side deepens cheek and chin wrinkles while lying face-down furrows the brow. The AAD recommends sleeping on one's back.

If you have trouble doing this, as I do, try dozing off with a large pillow perched on top of your body. Hours later, the weight of the pillow subtly reminds me not to turn over on my side.

ANTI-AGING PART II: THE SKIN DIET

The Fat Myth

As Meryl Streep, quoting Catherine Deneuve, once observed, "After a certain age, you can have your face or you can have your ass—it's one or the other. I have chosen my face, and I can just sit on the rest of it."

Translation: Avoiding all fat for the sake of your waistline will only make you look wrinkled and haggard. It's far more attractive to be a few pounds overweight. (The fact that Meryl Streep is has never prevented her from getting a part.)

A little extra baby fat will ease wrinkles and make you look younger and more vibrant. Doctors even claim that the body needs fat in order to lubricate itself and absorb vitamin A, which can prevent skin from premature aging. So sprinkle your salad with olive oil! Eat some almonds. Indulge in oily fishes, such as salmon, tuna, and mackerel, all swimming in "the good fat": DHA-omega 3.

Holy mackerel! You can eat mackerel. Your skin will reward you by looking dewier.

For beautiful skin, look for activities that ease the tension.

And if you stick with a diet that includes a lot of fish, hopefully your jeans won't punish you too much. (If they do, slip into your "fat" jeans.)

Seriously, if people are looking at your butt instead of at your youthful face, they're into you for all the wrong reasons. Trust me.

WHEN YOU GET SICK OF FISH, GO VEGETARIAN

Man cannot live on fish alone. Neither can woman. Some other digestibles that impart skin with a healthy glow include: tomatoes (they reduce the likelihood that you'll get sunburned); eggs (they help metabolize carbs); and green tea (it protects against sun damage and helps thicken skin and may even help prevent sunburn).

FORBIDDEN FOODS

Once upon a time, even before the dawn of Facebook and Twitter, there was a list of forbidden foods that dermatologists would circulate to their patients suffering from acne. Public Enemy Number One was chocolate, followed by potato chips, all fried foods, all spicy foods, all shellfish, and iodized salt. At the time, I remember thinking that the *only* things I ever ate were the items on the list.

Still, I followed instructions. After I received the list, I didn't eat any chocolate for two years, five months, one week, and thirty-seven minutes or until the "Thou shalt not eat chocolate" prohibition was proven to be total B.S. I swear that I ate Toblerone bars every single day for a month after the no-chocolate ban was lifted.

However, while chocolate has redeemed itself, some skin doctors still claim that food with

iodine tends to cause acne in both adults and kids. Unfortunately, it's not as easy as it sounds to avoid the additive in food because iodine is sometimes used in livestock feed. There is iodine in shellfish, regular fish, meat, and even eggs. If you suspect your skin bumps up when it bumps against iodine, read all labels and stay far away from iodized salt. (Sea salt is an excellent substitute.)

THE NO-ALCOHOL LOOK

After a couple of drinks, everyone looks more attractive—but, alas, the illusion is only temporary. In the clear light of day, heavy drinkers look haggard. Here is the ugly truth about America's number one vice.

Alcohol is a diuretic. It dehydrates the body and causes skin to lose its plump, firm appearance. That's pretty bad, but it doesn't stop there. Liquor is a vasodilator, which means it opens blood vessels. The elixir darkens the under-eye area and puffs up the face like a balloon. In large quanti-

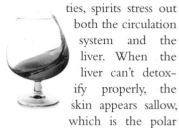

ties, spirits stress out both the circulation system and the liver. When the liver can't detoxify properly, the skin appears sallow, which is the polar opposite of "peaches and cream."

On the other end of the alcohol rainbow is redness. Alcohol can trigger rosacea. By dilating blood vessels, alcohol can make a red face turn crimson and stay that way—an effect that may require a dermatologist's touch to wrest under control.

If you have florid skin, swear off red wine and observe whether your skin reddens after consuming other intoxicants, such as white wine, beer, and vodka. Drinking cool water directly after an alcoholic beverage or sucking on ice chips may help dilute alcohol's uglifying influence.

I find that some advance planning can as well. I ask every bartender I meet from New York to L.A. to make my screwdrivers (vodka and orange juice) "light." I always say, "One screwdriver, and please go light on the vodka." By asking for (roughly) *half* a shot of vodka in each cocktail, I hope to keep the redness out of my skin and the alcoholic calories off my hips while not tipping all the way towards teetotalism (which is superb for the skin and body but not so fabulous for the personality).

A Few A, B, Cs

I try to drink a healthy cocktail mixture of skin vitamins each day.

A, C, and E, the "good skin vitamins," can be found in pills, food, drinks, and certain topical creams. Vitamin A (found in Retin-A) helps heal sun damage. Applied topically, vitamin A helps combat acne, rosacea, and seborrheic dermatitis. Vitamin C stimulates collagen and builds up the skin to protect it. Vitamin E enhances the effects of sunscreen and slows wrinkle production.

Uncommonly known, but unfortunately true: Ultraviolet light degrades vitamins A, C, and E, so in order to get the full impact, you have to apply them topically at night. (It's something to do while you're battling insomnia.)

Worried that smearing vitamin glop all over your face may depress sexy pillow talk? Perhaps you'd prefer to chew your vitamins instead. If so, here's a simple shopping list. Vitamin A is found in eggs, cheese, milk, meat, spinach, broccoli, cabbage, carrots, apricots, and peaches. Vitamin C is found in spinach, tomatoes, green peppers, potatoes, oranges, grapefruit, strawberries, kiwi, cantaloupe, and pineapples. Along with its luminous skin benefits, C keeps hair healthy. Vitamin E is found in soybeans, nuts, raw seeds, and wheat germ oil.

However you ingest it, here are the right amounts to get, and whatever you do, don't overdose on vitamin A. Just a little "A" is good for you. A lot could potentially damage your immune system.

Vitamin A, 1,500 IU a day

Vitamin C, 500 milligrams, twice a day

Vitamin E, 400 IU a day

ANTI-AGING PART III: SUN PROTECTION

Preserve Your Millionaire Skin
For such a pretty object, the sun is like Evil Incarnate for your skin, especially if you don't have a lot of melanin (color) in it. Don't let the sunshine in. Sun is the number one cause of wrinkles, plus for a certain percentage of the population, even mild exposure to it can cause moles (which have the potential to turn cancerous). Shunning the big yellow orb is best; but if you have to troll about outside, wear gobs of sunscreen with a sun protection factor (SPF) of at least 30. For the fair-skinned, an SPF of 45 is even safer. If the light is particularly blinding, wear a hat and sunglasses.

Must you wear sunscreen in the winter? Yes. Ultraviolet rays exist all year long, even in the cool winter months. Do you have to wear sunscreen in an office? Yes. Ultraviolet rays can pass through office windows and even car windows. While newer car windshields tend to block UV rays, you can still get them through the side and rear windows. And it doesn't take long.

There are two types of damaging rays. UVA rays tan, age skin, and increase the risk of skin cancer. UVB rays cause sunburn, but the degree of burn isn't always a reliable guide to how much UVA exposure you've received.

Smear sunscreen on your face, neck, arms, and hands before you leave your house each day. If you're concerned about how this product works with all of the other creams and potions you use, be sure to put on moisturizer first, sunscreen next, and makeup last.

Ironically, the new math of SPF protection doesn't work quite like the simple addition you mastered

in grade school. If you use a sunblock with a SPF of 45 and then cover it with makeup that has a SPF of 15, you are only getting the SPF equivalent of 45. The lesser SPF count in the makeup won't "subtract" from the original SPF count, but it won't add to it either. So why use makeup with SPF in it? You're better off just using the sunscreen. Start with moisturizer. Once that's seeped in, apply sunscreen. Then, finish with your makeup. Sunscreen works best if it has a chance to "bond" with your skin for about thirty minutes before you venture out in the sun.

ANTI-AGING PART IV: DENIAL

If you're going to lie about your age, destroy the evidence. By getting the ideal amount of sleep for your body, introducing skin vitamins and certain foods into your diet, and guarding your precious skin against the ravages of the sun, it *is* possible to roll back the years. There is also out-and-out denial, which you may or may not care for.

For anyone who has turned twenty-nine (I mean, for the

second time), denial sometimes has the benefit of making one feel younger than one is. Just as the "placebo effect" works some of the time in all sorts of clinical trials, I believe that denial as an anti-aging stratagem is worth exploring. Be forewarned, this tactic is not for the faint of heart. For starters, it helps to be a gifted actor. You really have to be able to adamantly fib about your age—a lot—in order to pull off the ruse.

"Did you know so-and-so [from your same class year] at high school?" You scratch your head. You just can't recall. "Do you remember the pop hit 'XYZ'?" (It happened to be the number one single from a particular era.) You close your eyes, pretending to think hard. No, you're pretty certain you've never heard the song before.

To determine if you've got the brass cajones to out-and-out deny your age, let's start by playing the "Where were you when . . . ?" game.

Where were you when . . .
John F. Kennedy was shot?
Martin Luther King Jr. was shot?
John Lennon was shot?

Where were you when . . .
Neil Armstrong walked on the moon?
NASA launched the Mars probe?
Pluto was downgraded from planet status?

Where were you . . .
during the Watergate trial?
on September 11, 2001?

Where were you when . . .
Elvis died?
Liz Taylor died?
the Berlin Wall fell?

Wrong in all cases! You were nowhere, because you weren't born yet, silly.

In Memory of My Great-Aunt Lynne

When my great-aunt Lynne died, she had a different age written down on all of her government-issued documents. It wasn't some mistake that happened when she first arrived in this country because she was born and raised here. Some in my family attributed Lynne's alternate ages to a deliberate act of vanity on her part. She must be obsessed with her appearance, they reasoned, because she looked so damned amazing for her age—whatever age that was.

Lynne looked like a taller, more real version of Doris Day and was by far the most glamorous woman I have ever met. She had platinum hair that she wore swept into a saucy updo, long, springy black false eyelashes that she plastered on every single day (that would constantly fall into her eyes), and ice-blue contact lenses. She had three husbands (my great-uncle was her third) and legs chiseled like a Rockette's. Her sister Trixie actually *was* a Rockettte.

I once asked Lynne how old she was and was surprised when she told me that nobody knew— not even my great-uncle. As a six-year-old, I found this fascinating. "But doesn't he ask?" I said, incredulous at my great-uncle's lack of curiosity.

"He asks," she said with a wink, "but that doesn't mean I tell him."

MILLIONAIRE SKIN AT ANY AGE

You don't need to raid someone else's trust fund to keep your skin looking young and fresh. And your life needn't be divorced from stress. But it's essential to put your skin on a rejuvenation regimen, which includes the proper amount of sleep, the right diet, and attention to preservation tactics.

New reports emerge every day about the health and beauty benefits of sleep. A skin diet that's high in certain kinds of fats can also keep you looking young. A minute spent guarding your skin from the sun each day is worth a pound of cures, lotions, and injections at the dermatologist's office. And finally, if you're sensitive about your age, there's always denial.

You're as young as you feel, and with a couple of small changes, you can soon feel as young as you look.

CHAPTER THIRTEEN

NEVER ASK FOR RECOGNITION IF YOU'RE ON THE BOARD OF A CHARITY

At your office, the prevailing philosophy is "Toot your own horn." At your volunteer stint, the prevailing philosophy is "Get on the horn."

Silly you for confusing the two.

"Get on the horn!" Chair Dragon Lady barks, when you report the pitiful number of tickets you've sold to the Charitable Ball at the twenty-strong monthly committee meeting.

"I got on the horn," you say in your defense, "but . . ."

"Well, get on the horn again!" she says in a voice that hints of one too many cigarettes.

"I feel like there may be something wrong with the list," you say. "The people I called just don't want to spend . . ."

"Then call your friends!" Dragon Lady snaps as she taps her long talons against the conference room table. *CLACKETY-CLACK. CLACKETY-CLACK.* "Sell tickets! TICKETS."

"But I don't have a lot of rich friends," you say.

"They don't need to be rich," Dragon Lady rasps. "They just need to buy tickets." Her voice sounds like it will erupt into a cough at any minute.

"Yes, but at $500 a seat, they—"

"Five hundred dollars really isn't a lot of money for a ball of this caliber."

"Maybe if it weren't just a ball," you say, "but a themed party, like a masquerade. . . . "

"We already did a masquerade last year," Dragon Lady barks, eyes glowering.

A mild murmur circles around the table. One of the wizened scions—there are several who sit on the Charitable Ball committee of twenty—raises a quivering pale hand in Dragon Lady's direction.

"Yes, Harold," she says.

"Maybe we *should* have a masquerade ball again, Lila," he says. "It was our most successful event ever."

"Yes!" you pipe in, "and we could call it 'March Masquerade.'"

The scion and Dragon Lady both attempt to stare you down into silence. If there were a tape dispenser on the conference room table, these two volunteer chieftains would be taping your mouth shut just about now.

"Or the 'Ides of March,'" you add, "if you think 'March Masquerade' is too alliterative."

"'The Ides of March' has been done to death," Dragon Lady snorts, tapping her nails against the table again. *CLACKETY-CLACK. CLACKETY-CLACK.* You can almost hear her dragging on an invisible cigarette as she mulls over the possibilities. *CLACKETY-CLACK.*

"I have an idea," Dragon Lady says, pulling her lips back to reveal a full set of huge yellow teeth. "Why don't we call it 'March Masquerade'?"

"Excellent idea!" Harold beams at her. "I knew you would solve it, my dear."

"Hello?" you feel like screaming. "THAT WAS MY IDEA!"

TOOTING YOUR OWN HORN IS UNSEEMLY

In the for-profit world, everyone toots his or her own horn. Self-promotion is considered a legitimate tactic for getting ahead. Between the loud singing of one's own praises and the symphony of self-congratulatory horn-tooting, it's amazing that any real work ever gets done. Yet it does.

But take note: Volunteer work is distinct from labor of the paid variety. And volunteering for a charity or a not-for-profit has a

markedly different set of rules than exists in the business world, even though many volunteers do hold corporate jobs.

As a volunteer, you have no power until you land a coveted chair position. And you will never secure that seat of authority if you are perceived as either truculent or too much of a spotlight seeker.

Your charge is to come up with ideas (if asked), back other people's ideas (even if not asked), and above all, to foster cooperation. If, by some bizarre coincidence, one of your concepts happens to be embraced by a committee and you are a newly minted volunteer, you must stay humble about your success.

The competition to get onto certain boards and charities is cutthroat; everyone on the board is beyond brilliant and has just

as much passion for the cause as you do (if not even more so); and no one has the patience to hear a junior volunteer blather about any credit that may or may not be due.

WHY VOLUNTEER?

Volunteering for a charity or a nonprofit allows you to work on a project that benefits the common good while mingling with the crème de la crème. Many of your fellow committee members are people whom you would never have the chance to meet in the course of your ordinary life. They tend to be business and community leaders, such as doctors, lawyers, members of the C-suite (CEOs, CFOs, and COOs), and successful entrepreneurs from diverse fields.

These people have access— access to the heads of companies (helpful if you're looking for a job); access to connectors (beneficial if you're looking to expand your networking reach); plus access to better parties.

You'll gain new friends in high places while you experience the true joy of making a difference. You'll also build your résumé, mas-

ter new decision-making skills, and get invited to elegant receptions.

Volunteering is your best entrée into the Inner Circle of business titans, future tycoons, and civic leaders. If you have the time and dedication to devote to a worthy cause, the effort will pay you back tenfold with a vastly improved social and business life.

But in order to excel as a volunteer and really make those connections work for you, it's necessary to earn the respect of others around the table who are devoting their time and energy to the cause too. And to do that, you need to understand and follow the Code of Good Volunteer Conduct.

The Six Cardinal Rules of Volunteering

You won't find these rules explained in *Robert's Rules*, the book that details parliamentary procedure and meeting behavior. Nevertheless, following these conventions is critical if you wish to have a bright future ahead of you as a volunteer.

For the uninitiated, scaling the charity ladder can be fraught with peril, and one false step can topple your chances for success.

Here, for your charity-scaling education, is a roadmap, complete with potential pitfalls and the path around them. Stay humble, and watch out for hidden quagmires and other menaces lurking near.

1. Quit Bickering: You Work for the Staff, Not the Other Way Around

Most charities and not-for-profit organizations have staff. The staff consists of qualified professionals who are paid real money to perform various tasks.

You, conversely, are just a lowly, unpaid volunteer. If you encumber, undermine, or wage war with the staff, its members will despise you. And someone to whom they report will get you kicked off the committee faster than you can scream, "No, honestly, I'm a super nice person!"

If you have never had the privilege of serving on a board, you may well wonder what a well-meaning do-gooder could possibly fight about with a staff liaison. Rest assured, there are countless potential items over which to quarrel, including meeting agendas, event management, event marketing, budgetary control, and recognition (more on that later). Occasionally, the battle will be over something intangible, such as the various differences between the not-for-profit and the profit world. Whatever the issue, from your standpoint, bickering with the staff is a no-win situation.

I once sat on the alumni board of a high school in New York City. At the time, some of the board members demanded to see a line-item budget for all alumni events and made quite a fuss about it.

But the staff felt that financial responsibility was (well) beyond the purview of the board. It was like being subjected to an endless loop of *Much Ado about Nothing*, as month after month, the disgruntled alumni would endlessly carp to staff liaisons seated in the same room about how the events

budget was being kept hush-hush, a state secret.

Did the river of alumni outrage usher in a new era of transparency? Surely, you jest.

The high school seized the opportunity to reorganize the entire board. Those who had vociferously complained about the lack of a line-item budget were politely nudged off the board pronto, while those of us who had joined the effort too late to understand what all the hoopla was about (or who just didn't consider "budget control" the issue of the century) stayed on.

Fight City Hall if you must, but never ever take on the staff! Attempt it, and you will lose. The staff rules the roost, while you are just an unpaid volunteer with a term limit.

Think of yourself as privileged to serve rather than the staff as being privileged to serve you. If you believe the staff is there to service your every whim, your future as a volunteer will be short-lived, indeed.

2. Zip It

Charities need engaged, wealthy patrons in order to survive, but unless you have enough money to write a check for a swimming pool or a new library, *your* opinion is not all that significant. Hence, you must rein in the urge to give it.

As a general rule, never offer an opinion on any matter unless you are specifically asked for it or until you rise to chair or a head-of-committee position.

No matter what, never speak your mind in an "open" board meeting. If you have a burning issue with an agenda item, the time to surface your problem is in a closed-door huddle *weeks before* the open meeting while there is still time to make your case.

Learn to work the back channels rather than the front channels. Identify who the real decision makers are on each project and try to persuade them to your point of view. And then, win or lose, resolve to abide by the majority decision. Because once the open board meeting occurs, your charge is to remain silent and just vote for "it"—whatever "it" is.

The open meeting is like a play: It's well rehearsed and no one in attendance will appreciate any surprises or filibusters. The staff liaisons, leaders, chairs, and committee heads are the performers. They wish to report on their teams' progress without incident or any second-guessing from the peanut gallery. (The peanut gallery didn't sit through countless meetings on the topic.)

Ask any pointed questions in an open meeting and you will be regarded as a troublemaker—and not just by the charity's employees, but by your fellow volunteers—which is the death knell to your future prospects. An open board meeting is code for "Keep thy mouth shut."

You may wonder what you're supposed to *do* in a committee meeting, if, in fact, you're not supposed to offer your opinion. Make it a habit to listen rather than speak. Strive to be a catalyst

who works well with the staff and facilitates its ability to get things done. Identify new volunteers to replace you when your term is up. Help get the word out about new staff initiatives. If you are raising money for a cause, be the hardest-working fund-raiser—the one who attends all the phone-a-thons or who tackles the hard cases, such as those who donated five years ago but haven't given a dime since.

Contact other volunteers who are also working the phones and, together, devise new strategies. In any volunteering scenario, teamwork works. Lone Ranger behavior doesn't.

Also, show up. As Woody Allen once said, "Half of life is showing up." On a charitable board, the percentage is considerably higher.

Trust that, if you keep showing up without speaking up, eventually, the day will come when people will actually want to hear from you. Chairs will term out, some actively engaged volunteers will leave the fold (as their real jobs demand), and there will be a need for you to fill in for them.

While you're waiting for your big break as a volunteer, move heaven and earth (and business meetings and dentist appoint-

ments) to attend those committee pow-wows and to be on those conference calls.

Never think of yourself as a seat-warmer. True, you may have to warm your seat for a year or two before anyone considers you someone whose opinions matter. But one day, perhaps when you least expect it, all of the physical chairs in the room will be pivoted in your direction, and the occupants of those chairs will want to hear from you. Lo and behold, your input will be needed.

You may be asked to step up and take charge, so you also have to be prepared. Read the memos. Ask questions. Stay engaged. Make friends on your committee. And wait.

Unless change is in the air.
If the charity is under duress and the current order needs to be toppled, you may be asked for your opinion considerably earlier— even if you're just a rank-and-file board member. Your ideas may also be solicited if there is some macro marketing change afoot. If, for example, the charity decides that all of its board members are too old and it needs new, fresh faces and "young blood," it could

be a real opportunity to give your opinion. But only do so if asked.

New administrations also tend to be more open to hearing from their newer members. Restrain yourself, unless someone specifically solicits your thoughts.

3. Don't Get Drafted into other People's Battles

Several of my acquaintances went on wild rampages against their alma maters when these institutions turned around and subsequently rejected their kids. This was the height of bad manners—on the part of the alumni.

In most high schools and colleges, there is a Chinese Wall between the admissions and the alumni relations department, and it's a bit naïve of alumni to assume that their kids will be automatically accepted just because they happen to be legacies. There are still pesky issues—such as how well those kids perform on standardized tests, how well the in-person interviews progress, the caliber of any recommendations received, plus the competition that the applicants face during that particular year. (Steep.)

Should you find yourself on the phone with a disgruntled parent whose kid was rejected from the school, simply take copious notes and lend a sympathetic ear. Then report the situation to the alumni relations office without delay.

When it comes to other people's battles with an institution where you are volunteering, maintain a compassionate but cordial distance. Schools reject candidates for a host of different reasons; and unless it's your kid who's rejected, you will never know the whole sorry story.

On a related note, I also believe that it's a smart idea to *not* write recommendations for other people's children—unless you know the parents well enough to politely tell them to butt out of the process. A few years ago, I was flabbergasted when I graciously agreed to write a letter of recommendation for the daughter of some close friends. After toying with the verbiage for days, I emailed my letter to the parents in a Word document. The parents brazenly rewrote my letter without my permission, added scores of accolades about their child, and had the unmitigated gall to send it back to me for *my* approval (and signature). I was furious. Not only had these ingrates taken it upon themselves to fabricate facts about their kid (a "prodigy," for sure), but they had the abominable manners to challenge the sentence structure, logic, and gentle pathos of a professional writer!

I called the parents and coerced them to let me send the schools my original letter, as drafted. And thankfully, the child was still accepted.

But ever since that unfortunate incident, I follow a different tack when it comes to writing recommendations for my friends' kids: I work in KGB-like secrecy. I will draft the letter, send it to the powers-that-be at the institution, and never allow the parents to even read the missive until long after the school makes its decision.

Does a volunteer have a grievance against a staff member or against another volunteer? Listen, nod your head, but don't sign up to wage any battles. As a volunteer, your job is to instill peace, not go to war.

In sum, don't take on other people's battles and never allow anyone to micro manage the recommendations you write about their children. Do you hear that loud, chopping noise? It's the sound of a helicopter parent, circling overhead. Tell the parent that you have not cleared the runway for his landing, and to fly, fly away!

4. Be a Jolly Good Fella: Never Criticize a Fellow Volunteer

Considering that many board members are people in positions of prominence, you'd be well advised to tone down any criticism of a fellow volunteer's performance. The tongue-tied slacker who sits in the room cynically biting his lip or rudely texting during a committee meeting might have a family foundation worth millions of dollars, and keeping him involved may be far more important to the continuing health of the charitable institution than keeping you so.

If someone does ask for your opinion, beware of sounding overly harsh. Everyone hates to be criticized, and everyone on the volunteer side is also "working" on behalf of the organization for free.

Surveys liberate you to say what you really think, but use tact.

If a particular board member thrills to the sound of his own voice (as many do), and his digressions threaten to derail a meeting, you might suggest that perhaps the discussion would be better saved for a future committee phone call, but say it only if you're chairing the meeting.

If a volunteer has an idea that may have sounded fresh during the Stone Age but has fossilized since, you might recommend putting his idea to a vote, and keep fingers and toes crossed that the collective intelligence in the room will quash the hackneyed notion. But don't rudely cut him off mid-sentence, snapping "Vote! Vote! Let's bring this to a vote!" Be diplomatic, and don't take it upon yourself to personally kill his idea.

If a board member has the kernel of a good proposition, and

you can think of a way to expand upon it to make it work even better, *that's* a worthwhile way to demonstrate your leadership potential. Stay detached from your own ideas and support other people's, and you will be considered a superb team player and a worthy volunteer.

A notable exception: surveys.
Sometimes, when bequests and other gifts are down and money isn't flowing into the charity as freely as it used to, a not-for-profit may seek to reflect on the reason. Some smart soul in the room will inevitably suggest taking a survey! A staff member, possibly with the help of a student or intern, will cobble one together that asks the constituent base what the organization could be doing better. If

you are displeased with any aspect of your volunteer experience, this survey is the *one and only time* that you have the freedom to openly express yourself.

However, remember that while a survey may grant you carte blanche, in the words of a famous lyric, "Freedom's just another word for nothing left to lose." But in this case you actually *do* have a lot to lose—your reputation as an upstanding volunteer!

Never name names. Bend over backwards to position your grievance as the one and only thing that could make the absolutely fabulous experience of volunteering even better. If there is an option to leave your name off the survey, do so. (Chances are excellent that the staff will still be able to deduce who wrote it, but they are less likely to hold your grievance against you.)

5. Your Charge Is to Fill Slots, Not to Carve Out New Shapes

The Boston College Center on Wealth and Philanthropy estimates that individual charitable giving in the United States during 2009 amounted to $217.3 billion.[18] Fund-raising raises its own special set of challenges because it entails calling on wealthy people who feel a certain sense of entitlement. Some of the people you approach will believe that they deserve a special arrangement. Pass on their requests to the forces-that-be, but don't cut any special deals with the philanthropist unless you have the specific approval to do so.

A woman I know was shocked when her charity of choice turned down a generous offer of a quarter of a million dollars over several years versus $100,000 in year one. How could they be so short-sighted, she wondered? Easy. They were filling a slot.

Don't look for massive creativity from the gurus of fund-raising. They need to fill pledges. This year, it's 5 pledges of $ A, 30 pledges of $ B, 300 pledges of $ C, and 1,000 of $ D.

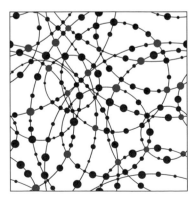

Raising buckets of money is important, of course, but the funds will be appreciated even more when they come in pledges of the right denominations! Again, if you are wealthy enough to write a check for a swimming pool or a new dance studio, you might discover a lot more latitude and creativity on the part of the fund-raising aficionados, but if you're not, just try to give the charity *exactly* what it wants if you can afford to do so—no more and no less.

If you have enough money to donate a swimming pool, you can be more creative with your donations.

If you're the one making the phone call on behalf of the institution, always recommend that the patrons follow the bequests that the institution actually desires. Never try to reinvent, restructure, or reinterpret the fund-raising pyramid. (Many fund-raising challenges are, in fact, laid out in the shape of a pyramid. The pyramid is sacrosanct. Perhaps the first pharaoh was a fund-raising guru who divined that he *couldn't* take it all with him.)

Don't worry about being "creative," and whatever you do, never encourage others to be. You can still have fun and meet a lot of genuinely nice and incredibly successful people while you're busy filling in the slots!

6. Recognize That You Won't Always Get the Recognition You Deserve

By definition, volunteers don't get paid for their services. That makes getting acclaim all the more important. And yet, praise is a zealously guarded commodity.

Did you raise more money for a particular outreach than anyone else? Did your event attract more donors in the coveted 20–34-year-old age group?

Did your charitable auction generate cooler prizes, more bidders, or more buzz among the charity blogging set?

Don't automatically assume that you will receive the accolades you deserve. You may think that you merit a chair title as a reward for your diligence. But others may disagree. (And still others may be competing with you for the very title you feel you've earned.)

In charitable circles, people can be surprisingly *uncharitable* about all attempts to toot one's own horn. Therefore, the more you vie for a title on a not-for-profit board, the less likely you are to obtain it. To suggest that YOU have the ideal qualifications for a particular position will only raise the hackles of other equally qualified board members who will then question why THEY are not running against you for it. (Don't even think about campaigning—or watch your chances for a title sink faster than the *Titanic* that brought down their ancestors.)

Strive to offer fresh-squeezed ideas that will be embraced by the chairs of the committee without angling for special kudos. Is there an effort that no one else wants to touch? Raise your hand and volunteer to take it on.

Befriend staff members by having lunch with them or meeting them for a drink occasionally, and you will have a brilliant career as a volunteer ahead of you. Also, if you have the wherewithal, don't be afraid to throw excellent parties and invite the staff. You'd be surprised: It's not every day that volunteers treat staff members as if they are their close personal friends. Never forget to thank the staff profusely for all of its hard work.

Above all, when someone *other than you* comes up with a good idea, be it another volunteer or a staff member, be sure to croon his or her praises really loudly. If you can be generous in this way, that is, magnanimous in extolling other people's virtues and not just with a dollar, it will make staff members sit up and pay attention to you, and sometimes they will even suggest you for special leadership roles.

Just do yourself a favor and never pat *yourself* on the back, belt out your own praises like a tune in the shower, or nominate yourself for any volunteer positions. Staff members often frown on self-nomination (and everyone I have

Good volunteers sing other people's praises.

ever known who has attempted it has failed to be nominated for anything).

Lastly, never badger other volunteers who sit on the board to "toss your name into the hat" for special awards and titles. You have to be a good-enough volunteer so that someone finds you worthy of recognition—other than yourself.

THE VOLUNTEER CODE

As a volunteer, you join a band of people with a zeal to help others. There is a selflessness about volunteerism that helps dampen most aggressive acts of self-promotion. Along with staying humble, don't forget to:

1) Cooperate with the staff
2) Hold back your opinion until people specifically ask for it
3) Make peace, not war by refusing to take on other people's battles against the institution
4) Compliment your fellow volunteers instead of carping about them
5) Work within the fund-raising pyramid rather than reinventing it
6) Credit others instead of mongering credit for yourself

There is no star system in the volunteer arena. However, if you work tirelessly to promote the cause rather than your own self-aggrandizement, and champion other people's ideas over your own, slowly but surely, your volunteer star will rise.

CHAPTER FOURTEEN

SHOW SOME CLASS

Before the unfortunate incident with the flight attendant, you had fancied yourself quite the road warrior.

It was only your third business trip overseas, but this time, you believed you had come prepared. Not only had you packed five French–English phrase books, you had also taken the precaution of downloading the Babelingo application onto your trusty iPhone. With any luck, you thought, Babelingo would save you from having to pull out your rusty high school French and embarrassing yourself in front of the clients. With this electronic translator at your fingertips, you could simply find the key phrase in English while Babelingo would display it in French. Then your clients could type out the answer in French while Babelingo would display it for you in English.

Ou est Starbucks? Tap. Tap.

Make a right and it's three doors down on the left. Tap. Tap. Tap.

With Babelingo by your side, what could possibly go wrong?

"Excuse me," says the flight attendant, poking her big blonde bob into the open overhead bin above your seat in coach and fishing out your beige Burberry. "Is this your coat?"

"Yes. . . ."

"It needs to go up front."

"I'm sorry," you say, "but my Babelingo is in that coat. I need to hold on to it you see."

"Didn't you hear the announcement?" she asks in a steady, overly patient manner, as if talking to a rather large, impossibly spoiled child.

"I—I—I was reading the *Wall Street Journal*," you say. "I must have zoned out."

"Either the coat goes up to the front or

it will need to be removed from this plane," she says. "The plane is completely full. We need to make room for *everyone's* belongings."

"But MY coat doesn't take up very much room."

"We need the overhead bins for LUGGAGE."

"But that's where I wish to STORE MY COAT!"

"There's plenty of room for your coat—in the front of the cabin!"

"But I have very important items in those pockets."

"Well, take them *out* of the pockets," she says. "Your coat needs to go up front."

She holds out the coat to you like a beige bullfighter's cape. Accepting it from her with extreme reluctance, you proceed to remove your iPhone, wallet, map, house keys, two loose spearmint Lifesavers, work ID badge on blue cord, felt tip, gloves, sunglasses, dry-cleaning receipt, and other sundries, and place them on your lap. Shards from the aluminum wrapping that used to house the breath mints add to the detritus. Continuing to rummage through your coat pockets, you extract two small dust balls from the inner lining plus three

paperclips, which you add to the unsightly heap balanced on your thighs.

"Did your briefcase explode?" your supervisor Mr. Bucks asks, suddenly appearing out of nowhere from the line of passengers entering the cabin, and seating himself beside you. "You look a mess."

"Where's *your* coat?" you ask him, finally handing your empty garment to the victorious flight attendant.

"Up front," he says. "Why? Didn't you hear the announcement?"

THE COMMON GOOD

It's easy to be rude and perfunctory; modern society practically encourages it.

When every seat is filled on an airplane, it's tempting to ignore the flight attendant's impassioned pleas to stow only your luggage in the overhead bins, then stuff your winter coat up there as well. But once you have reached a certain station in life, you are expected to have manners.

Manners defer to the common good over individual gain. This has been true ever since the invention of etiquette.

According to *Etiquette in Society, in Business, in Politics, and at Home*, the watershed book written in 1922 by the late great Emily Post, we owe the word "etiquette" to the master gardener at Versailles, who complained to King Louis XIV that the newly seeded palace gardens were being continually trampled upon.

To keep trespassers off the grass, the greenskeeper put up warning signs or "etiquettes," which indicated the path along which to walk. When the courtiers ignored these directions, the gardener complained to the king, who issued an edict commanding everyone to "keep within the etiquettes."

Each courtier trespassing on the grass could have argued that *his* feet weren't the ones destroying the garden. But Louis XIV was too formidable a force for that, and by instructing everyone to stay off the grass, the common good was aided at the expense of individual gain, so that all could enjoy the beauty of the Versailles gardens.[19]

Whenever you are tempted to put your personal comfort ahead of everyone else's, remember Louis XIV's edict to "keep off the grass." Louis, the "Sun King," was not only rich and powerful but also respected by those who were in the habit of plotting against monarchs.

Similarly, when you place the common good ahead of your own individual gain, you will distinguish yourself. At work, you'll display leadership abilities and team spirit. In social settings, you'll show yourself to have good breeding. Even when you're *not* at the office or at a party, it's usually a smart idea to defer to the common good. Practicing exemplary etiquette builds self-confidence and helps create a more pleasant atmosphere for everyone concerned. With the self-confidence that you attain, you'll demonstrate

After the master gardener at Versailles put up warning signs or "etiquettes" to stay off the grass, the term "etiquette" became synonymous with the word "decorum," or the observance of the formal requirements governing behavior in polite society.

that you're a person who feels at ease. Comfortable with yourself, you'll be adept at putting others at ease. People will enjoy having you around, which will augur well for you—both at the workplace and in your social life.

ETIQUETTE 101

In case you're not an etiquette buff, here are the "monarch notes," so to speak.

After the monarchy was deposed in France, etiquette became all the rage in America, an ironic twist of fate since many of etiquette's rules were based on customs derived from a European aristocratic society that the new middle class had helped to displace. In nineteenth-century America, a command of propriety helped distinguish the middle and upper classes from the working classes, who often didn't have the time, money, or inclination to follow the rules. From the 1870s until the end of the nineteenth century, the American market was flooded with etiquette books, which outlined the tenets of "polite society" to a consumer-driven one that had been recently energized by the industrial revolution. By all accounts, the number of articles that appeared about place settings alone was staggering. There was also plenty of instruction on all other matters of decorum, including the practice of calling on people, extended visits, courtship, carriage riding, ballroom demeanor, formal dinners, and polite conversation.

Today, superior etiquette instruction is harder to find. The grand diva of etiquette, Emily Post, died back in 1960. And some of the old conventions seem quaint, almost fusty, in the age of technology, texting, and Babelingo. And yet, the fact that so few people know the rules can help you distinguish yourself even more from all of the rudelings and ingrates.

During the nineteenth century, hundreds of etiquette books were published in America, a record by today's standards.

Consider, every time you chat with a boss in an elevator, approach a worker in a cubicle or office, take out a client for dinner, R.S.V.P. to a cocktail party, stand in a buffet line with either colleagues or friends, or invite anyone to join you socially, you are demonstrating your mastery of etiquette—or the lack thereof.

Are you passing life's etiquette tests or flunking them? The quiz below depicts six common conundrums. Why not conduct a quick reality check and see how your own behavior rates? Are you the next Mr. Manners or the current Ms. Neanderthal? The section that follows the quiz will provide more gloss about why a particular answer is correct.

Whether you're trying to prove that you are capable of taking on greater responsibility at the office or are angling to become more socially upwardly mobile, demonstrating that you understand today's modern etiquette rules can only help you in your quest.

Little touches make a big difference. Open a car door for someone and help prove that chivalry isn't dead.

ETIQUETTE QUIZ. GOOD LUCK!

1. *Your best friend's significant other has just died. You've already sent your friend flowers and a heartfelt condolence letter. Now you'd love to invite him to a few low-key parties to help take his mind off his grief. But when you leave him a voicemail message, he doesn't call you back. What's your next move?*

A. Give him a little space, then call him in a month to invite him out again.

B. Take it personally. You appreciate that the circumstances are horrific, but he should honor protocol anyway, dammit.

C. Send him a handwritten letter saying that you're thinking about him and suggest that he call you when he's ready to get together.

2. *The presentation is so mind-numbingly dull that you can feel your eyes rolling into the back of your head. Help! What if your eyes get lodged up there permanently? Then no one will ever know whether your eyes are blue or brown, plus you won't be able to see anything ever again. You no longer know if you're awake or asleep. Is it okay to leave the room to figure out whether you are or aren't?*

   A. No, but if you want to stay engaged, you can ask the speaker a question (if interrupting him won't be perceived as rude).

   B. Leave already. Life's too short to be bored to death.

   C. Yes, it's perfectly acceptable to slip out of the room. But wait for a natural pause in the speaker's conversation. Then withdraw quietly without drawing attention to yourself.

3. *While standing on line at Starbucks, you notice that some of the people behind you get served their drinks long before you get yours. Should you complain? Why or why not?*

   A. Don't raise the issue. A "last in, first out" policy may seem unjust, but that's no reason to make a fuss. Especially since those who *were* served first have already left the premises.

   B. No. The people in back of you are regulars and you aren't, so it's almost a "House Rule" that they will be treated better.

   C. Vehemently complain, and while you're at it, insist on speaking to the manager. Your drink cost two dollars more than the drinks of the three people behind you who were served first. It's a travesty of justice!

4. *During a foray to the office kitchenette, someone who you barely know asks if you enjoyed your recent ski trip. You're flummoxed about how he even learned of your vacation, then realize that he probably overheard you gabbing about it through the tissue-thin cubicle walls. You:*

   A. Mumble something about how your vacation was "fantastic, thank you," and skedaddle. No point in encouraging a would-be stalker!

   B. Pretend that you're the TV detective Columbo and pin down your officemate with a series of seemingly innocent questions. Then ask how he found out about your trip to confirm whether your suspicions are accurate.

C. Thank him for inquiring about your trip, and then silently resolve to conduct all future personal calls outside the office.

5. *You are finally invited to a party at a posh Hamptons "cottage" by the ocean. Picturing that the guests will include some famous Hamptons A-listers, such as Steven Spielberg and Billy Joel, you devote a whole week to plotting out your wardrobe and sharpening your conversational aptitude. Alas! The party for 100 is under-attended, and the most impressive person there is . . . YOU? How do you recuperate from the shock?*

A. Seek empathetic ears. Be sure to gossip with some of the other guests about what a colossal disappointment the party was.

B. Be proactive. Email the host directly afterwards and offer to help him throw a bigger bash next time. If you and he align forces, you can practically guarantee that he'll get the numbers up.

C. Strive to be the consummate diplomat. Write the host a handwritten Thank You note saying how much fun you had, even though if lies have color, this is a gray one bordering on black.

6. *The host at a fancy dinner party announces that everyone should take their seats. How precisely should that be accomplished these days?*

A. Everyone stands and waits for the host to sit down first. Then, all sit down in unison.

B. Men remain standing until the women are seated. If seating is tight, the gents help the ladies sit by pulling out their chairs.

C. There is no special decorum. Everyone takes his or her place without further ado.

QUIZ ANSWERS

See the discussion that follows.

**1. C.   2. A.   3. B.   4. C.
5. C.   6. B.**

B.E.H.A.V.E., OR MANNERS 101 FOR THOSE WHO WERE NOT TO THE MANOR BORN

I recently taught an etiquette seminar at the New York Athletic Club. There were a lot of experts on the roster that day who had been brought in to speak to a Gen-Y crowd about soft skills, such as interviewing, networking, and business writing. I bumped into my friend Andrea Nierenberg in the vestibule where some of the seminar leaders were waiting for their turn at the podium. Andrea, an author with four published books about networking, had been kind enough to blurb my latest book on business etiquette. (A "blurb" is a glowing book review.) Andrea's kind sentiment had not only been beautifully written, it had been the perfect length—ultra short. As a result, it graced the cover of my new book.

And how had I repaid this kindness? Sorry to say, I hadn't.

Directly after my book was published, I had completely forgotten to send Andrea a copy. My behavior had been truly thoughtless—and for an etiquette maven, nothing short of abominable.

At the conference, Andrea alerted me about my oversight with these words: "If you would just remember to send me a copy of your book, I would blog about it."

Her unbelievable generosity in the light of my callous neglect made me feel like a real Neanderthal.

Fortunately, I was able to rectify my gaffe on the spot because I happened to be carrying extra copies of my book with me that day. I handed Andrea a volume—along with a sincere and heartfelt apology.

It is my observation that 90 percent of etiquette gaffes can be remedied almost as easily. Unlike most of the other etiquette pundits out there, I believe that you *always* have a second chance to make a first impression. Indeed, etiquette provides you with the very tools that you need to remedy the most atrocious of gaffes. Of course, there *is* the embarrassment factor. (High.) Once you have stuck your foot in your mouth, you have to first remove all five toes, then stand on the offending appendage for a while so that it will stop cramping up, then jump around on it for long enough to get your blood circulating up to your brain so that you can strategize on how to fix the problem.

Given a choice, it's certainly preferable *not* to insert your foot in your mouth in the first place and to always do the right thing like a modern-day Emily Post. But failing that, etiquette at least gives you the solutions to correct most everyday uh-oh moments. That's why I believe that it's essential to first hone your etiquette skills, and then take them out whenever you interact with the species known as "human beings." It's unrealistic to think that you will skate through both your business and personal life without ever offending anyone. Trust me, if you are alive, you will offend numerous people! But at least when you do, etiquette will provide you with the pick and shovel for digging yourself out of the mess.

Andrea, who was one of the keynotes that morning, has all sorts of amazing tricks that she uses to help people become more proficient at networking. She's a big believer in acronyms and turns cute words such as *Charm* and big, horsey words such as *Networking* into acronyms, with each letter standing for something vital that one should immediately put on her to-do list. I heard Andrea speak that day and was quite inspired by her acronym for *Networking*.

So in deference to Andrea, I thought I would turn the word *Behave* into an acronym—as a memory jog for the six behaviors that I believe are the underpinning of all modern etiquette today. These six rules apply to both business and social situations, as I feel that distinguishing oneself in the business arena never hurt one's prospects in the social realm or vice versa. So here it is, my first etiquette acronym, ever.

B is for Boundaries. Respect other people's boundaries.

E is for Enthusiasm. Keep up your enthusiasm.

H is for House Rules. Be sure to follow House Rules, especially when you're a guest.

A is for Awareness. Stay aware of how your behavior impacts others and modify it if necessary.

V is for Value. Show people that you value their contributions.

E is for Extra. Go the extra distance with people whenever you can.

B IS FOR BOUNDARIES

At the heart of etiquette is a respect for boundaries—yours, certainly, but especially other people's. When you acknowledge other people's limits of endurance, you understand that each situation is slightly nuanced, and you take your cues from *the other person* about how to behave on a case-by-case basis. To return to the first question on the quiz, if a friend has died, you need to honor the key mourner's wishes. Each person grieves differently. The key mourner may desire your com-

panionship—or not. That's why, after reaching out to him once and being rebuffed, it's far more considerate to write him a hand-written note suggesting that he contact you when he's ready to socialize. In this way, you allow him to grieve at his own pace, rather than at one you might find more acceptable.

Good manners mandate that other people's expectations take precedence over your own. Therefore, if a hostess specifically asks you not to smoke a cigar while sitting outdoors on her pristine terrace, you should not argue that the fresh air will waft the stench into the stratosphere and that all the hoopla about the danger of secondhand smoke is the reason you smoke in the first place! A respect for other people's perimeters and desire for some "breathing room" explains why you obligingly move your elbow to give a complete stranger more space on the shared armrest at a movie theater.

Do you require the assistance of someone who works in an office cubicle? It's only polite to acknowledge his boundaries by imagining that there is an invisible "wall" around him. While you're at it, remember to knock on the wall. Make it a habit to honor the privacy of your fellow workers. Doing so will help position you well for a leadership role down the road.

E IS FOR ENTHUSIASM

Being critical, cynical, and jaded never did any wonders for anyone's personality. Enthusiasm, by contrast, has proven magnetic properties. People actually *want* to be around an enthusiastic person. Enthusiasm is a draw. It's so charming, and yet highly unusual in most people over the age of four. Splash on some rah-rah spirit today. If you don't actually feel gung ho, feign it.

Are you trapped inside a conference hall developing hemorrhoids while someone's plodding speech waxes prolific? Do try to remember that not everyone can be the next Winston Churchill. In study after study, the fear of speaking in public ranks as number two on everyone's bugaboo list—a fear that seems perfectly justified based on most speakers' lousy perfor-

mances! Let's be honest: Deadly dull speeches are the norm rather than the exception. If you happen to be stuck listening to one, your only option is to stay put and do your best to at least *look* animated. Pretend you're a reporter whose job is to summarize the person's talk and listen hard for any pearls of wisdom. If no pearls are forthcoming, then imagine that you will be tested at the end on your retentive abilities, and force yourself to keep listening. Sometimes, in order to stay engaged, it helps to ask the speaker a question. (But don't do it if you feel that his whole talk will unravel, or if the speaker has specifically asked audience members to hold all questions until the end.)

As a general rule, if you show some exuberance, it will enhance your popularity. When you first meet someone new, always remember to smile and say hello. Then, devote most of your energy to taking an interest in what he or she has to say rather than in endeavoring to be fascinating yourself. If you do this each and every time that someone new enters your life, most people will love being around you and your likeability factor will soar. This can only help you in business and socially.

Make no mistake: Life is a popularity contest. Business too.

H IS FOR HOUSE RULES

When you're a guest of the house, you need to play by its rules.

To return to the question on the quiz, the system at Starbucks is "first come, first served" *except* where regulars are concerned. Once the person behind the counter recognizes you and knows your drink, she will automatically make it for you, regardless of the call order for the rest of the patrons. Think of it as the "frequent buyers' loophole" if that makes it more palatable. It's a house rule that must be accepted without complaint.

In movie theaters, there is a no-texting-or-talking-during-the-film regulation. In casinos, there is a no-counting-the-cards law. In bars, cabs, and hotels, tipping is mandatory (and 20 percent is standard). In airplanes, the

flight attendant and pilot are your benign dictators for the duration of the flight. When tooling around Versailles, stay off the grass.

If you are a guest at someone's home, must you always abide by your host's wishes? Of course, silly. How else can you possibly guarantee a return invitation?

A IS FOR AWARENESS

"He who knows others is wise. He who knows himself is enlightened," wrote Lao Tzu, the father of Taoism. Many other philosophers agreed with this notion, including Socrates who is often credited with crafting the exponentially catchier "Know thyself."

Stay aware of your surroundings and monitor how your behavior influences others. If someone at the office has unearthed a personal detail about you that you never shared with him, ask yourself whether it's probable that someone else told him about it or if it's even likelier that he overheard you discussing it. In the latter case, resolve to keep your voice down in the future. (There's no need to apologize for the fact that he overheard you. In fact, doing so could make your colleague feel self-conscious about raising the topic.)

Stay particularly attuned to your behavior in confined spaces. If you are blessed with the gift of gab, don't unwrap your gift in an elevator. If you tend to stuff numerous items into a large backpack each morning, peel the nylon shell *off* your back before you enter any elevators so you won't inadvertently knock into people with it (or be mistaken for a tortoise). If you are allergic to throwing out

paper, be especially vigilant about cleaning up your desk before you leave the office each night and keep all surfaces clear of clutter.

Practice mindfulness. As the Italian author Pietro Aretino once said, "I am, indeed, a king, because I know how to rule myself."

V is for Value

Way back in 1936, Dale Carnegie wrote that everyone craves sincere appreciation. By all accounts, nothing has changed all that much in the intervening years. Studies show that at the office, workers enjoy morale-boosting pats on the back almost as much as raises. Look for ways to show the people around you that you value their contributions.

Let's return to the host of the dismal party in question five of the quiz. Perhaps he feels humiliated about the poor party turnout and is loath to throw another bash for the rest of eternity. When

At a formal dinner, men pull out chairs for women.

you reach out to him with a hand-written note that expresses your sincere appreciation, he can't help but feel more sanguine about his foiled party and significantly better about his hosting capabilities. When you make someone else feel appreciated, all of your efforts will boomerang back and reflect well on you. Why? Because people are only human: We gravitate to those who appreciate us and tend to like those who like us back.

E IS FOR EXTRA

Go the extra distance. At a formal party, such as the one cited in question six of the quiz, the men need to remain standing until the women are seated. While the gents are standing, they should make themselves useful by pulling out the chairs and helping their female dinner partners into them. If there is anyone elderly at the meal, the men should offer to help that person sit, even if the senior is another male.

If someone at the table can't hear a word you're saying due to partial deafness, extend yourself by bending towards him and repeating what you said more loudly than before. Extra touches

can also be expressed by the wine you bring to the party as a small token of your appreciation and the handwritten Thank You note you send afterwards to the host. Compliments are other miscellaneous kindnesses that you can offer people that are free of charge. Just make certain that your sweet words always have the stamp of truth to them.

Give the gift that will never be returned: a beautifully crafted Thank You note.

HOW A COMMAND OF MANNERS CAN HELP YOU GET AHEAD

It doesn't matter whether your parents were monarchs or milkmen, sultans or seamstresses. You might be seated in the coach section of an airplane or in business class. In order to attain class, it helps to demonstrate that you already possess it. An ad that appeared in *The American Maga-*

zine back in 1921 for *The Book Of Etiquette* put it this way:

What Etiquette Does

To the man who is self-conscious and shy, etiquette gives poise, self-confidence. To the woman who is timid and awkward, etiquette gives a well-poised charm. To all who know and follow its little secrets of good conduct, etiquette gives a calm dignity that is recognized and respected in the highest circles of business and society. [20]

Good manners can open doors that the best education and contacts cannot. Master the six tenets of B.E.H.A.V.E., and you will be welcomed with open arms almost anywhere.

CHAPTER FIFTEEN

NAME YOURSELF IF YOU HAVE TO

Hunkered down in your cubicle, you sip your latte and fervently review your presentation notes until you hear a quiet footfall directly behind you on the beige industrial carpet. A dark shadow splays across your desk.

"AAAH!" you scream, spinning your chair around to see the unflappable, handsome Mr. Bucks just three inches away from you. A drop of latte splashes on your face.

"I have that effect on people," he laughs. He holds an official-looking blue document in his right hand. "So tell me," he says, briefly glancing at the page, "do you have any idea who 'A. J. Thomas' is?"

"That's me," you say, suddenly straightening up in your chair. "Why?"

"Are you sure?" he says, peering into your eyes. The look on his face is inscrutable; you can't tell whether he's angry or being playful.

"I'm positive!" you say. "Why?"

"Because when I hired you, you told me your name was 'Alex.'"

"My name is 'Alex,'" you say.

"Because I quite like the name 'Alex.' And I'm not sure how I feel about the name 'A. J.' When did you change your name to 'A. J.'?"

"I didn't change it, exactly. I just decided to use my initials when I applied those campaigns for the marketing award," you say.

"Why? Why would you do such a thing?"

"It just seemed more professional," you say. "Plus the application asked me for the contact information about a billion times and 'A. J.' was shorter to type."

"So I should call you 'A. J.' from now on then?" Mr. Bucks asks.

"You can call me 'A. J.' or 'Alex,'" you say.

"You don't think that might get confusing?"

"I promise to respond to either."

"Good answer," he says with a grin. "Because A. J. is getting a raise. But I'm not so sure about Alex. . . ."

"Mr. Bucks, I SWEAR that 'A. J.' is just a nickname that I used to . . . "

"Just kidding!" he laughs, shaking your hand vigorously and handing you the blue document. "Congratulations on your first award, A. J."

What's In a Name?

A name can make you sound like a prince or a pauper, a businessman or a bum. A great name can position you for greatness. Depending on its rhythm and its spelling, a name can sound aristocratic, presidential, poetic, or even humorous. Does your name convey every-

thing you want it to—both about you and your ambitions?

If you have any doubts about your name, feel free to blame your parents. If you don't like your name, it's definitely their fault! Some parents know how to plan for their progeny and some parents don't.

But just because you weren't given an inspired name at birth doesn't mean you have to suffer without one for your whole life. At a certain point, you simply have to take matters into your own hands—and name yourself.

You'll be in good company. Actors do it. Rappers do it. Even three presidents of the United States did it. Did you know that

Before you legally change your name, first see how you like it on your stationery, business cards, and other documents.

fashion mogul Ralph Lauren used to be Ralph Lifshitz? That philosopher Ayn Rand was born Alisa Rosenbaum? And Ringo Starr was born Richard Starkey?

One easy way to rename yourself that won't involve lawyers is to give yourself a memorable nickname.

Nicknames that connote wealth often end in "y," such as Missy, Miffy, Muffy, Buffy, Biffy, and Sandy. Other nicknames sound studly, such as Jock, Atlas, Aaron, Chad, Hunter, and Chase. Other names sound professional, such as A. J. or Jones.

Don't fret if the nickname you give yourself has zero relation to your birth name. You can't pick your parents, but you can pick your name.

THE MIDDLE NAME TRICK

Does naming yourself make you feel like an imposter? Give yourself an opportunity to grow into your new name by adopting it first as a middle name. You might select a nickname with the same initial as your real middle name and allow the alias to secretly marinate for a few weeks. Then, only

when ready, try swapping your new middle name with your first name. Since most people haven't the slightest clue what your real middle name is, they are unlikely to quibble with your nickname's authenticity.

Start by seeding your new nickname with your oldest friends on the planet. Tell them that you'd prefer for them to start calling you by your "middle name"—for whatever reason, "Jock" has grown on you over the years.

Or the next time an old chum visits, take him or her out with instructions to call you by your new chosen name and to tell all mutual friends that it was your nickname when you were in col-

lege. (Don't fear the gossip mill—the more buddies you have acting as "name enforcers" on your behalf, the more likely your new handle will stick.)

Or start a Facebook page with your new name and tell your friends that Chip is on your birth certificate (but when you were a kid you preferred to be called Jim, which is really your middle name).

THE NAME GAME

Another gambit is to nickname yourself after a fond childhood memory. Then when people ask how you got the cute name, you can recount the story. For example, if you were the tallest kid on your softball team and friends always called you "Stretch," it's not such a stretch to ask your adult friends to follow suit.

Nicknames that seem like they belong to baseball players such as Chuck, Derek, or Gordy have the potential to make you sound rich. (Top baseball stars fetch an annual salary of approximately $25 million.)

Landed gentry names—such as Finn, Covington, Hutton, or Dexter—that sound as if your family landed a long time ago and immediately started building a plantation work too. Nicknames that imply a long family line of WASPS from Kennebunkport to Newport are always in vogue with the upper echelons. Junior and Trey are solid options, while "Quarry" is a dynamite name that implies the fourth.

Short, pithy names of famous British kings, like Hank for Henry, have a regal touch. Speaking of kings, it's hard to go astray with impressive titles, such as King, Admiral, or "The Commodore."

On the upward trend today are appellations that are also cities, like Paris and Troy. (Although with a name like Paris, you might want to first ask if you truly want Paris Hilton's legacy associated with yours.)

Some sobriquets to shy away from are those of large jewelry stores like Tiffany and Cartier.

Jewelry: the perfect backdrop for your new name.

Those names are played out and, at any rate, always had flashy overtones that made old-moneyed types wheeze. Fortunoff (or any other jewelry store that's out of business) has unlucky name karma. Lesser-known jewelry stores (think Zales) that are found in malls are even worse. As a general rule, anything that has proven mass appeal clashes with the dogged pursuit of class. Never call yourself Costco. Steer clear of the first name Ford unless you want to go hog wild and change your last name too.

Hippie names that bring to mind one's parents or grandparents getting it on at Woodstock also interfere with the quest to look rich. Plutocrats rarely brag about sex, and images of thumping, vibrantly colored love buses might distract those in a position of power from noticing your finer qualities. Some hippie names to avoid—especially since you do have a choice—are Sunshine, Rainbow, Moonbeam, Meadow, Skye, Harmony, and Apple. (Sorry, Gwyneth.)

Names that convey virtues, such as Amity, Prudence, and Temperance, work only if you happen to possess the virtue. Otherwise, there could be a backlash. Are you considering naming yourself Chastity? Be careful what you wish for.

By its nature, a nickname is a foreshortening. So why not take out an imaginary pair of scissors right now and trim all extraneous letters from your name until you arrive at the world's most elegant initials— your own. (If you can visualize these initials monogrammed on a set of fluffy towels or crisp linens, all the better.) For example, if your name is Thomas James Williams, you can't go astray if you start calling yourself "T. J." "P. J." as a nickname is also immensely popular. And who can forget T. S. Eliot and the beginning of his poem "The Naming of Cats"?

The Naming of Cats is a difficult matter,
It isn't just one of your holiday games;
You may think at first I'm as mad as a hatter
When I tell you, a cat must have
    THREE DIFFERENT NAMES.

Keep in mind that while cats apparently must have *three* different names, cats also have nine lives. Shirley MacLaine aside, most mortals have only one life.

And fortunately, it only takes one great nickname to reverse much of the damage your parents inflicted on you through poor name choice.

Once you arrive at a nickname, allow it to gestate for several days and then decide if it still appeals to you. There's no need to rush into anything. It's perfectly normal to find yourself toggling between a couple of different monikers. Advertising copywriters often take months to name a new product, and in this case, the product that you're branding is YOU.

How will you know if you've selected the right name? If you feel goose bumps, that's a positive indication. Your new name should energize you, sparking you with the passion that you'll need to slowly begin introducing it to your circle of friends. In this situation, remember that patience is a virtue and it helps to acquire some fast.

With Friends Like This . . .

Be forewarned, for your friends, the idea of calling you something completely different may be surprisingly difficult for some of them to accept. At first, they may resist. Greet their skepticism with tolerance, and try not to get frustrated when they forget to call you by your new handle. Simply issue gentle reminders. Prepare for some jokes as well. One or two of your friends may start referring to you as "the friend formerly known as _____." (If so, don't forget to laugh with the rest of the crowd.)

Always sign your emails, as well as any handwritten correspondence, with your new name. Practice your new signature and be sure to take it out once in a while.

If you've changed one of your initials recently, why not subtly remind your friends?

A NAME MAKEOVER

Even if you never pull it out at a charity function or a fancy soirée, it's worth knowing what your nickname would be if you chose to adopt it. Below, find some creative ways to unlock your nicknaming muse.

Current :   Given Name   Middle Name   Last Name
          _____   _____   _____

Are there any moguls whose names you covet? Would you feel considerably richer if your name happened to be Bill, Warren, Donald, or Ingvar? What about Martha or Tyra? Jot them down on the lines below.

1. Mogul names I like:

_____

_____

_____

What character from a novel do you most admire? Is it Rhett, Jay, or Holden? Anna, Emma, Hermione, or someone else?

2. If I were a hero or heroine from a novel, I would be:

_____

Is there a TV character with whom you identify? Is it Lemon, Zoe, or Lavon? Rachel, Peach, Blake, or someone from a whole different genre?

3. If I were a TV character, I would be:

_____

If you could come back as a famous historical figure, who would it be? Would it be Abraham, Dwight, or Ronald? Eleanor or Jacqueline? Alexander, Napoleon, or Winston? Cleopatra, Margaret, or Fergie?

4. If I were a famous historical figure, I would be:

_____

Are you a blonde, brunette, or redhead? If so, what names, if any, do you associate with those colors? For example, a "blonde" name might

be Barbie or Bob. A "brunette" name might be Veronica or Reggie. And a "redhead" name might be Ruby or Ross. Names are highly subjective. Go wild.

5. Blonde names, Brunette names, Redhead names:

_____

_____

_____

Are you considering names that start with a particular letter in the alphabet? In Jewish tradition, naming a newborn after the living is considered bad luck. Infants are named after the deceased; or at the very least, the deceased's first initial is used. Thus, if your grandmother's name was "Samantha," your name might be "Sandra." Of course, if you are Jewish, your given name probably already memorializes a relative, and the great thing about self-created nicknames is that they needn't conform to all of the rules.

6. Names that start with letters I like:

_____

Do you dream of having a first name that sounds like a last name? Do you wish you had been named Dawson, Porter, Logan, Taylor, Bailey, or Campbell? Your nickname can be anything you want it to be.

7. Last names as first names:

_____

_____

_____

It's the magical moment of transformation. First, take a deep breath. Now, review your list. Are any nicknames repeated on it? If so, that could be a sign that you've found yours. Are there any names that repel you? Cross them out. Is there a name that particularly resonates with you? Try pairing it with your last name.

And my nickname of choice is:

_____

The Pygmalion Effect and the Power of Intention

Once an expectation is set, even if it isn't accurate, we tend to act in ways that are consistent with that expectation. Surprisingly, the result is often that the expectation comes true, as if by magic.

In his paper "Social Theory and Social Structure," Robert Merton, a professor of sociology at Columbia University, referred to "The Self-Fulfilling Prophecy or Pygmalion Effect." It's the combination of three vital powers that you bring to bear to help you fulfill your destiny:

1. The power of identifying a clear goal
2. The willpower to figure out your best course of action, the path that you need to take
3. The power of action—every step you take towards reaching your ambition

Start now by writing down your new sobriquet. Put the piece of paper somewhere where you'll see it every day, perhaps on your desk at home or nightstand. Then, behave as if the name that you've created isn't some fictitious person but a reality.

Change your voicemail message to reflect your new identity. When your phone rings, greet your callers with your new first name (along with your old last name, of course, so that they won't hang up). Send out holiday cards under your new alias. Don't forget to contact your schools' alumni associations and let them know of the change. And slowly but surely, your nickname will begin to manifest and shape the way that you and others see yourself.

You might also jot down the qualities your new self possesses. Here are some magnetic qualities. Which of them best complement your new name? Pick three:

○ ambition
○ charisma
○ charm
○ confidence
○ intelligence
○ luck
○ optimism
○ playfulness

○ poise
○ pragmatism
○ resilience
○ self-reliance
○ sense of humor
○ success
○ tenacity
○ wisdom

Excellent work.

Now start to think of this new persona—comprised of your new name plus the appealing traits associated with it—as YOU. Only you can actually make yourself over into the type of success story that will make you irresistible to those whom you court. The real power of transformation is in your hands.

So take action. Pick up the phone, craft some engaging emails, and spread the news. Tell your friends about your name change. Then, break it to your parents. Finally, unleash it on the relatives.

Once you begin to adopt the characteristics of your new persona, you might try designing some stationery with your new name followed by a calling card. Create a new Facebook page. Whenever you're invited to a party, remember to R.S.V.P. with your new handle. Take advantage of all introductions. Each new person that you meet has no preconceived notions about you so you're free to truly celebrate your new identity. Ever so slowly, the new entity that you created will start to take on a life of its own.

What's in a name? Everything.

Engrave—and get the word out about your new "look rich" name.

BEFORE THEY WERE HOUSEHOLD NAMES, THEY WERE . . .		
BEFORE	**AFTER**	**PROFESSION**
Alisa Rosenbaum	Ayn Rand	Philosopher
Benjamin Kubelsky	Jack Benny	Comedian
Brian Hugh Warner	Marilyn Manson	Rock Star
Cassius Marcellus Clay, Jr.	Muhammad Ali	Boxer
Cherilyn Sarkisian	Cher	Singer

BEFORE	AFTER	PROFESSION
Clive Staples Lewis	C. S. Lewis	Writer
Dante Terrell Smith–Bey	Mos Def	Actor/Rapper
Eldrick Tont Woods	Tiger Woods	Golfer
Elmore Rual Torn Jr.	Rip Torn	Actor
Emmanuel Rudnitsky	Man Ray	Photographer
Eric Arthur Blair	George Orwell	Writer
Ferdinand Lewis Alcindor	Kareem Abdul-Jabbar	Basketball Player
Francis Lee Bailey	F. Lee Bailey	Attorney
Gil Schwartz	Stanley Bing	Writer
Hiram Ulysses Grant	Ulysses S. Grant	President of the U.S.
Lawrence Peter Berra	Yogi Berra	Baseball Player
Arthur Leonard Rosenberg	Tony Randall	Actor
Leonard Alfred Schneider	Lenny Bruce	Comedian
Leslie King, Jr.	Gerald Ford	President of the U.S.★
Malcolm Little	Malcolm X	Civil Rights Activist
Norma Jeane Mortenson	Marilyn Monroe	Actress
Ralph Lifshitz	Ralph Lauren	Fashion Designer

BEFORE	AFTER	PROFESSION
Richard Starkey	Ringo Starr	Drummer
Robert LeRoy Parker	Butch Cassidy	Bank Robber
Robert Weston Smith	Wolfman Jack	On-Air Personality
Roy Harold Scherer, Jr.	Rock Hudson	Actor
Sally Lowenthal	Sally Jessy Raphael	Talk Show Host
Shawn Carter	Jay-Z	Rapper
Steven Demetre Georgiou	Cat Stevens	Singer**
Terry Gene Bollea	Hulk Hogan	Wrestler
William Blythe III	Bill Clinton	President of the U.S.***

* Gerald Ford was born as Leslie King, Jr., named after his father. Rumor has it that Ford's father was abusive, causing his mother to divorce him in 1913 shortly after Ford's birth. Two and a half years later, Ford's mother met and married Gerald Ford Sr., and Ford's family began to call the young boy "Gerald Ford Jr." rather than Leslie King Jr. The name change was made official when Ford turned twenty-two.

** Today, Cat Stevens is known as Yusuf Islam.

*** Bill Clinton was born William Jefferson Blythe III three months after his father died in a traffic accident. When Bill was four years old, his mother wed Roger Clinton.

THE EIGHT GREAT TRUTHS OF NICKNAMING YOURSELF

1. **Name drop.** If your first name is unusual enough, sometimes you can get away with making it more glamorous by dropping your surname. "Apollo Loomis" may sound more chic as "Apollo."

2. **Three is a fetching number.** When it comes to names, there is a magic about the number three. Nicknames of one syllable sync beautifully with last names of two syllables, and nicknames of two syllables pair up nicely with last names of one syllable. For example, Jock Knightly sounds pleasing to the ear, as does Lily Dale.

3. **Make sure your new nickname doesn't fight with your old surname.** Nicknames that convey a definite ethnicity may clash with a surname of a different ethnicity, but not always. For example, "Diakelmad Cohen" may trip an American ear whereas "Di Cohen" won't. By the way, in case anyone asks you at a cocktail party, "Di" is from Chinese and means, "to enlighten" and "Diakelmad" has a Palauan root that translates as "never die."

4. **It's harder than it looks to be a Dick.** One needs a special swagger to carry off a nickname that conveys a body part such as Dick, which, from the German, is a short form of Frederick or Richard. The name Fanny will also draw its fair share of ribbing and commentary. If your name happens to be Fanny Brice, chances are you'll shrug off the teasing good-naturedly. However, if the funny bone skipped your body, you may not want so much attention focused on thy Fanny.

5. **Don't tempt fate.** If you believe in karma, you may want to avoid using a name that's most famous for something negative, such as Electra (she had a fixation with her father), Pandora (her curiosity got the better of her and she opened a box, releasing all the evils of mankind), or for that matter, Adolf.

6. **Shun names that make it easy to go phish.** Never use any words in your name that are prompts for when you forget

your password. Stay away from your mother's maiden name, the name of the street where you grew up, and your first teacher's name. Personal identity theft is the fastest-growing crime in the United States, and you don't want to give these hackers any ammunition that can help them retrieve your credit card number, bank account, or ATM password.

7. **Experiment with what your parents gave you.** Sometimes spelling your given name a bit differently can yield surprisingly fresh results. For example, Vicki or Vickie are the most common spellings for the shortened form of Victoria, but the name can also be spelled Vicky, Viki, or even Vikki. Or go back to the Latin and spell it Vici, as in *Veni, Vidi, Vici.* ("I came, I saw, I conquered.")

8. **Sometimes a tall tale is better than the bald facts.** If someone asks how you got your name and you invented it, you should also concoct a clever story to explain it. "I read in this book that I should try nicknaming myself if I wanted to hang out with a classier group of people" is probably *not* the story you want to share!

The Last Word on First Names

If a radical departure from your given name seems like too daunting an adjustment, think of ways to tweak the name you were given to make it more upscale.

On the Britcom *Keeping Up Appearances*, the social climber Hyacinth Bucket coerces friends and neighbors to call her "Bouquet." "Barbra" Streisand was born "Barbara Streisand." Perhaps by dropping a syllable, swapping your middle name with your first, or going the initial route, you too can achieve a posh name, which will help you in your quest to achieve your ambitions.

William Shakespeare was a bard and a scholar. But he was seriously wrong about something. A Rose is not a Rose by any other name. And neither is a Lily, a Daisy, a Heather, or a Snapdragon.

CHAPTER SIXTEEN

FOSTER AN ECCENTRICITY

In the kingdom of eccentricity, in the principality known as Southampton, Long Island, your friend Hadley is the first person to expose you to the secret life of the court.

"Sitting on Gin Lane waiting for the gin to pour," she texts. "But it's only 1 PM, too early."

Visions of crashing exotic bashes held on manicured lawns dance through your head. You picture yourself crawling through a privet hedge in order to avoid the attendant holding the guest list.

"Need some company?" you text back.

"Want to come play?"

"How soon?" you text.

"Don't get too excited," she writes. "My whole family's here, and trust me, they are a peculiar bunch."

You thought Hadley might have exaggerated, but if anything, she understated the situation.

Each member of her family has at least one glaring eccentricity, if not several piled one on top of the other, almost turning their owner into a caricature. And yet, there is no intended irony about the behavior.

Hadley's older brother walks with a slight limp, even though he has never had a sports injury or a war accident. Tall, broad-shouldered, and handsome in a milquetoast kind of way, the limp is the most pronounced thing about him. His right leg strides in a normal enough manner, but his left leg shuffles, and both legs don't seem like they belong to the same

set. He hobbles out to the train station to greet you and drives you back to the gracious thirty-room Tudor, or what the immediate family refers to as a "cottage."

Sitting outside on the white wooden swing set with Hadley, you both attempt to diagnose her brother's curious ailment. "Brother Harry has *not* recently pulled an Achilles tendon or a muscle," Hadley says, idly twisting a strand of her hair as she tries to uncover the genesis of his limp. "He was *not* born with one leg shorter than the other. He does *not* have a clubfoot."

"So why *does* he limp do you suppose?" you whisper, pushing your feet off the mud under your swing, pointing your legs like a human arrow, and arching high over a nearby crabapple orchid.

"It's totally psychosomatic," Hadley says, propelling her own swing to join you in the air. "He developed the limp at around the same time his fiancée jilted him and has never walked right since." As if on cue, brother Harry limps out to the back lawn to summon you both to cocktail hour, to be held at precisely ten minutes of six on the front porch.

Hadley's retired father, Steven, has sustained some sort of accident, probably a hunting mishap, which made him deaf in one ear. Sit on the wrong side of him and he can't hear you, forcing you to bend halfway across the expansive white wicker lawn table so he can read your lips. At the same time, he seems deeply paranoid about discussing whatever it was that he used to do for a living, so he keeps his voice dialed down so low that you can't hear him. The combination of not being able to hear a word he says but having to shout every word of your own makes for a most taxing conversation.

"It's a beautiful day," you scream. "THANK YOU SO MUCH FOR HAVING ME OUT."

"What?" his lips suggest.

"I said, it's a beautiful . . . "

"Speak up!" he says in a muffled tone, soft as Egyptian cotton.

"Oh, let me just move over here." You jump over to the wicker lawn chair on the other side of Hadley's father. But then he turns his good ear away from you as he addresses his daughter.

"Hadley, will you please tell your friend to talk louder."

"Yes, Dad!" And then to you, "Oh, don't mind him, he's just deaf in that ear."

Meanwhile Hadley's grandmother, who, apparently, has never seen a heating bill that she agreed to pay, trolls around the porch wearing the identical black skirt, black top, and hot pink leggings combination that she wears every day. If you had to speculate, you might guess that she hadn't taken a bath for a few weeks even though the water's free.

Every time she wafts by on the porch, a plume of unsavory aromas in her wake, you have to hold your breath and politely pivot your nose away from her. This makes you feel a tad eccentric yourself.

"Told you," Hadley says, winking.

The Etymology of Eccentricity

"Eccentricity" is defined in the *American Heritage Science Dictionary* as "a measure of the deviation of an elliptical path, especially an orbit, from a perfect circle." But the amount of devia-

tion is no cause for alarm. The planets (nine or eight, depending on whether you count Pluto) will all continue to orbit the sun elliptically, rather than in perfect, concentric circles.[21]

According to *dictionary.com*, "Eccentricity usually suggests a mildly amusing but harmless characteristic or style." Here, in the circles with which we are more concerned, there is an implied deviation from "normal," one that is both "harmless" and "amusing."[22]

The Connection between Eccentricity and Wealth

By most accounts, eccentricity and money go hand in hand. Dame Edith Sitwell wrote, "The man of genius and the aristocrat are frequently regarded as eccentrics because genius and aristocrat are entirely unafraid of and uninfluenced by the opinions and vagaries of the crowd." *Wikipedia*, too, notes that "eccentricity is . . . believed to be associated with great wealth," while *Merriam Webster Collegiate Dictionary* nods to the implicit tie between eccentricity and high net worth with one of its examples under the word *eccentric*, i.e., "an eccentric millionaire."[23]

Eccentricity is a statement about one's individuality. Sometimes it arises through the extraordinary isolation that the truly wealthy enjoy. The cloistered life can lead to a certain quirkiness, as third and fourth cousins, thrice removed, hob nob only with each other on 300-acre estates located in the remote reaches of Nantucket, Northeast Harbor, Newport, and beyond. The endless play with kin and clan often has the result of keeping family quirks *in* the family. There is a tolerance for idiosyncrasies within these circles that runs deeper than that afforded to outsiders.

But don't despair. Just because you don't happen to own an estate doesn't mean you can't develop an eccentricity that might suggest estate ownership. And doing so may help usher you into the Inner Circle with considerable speed.

True eccentrics don't give a hoot what the world thinks of them. They don't feel a burning need to conform. By showing that you've got a little bit of the eccentric in you, you'll demonstrate that you have gumption rather than coming off as a pandering sycophant. This is bound to make you more palatable to a tribe who generally distrusts boot-lickers. Naturally, some peculiarities are more acceptable than others, and some are intolerable under any circumstances. You shouldn't aim to smell moldy (even if there are plenty of rich people who do) or collect cats like others collect sweaters. Your eccentricity, whatever it may be, can't be deemed offensive by the very group that you're trying to infiltrate.

If you're looking for inspiration, examine the chart detailing several wealthy real-life eccentrics and the nature of their idiosyncrasies.

Wealthy people live large. And some of their oddities, while benign, can take some getting used to. Imagine being invited to one of Francis Egerton's lavish dinner parties for dogs. If you were a dog owner, you wouldn't want your pooch to be underdressed. You'd have to purchase your pet an extravagant outfit for the party.

The playwright Oscar Wilde, it's said, wore flamboyant clothing and walked a lobster on a leash while attending Oxford Univer-

Oscar Wilde understood the importance of looking dapper.

sity. Had you been friends with Oscar, you would have had to screen out the stares of curious onlookers while making certain that one of those lobster claws didn't poke you in the ankle. And clearly, ordering cooked lobster at a clambake would have been frowned upon by both the writer and his beloved pet.

WHAT'S YOUR PREDILECTION FOR ECCENTRICITY?

Not everyone has what it takes to become an eccentric. Following

are a few questions to test your proclivity to eccentricity.

1. A friend ardently describes a statue she saw of a giant stuffed bear with its head carved open. Your first thought is:

    A. Eeeew! That's art?

    B. No judgments till I see it.

2. An acquaintance drags you to a vintage clothing store. You feel that the clothes:

    A. Help you connect to your last life, and possibly, to the one before that, so you buy an item or two for fun.

    B. Remind you of moldier versions of what you can find in your grandmother's closet. Mission aborted, you dash to a department store instead.

3. You view "alone time" as:

    A. A chance to spend time with someone fascinating: yourself.

    B. Proof positive that you need more friends.

4. Someone calls you "eccentric" to your face. You think:

    A. What a wonderful compliment.

    B. What a horrible insult.

The potential eccentric answers as follows: 1B, 2A, 3A, and 4A.

Person	Eccentricity	Legend Has It	Profession
Francis Egerton (1756–1823)	Throwing lavish dinner parties for dogs.	He wore each pair of shoes only once.	Eighth Earl of Bridgewater
Emily Dickinson (1830–1886)	Wore all-white clothing all the time.	She never left the house. Her friendships took place via letter.	Poet
William Spooner (1844–1930)	Inventing spoonerisms. A "spoonerism" is the swapping of letters, vowels, and words in a sentence, i.e., "We'll have the hags flung out" (for "flags hung out").	People went to his lectures just to hear him make a mistake.	Professor at Oxford University
Salvador Dali (1904–1989)	Wore long hair, sideburns, coat, stockings, and knee britches, in the fashion of a century earlier.	He said, "At the age of six, I wanted to be a chef. At the age of seven, I wanted to be Napoleon."	Surreal Artist
Doris Duke (1912–1993)	Disguised in a wig, she would sneak into a jazz club and play piano for hours.	She owned two pet camels.	Philanthropist [24]

ON CHOOSING YOUR OWN ECCENTRICITY

To become a self-invented person takes pluck and a devil-may-care attitude. But there are rewards. Most eccentricity—as long as it's truly harmless—is a quality that's appreciated.

Gone are the ho-hum and humdrum days, each one barely indistinguishable from the next. Onlookers will now have countless stories to share about the beloved eccentric in their life—you. Zany people, after all, tend to be interesting and make life richer for all, just by their wacky presence.

Still, like fine wine, a well-calibrated eccentricity matures slowly. It's best to tap into your own peculiarity and not rely on anyone else's, lest you come off as a grade-C character actor.

A smarter tack is to take some odd tendency that you already possess and exaggerate it ever so slightly. Never aim to become more distinctive. Just try to become more *yourself*. Nurture the lovable quirkiness that makes you, *You*, and let *that* quality ripen over time.

My friend Kerrie collected ticks as a child. It's a miracle that she never contracted Lyme disease. My friend Phillip travels to certain disaster sites to assess the damage. If a bridge has collapsed or a hurricane has swept through the area, Phillip makes it a point to visit the scene. He's not making the journey for any business reason but rather to enhance his own, unbiased, personal understanding of the situation.

My glamorous friend Elizabeth, whom you already met in Chapter Three, takes three or four showers a day even though she's neither a pottery maker nor a construction worker. Truthfully, she probably doesn't get all that grimy, as she is a confirmed lady of leisure. And while I believe that her eccentricity may be too

Doris Duke had two pet camels. Hopefully, they were well behaved.

time-consuming for others to adopt, at least Elizabeth's quirk has the benefit of ensuring that others enjoy the time they spend with her. Nurtured properly, your idiosyncrasy can too.

Here are some worthwhile eccentricities to consider adopting: wearing dark sunglasses indoors; incorporating certain dandy-like elements into your wardrobe; finding a pet cause that no one else cares about; nurturing an exotic pet; and embracing a countercultural outlook.

We'll have a chance to peruse these five more in depth, but remember that the whole point is to choose an eccentricity that will fit your personality, and then further define yourself by exploring it. A well-tended eccentricity makes you more authentic to yourself, not less so.

Man as art—Dali, wearing the flamboyant mustache style he popularized.

Wearing Dark Sunglasses Indoors

A worthwhile eccentricity has provenance.

Ever since the then first lady of style, Jacqueline Onassis, showed the world how to pull it off, there has been a certain celebrity allure

to wearing dark sunglasses. To dial up your own appeal from merely glamorous to eccentrically glamorous, patently refuse to remove your sunglasses whenever you're inside. For added credibility, blame your stubbornness on something unprovable—perhaps it's eye sensitivity, a migraine, or an allergy to freshly mown grass that makes your eyes water.

Naturally, the 24/7-sunglasses habit is easier to master when you know for a fact that you look positively dashing in your specs. For inspiration, look to some modern-day celebrities to see how they get away with it. Check out performance artist Lady Gaga, model Kourtney Kardashian, and the princess of pop, Mandy Moore, who have all broadened their considerable charms by looking beyond hot behind the most enormous sunglasses. Matinée idol George Clooney and studly soccer legend David Beckham prove that sunglass style isn't reserved solely for those of the female persuasion. However, if you're going to sport this look 24/7, be sure to select a lens shape and color that shows your face to its best advantage. While the prevailing wisdom used to be, "go with your facial shape," most fashion icons today feel that going *against* type is more flattering. If you have a square face, soften it with oval glasses or aviators. If your face is round, don rectangular frames to subtly elongate and widen it. Is your face oval? Congratulations! You have freedom of choice. Most styles will work well on you because your

facial proportions are already perfect.

Meanwhile, a lack of contrast is considered the spiffier fashion choice for eyeglass frames and lenses. Try to more or less match your hair shade. Blondes and redheads look fetching in light-colored frames and lighter-colored lenses; dark-haired beauties look irresistible in black frames with witchy dark lenses.

One caveat: Looking eccentrically glamorous in giant shades can sometimes backfire. In low light, you may not be able to see. Try to develop a feel for where the priceless antiquities are housed in your host's mansion, and do your best not to knock into them with your elbows.

INCORPORATING CERTAIN DANDY-LIKE ELEMENTS INTO YOUR WARDROBE

The fastest way to broadcast yourself as eccentric is to emulate Salvador Dali and wear something that is painfully out of touch with modern sensibilities. For best results, turn back the clock at least one century. If you're a man, your wardrobe items might include a walking stick (particularly if you're young and don't need one); a pocket watch (with its telltale gold chain looping outside the vest so it can be readily spotted); a pipe (so you can resemble a modern-day incarnation of Sherlock Holmes); an ascot; or a fedora. A pince-nez, a monocle, or a green carnation are other options.

While there are female dandies (known as "quaintrelles"), the only way to spot one of them is via their enormous hats, which may cut down on peripheral vision too much to be practical.

Is there some story you can share about the dandy-like item you are wearing? If the tale hearkens back to a particular family member whose wealth level and status can neither be proved nor disproved, all the better.

"My great-great-great-great-grandfather, who died during the unfortunate crossing of the *Titanic*, left his son this pocket watch with the proviso that it be passed down to anyone in the family with the middle name of 'Herbert.'" (Of course, any tall tales are best told by gifted raconteurs.)

There is a longstanding connection between dandyism and aspiration for greater wealth. In the late eighteenth and early nineteenth century England, a dandy was a self-made man who strove to imitate an aristocratic lifestyle despite coming from a middle-class background.

The model gallant was British-born Beau Brummell, who, in his youth, was an undergraduate student at Oriel College, Oxford, and

A vintage item is even more valuable when it happens to come with a story attached.

Go easy on the number of vintage items in your wardrobe. Generally, one is plenty.

however, ultimately did. His lavish spending habits forced him to flee to France in 1816 to escape debtor's prison—a fate far worse than death for a natty clotheshorse.

If you wish to experiment with dandyism, my strong recommendation is to sport only one dandy item at a time. Wearing one vintage item whispers "stylish"; wearing two or more shouts "imposter," or worse—"thrift store victim." Also, if you work in a highly structured Fortune 500 company, it's not a good idea to wear vintage clothing to the office. (Your colleagues will automatically assume that your ideas are as recycled as your clothing.) Foster your eccentricity on weekends only.

FINDING A PET CAUSE THAT BROADCASTS YOUR SPECIALNESS

Adopt a pet cause that's vitally important to you but to few others. Then discuss it any time the opportunity presents itself. For the purposes of cultivating an eccentricity, the undertaking should be small and eminently achievable. If your pet project can bring a smile to someone's face, that's the ideal.

later became an associate of the Prince Regent. Chiefly famous for being famous, Brummell was immaculately outfitted and led the movement from wearing breeches to snugly tailored pantaloons. Even in faraway France, his fashion sense was copied and much admired. Beau Brummell was also a gifted conversationalist, which never hurt his aspirations to lift himself up to a higher social plane. Being a spendthrift,

There is a socialite in New York who has spent years trying to get a James Madison monument built. Apparently, he's the only U.S. president who doesn't have one. Yet.

Along the same theme, you might try to get a national holiday created *expressly* for James Madison. Yes, he was a U.S. president, so technically, when we celebrate Presidents' Day, we are honoring Madison as well. But everyone knows that Presidents' Day used to be two holidays: Washington's Birthday and Lincoln's Birthday. Why should Washington and Lincoln get all the respect? James Madison was important too!

Are you feeling ambitious? Why not petition Hallmark to create "Happy James Madison Day" cards? Or create James Madison Day bumper stickers and sell them online.

If presidential memorabilia isn't your thing, you could try to create a national holiday for all twelve signs in the Chinese zodiac. Happy Dragon Day! Or work on creating a special commemorative stamp for someone non-obvious but who deserves to be celebrated. Or devote yourself to something environmentally

lofty, such as bringing palm trees to a large northeastern city.

With any of these tactics, the trick is finding others who are willing to lend their name, time, or money to the cause. Start a Facebook page and a blog about your pet cause. Tweet about it regularly. And gradually, you'll surround yourself with like-minded individuals who, by sharing their pool of knowledge, can help the idea take root.

A Bird in the Hand Is Worth Two in the Cage

True eccentrics are a bit odd, and sometimes their difference extends to their pets: Oscar Wilde's

pet lobster, Doris Duke's two pet camels. My grandmother, may she rest in peace, once kept a tortoise in her bathtub. Legend says that eccentric millionaire Sir "Union" Jack Hayward once took a goat as his guest to a cocktail party.

In the movie *Bringing Up Baby*, the Susan Vance character played by Katharine Hepburn owned a pet leopard. What was Susan Vance's career? She was a flighty heiress, of course.

If you ever become really wealthy (or marry money) you might consider doing the humane thing by setting up a trust fund to take care of your beloved animal after you die. But until then, you may want to consider getting an unusual pet and just taking very good care of it yourself. Do not adopt a pet that's illegal or any animal that's so frightening that having it around will defeat the whole purpose of owning it in the first place. There is never a compelling reason to adopt a pet skunk.

By all accounts, teacup pigs, mini pigs, teacup potbelly pigs, and pixie pigs are becoming popular pets, despite the fact that an adult can weigh between thirty and sixty-five pounds, belying the name "teacup." Take note: Pigs need daily leash-led walks in order to stay svelte. Something else to consider: If you move apartments, you may have to create a pet résumé for your animal, and "exotic" may not be a bonus.

DARE TO BE COUNTERCULTURAL

"Countercultural" is a sociological term used to describe the values and norms of behavior of a cultural group or subculture that runs counter to those of the social mainstream. I have several friends, all born and bred in the North, who insist on referring to the Civil War as the War of Northern Aggression. If my friends had been born in the South and felt this way, it might simply be attributed to a regional difference. But that they were born in the North with no known affiliation to the antebellum South makes their verbiage notably eccentric.

Personally, I hate to drive cars. It's partly because I learned to drive as an adult and am therefore wretched at it. But with today's emphasis on maintaining a low carbon footprint, I find that I now know quite a few folks who don't drive very much either. There are approximately five times a year when I really wish that I enjoyed driving enough to actually do it, but the fact is I don't. Instead, I concentrate on being a good passenger so that I can secure rides when I really need them.

I have friends who follow all sorts of bizarre diets for nonmedical, nonreligious, and non-vegan reasons. I have other friends who consider themselves to be part of a special club because they are only children. These days, it's so easy to find others who will share your affiliation that there's

really no reason *not* to explore something unusual, especially if doing so makes you feel happy.

Don't pop a pill. Instead, take the opportunity to find your personality—along with your joy.

WHY POSITIONING YOURSELF AS AN ECCENTRIC HELPS INGRATIATE YOU WITH THE WELL-TO-DO

Eccentrics are nonconformists. By not seeking approval, you will distinguish yourself from others trying to climb into the group. You will be like a breath of fresh air in these stuffy circles. And perhaps inadvertently, you will make people laugh, which will also help lower their guard.

Since the Renaissance, many courts have had a clown. By taking on the role of the local eccentric, in essence *you* become the court jester. But unlike some of those clowns of old, your brand of humor won't be directed at the ruling "monarch." Instead, many of the jokes will be at your expense, but in a lovable way.

You don't have to wear clown makeup or slip into a giant outfit with polka dots. Even without colorful garb, your eccentricity will have those around you treating you as if you're an amusing entertainer. You won't be paid for your efforts, but at least you'll always have a seat at the table. And if you pursue your eccentricity with a lack of self-consciousness, you will be embraced even more readily.

CHAPTER SEVENTEEN

THE MIRACLE
OF DATING UP
(Yes, It Can Happen to You)

You're seated in the airless jury duty pen with two hundred other victims, waiting for your name to be called. Beside you is your reading material for the week: a book destined to bring enormous wealth into your life called *The Attractor Factor*, another book called *How to Marry the Rich*, and a third called *How to Marry Money*.

As you open *How to Marry the Rich*, a notice from your landlord tumbles into your lap like an omen. The tone of his letter is vitriolic, which you especially do not appreciate as your rent is only two months past due—an improvement from months past. *What an ingrate!*

You stuff the notice back inside the book, making a silent mind bet. If you do not get called for jury duty by 2 PM today, you will text your landlord your sincere apologies and pay him all the money past due. Even if you have to starve yourself for three months.

You are just contemplating whether you should fill out the diagnostic on your "Attractor Factor IQ" or read chapter 3 of the surprisingly cheery *How to Marry Money* when the green-eyed tax attorney you met at the charity event a few months earlier suddenly appears and sits down beside you. Coincidence?

"Catching up on some reading?" the lawyer asks, putting on a pair of tortoiseshell spectacles and picking up your copy of *How to Marry Money*. "Heady stuff!"

"A friend's getting married," you mumble.

"To 'Money'?"

"Actually, his name is Stanley," you say, quickly stuffing *How to Marry Money* back into your tote.

"Not 'Rich'? Because if it's to Rich, I think congratulations are in order."

You toss *How to Marry the Rich* back into your sturdy tote bag, as you feel the room spin. Damn these old federal courthouse buildings with their lack of ventilation. This one smells like the inside of a tomb.

"She's tying the noose," you say.

"That's quite a malapropism," the lawyer says, green eyes glinting behind sexy spectacles. "Because the expression is 'tying the knot.'"

"Not the noose?"

"A noose is something one uses to hang oneself."

The lawyer picks up your copy of *The Attractor Factor* and thumbs through it, stopping at some of the parts you've underlined in red and laughing out loud. White teeth like a wolf, a laugh like a green-eyed hyena.

"In all seriousness, do you think books like these actually work?" the lawyer asks, flipping to *The Attractor Factor* IQ diagnostic. "I mean, you went to college, didn't you?"

"My mother bought them for me. *She's* the one who thinks they work."

"But you're the one who's reading them."

"I just do what I'm told."

"So is this your retirement plan, then? *The Attractor Factor* and *How to Marry Money?*"

"I've also been reading a book called *Live Like a Millionaire,*" you say.

"Well, aren't you prepared for life's contingencies!"

You really wish the lawyer's eyes weren't quite so green. They're hard to look at this early in the morning.

"Better than buying a lottery ticket every week, my other strategy," you say. "To save money, I've been avoiding my landlord. And to not spend any, I've been subsisting on macaroni and cheese."

"How do you feel about pizza?"

"Well, it's no macaroni and cheese, but . . . "

"No. I mean with me."

"I don't have a huge problem with it. But it's only nine thirty in the morning."

SYNCHRONICITY

Synchronicity can be defined as the coincidental occurrence of events that seem related but cannot be explained by conventional mechanisms of causality.

The Swiss psychologist Carl Jung coined the term in the 1920s to explain the stuff that can't be explained. If two people who are unaware of each other, living at polar ends of the earth, happen to invent the identical gadget at the same time, that's an example of synchronicity. If, after years of being out of touch with someone, you suddenly have a dream about him and then run into him the next day, that's another example of synchronicity in action.

There's no particular reason why you should expect to bump into a richling at the very moment when your fledgling bank account dictates that you urgently need someone to treat you to lunch that afternoon, but if it happens, why not be prepared? Learn to allow that coincidences do happen, and anticipate the unexpected.

LITTLEWOOD'S LAW

Lest you think that synchronicity is only experienced by the lucky few once in blue moon, a mathematician named John Littlewood would have begged to differ. He coined the phrase *Littlewood's Law*, which states that individuals can expect miracles to happen at the rate of about one a month.

A professor at Cambridge University, Littlewood defined the word "miracle" as an exceptional event, which occurs at a rate of one in a million. By that criterion, it sounds like a miracle might happen infrequently—except that he also determined that human beings experience *one event per second*, the vast majority of them, unexceptional. (Reading a sentence of this book is an event; texting your buddy is an event; writing an item on your to-do list is an event.)

Littlewood figured that a human being was alert for approximately eight hours a day. As a result, he said, in thirty-five days, a human will have experienced *one million events*. By this definition of "miracle," one will take place every thirty-five days, actually making it a commonplace occurrence, indeed.

Whether you believe that miracles happen once a month, once in a lifetime, or that the definition of the word "miracle" should be changed to bring it more in alignment with reality, it still never hurts to be prepared.

With a little advance work, there's no reason why you can't take a chance encounter with someone you've had your eye on for months, and hit that particular miracle out of the ballpark.

THE ACCIDENTAL DATE

With all of the literature that exists about meeting someone well-to-do, there's a dearth of information on *what to do* once you actually find yourself sitting next to the person. And while it's true that each situation is unique, there are certain commonalities. For starters, you never want to appear desperate. When opportunity finally knocks, try *not* to be observed reading a book about meeting a millionaire!

You also don't want to seem as if you're down and out. In the same way that employers would prefer to hire someone who's already working, most wealthy singletons would prefer to date someone who seems like they're comfortably off. Think of it as a paradox. The less you appear to need the person's financial backing, the more likely you are to receive it.

Superior preparation and diligent but measured follow-through will help reap big rewards. Lastly, it's always smart to remember that, just like an attractive job offer, you only need one.

Why Dating Up Is Like Going on a Job Interview

I've read that going on a job interview is a lot like going on a date. But the analogy works even better backwards. Going on a date—particularly the first date—is a lot like going on a job interview. And if the prospect happens to be both physically and financially attractive, the stakes are even higher.

Similar to acing a job interview, there are five strategies you can hone that will steer you through the first date and help guarantee a callback appointment. These are:

1. Dress for success
2. Keep up-to-date on your field research
3. Do your homework
4. Ask revealing questions
5. Stay top-of-mind

Dress for Success

You'd never venture to a job interview without looking poised and presentable. You shouldn't go on a date without looking spiffy either.

That sounds utterly reasonable, you think, *but what if I don't happen to have a date?*

In that case, you should *still* dress up—on the off chance that one will appear in the nick of time. Synchronicity happens. Be prepared.

Previous chapters have disclosed the specifics of how to dress luxuriously on a threadbare budget. But dressing for success is also a philosophy—one you should adhere to, regardless of the vicissitudes of the weather, your schedule, or your mood. In the words of the old lottery campaign, "Hey, you never know."

When you bump into the person of your dreams today, will you be looking and smelling your best? Or will you be sporting the grunge look, just because you don't happen to have a client meeting back at the office?

Will you be toting a smart briefcase or handbag? Or will you be porting a grody, worn totebag with the logo obliterated and the handles worn down with stitches missing? Will you have packed light so that you can walk, unfettered, in a sprightly manner? Or will you be hauling almost as much baggage as a traveling hobo?

If you recognize that synchronicity works in strange ways and does not necessarily take time off to coordinate with your jury duty schedule, you won't allow yourself to slum. Imagine that each chance encounter is a preplanned interview instead of a random occurrence. And be sure to dress up for the occasion.

The French writer Chamfort once observed, "A woman on the way to her execution would yet demand a little time to put on her makeup." If you choose not to wear any and then bump into someone eligible, it's a wasted opportunity. The no-makeup look is extremely unappealing, unless your prospect happens to be a zombie. Consider: If you traipse about without makeup, people will be able to see straight into your pores. Lipstick, mascara, powder: Don't leave home without them!

Hair needs to be kempt. "Bedhead" is not a look, but a symptom. Bedhead announces to the world that you've given up before the day has even begun. And honestly, you shouldn't because, according to *Littlewood's Law*, you're due for a miracle any day now.

Oscar Wilde once said, "There is no greater aphrodisiac than money." That's a valid belief if you happen to be blessed with wads of the green stuff. But if you wish you had more of it, there's nothing wrong with investing in some over-the-counter aphrodisiacs. Wear some perfume or a hint of cologne. Pop a breath mint. Put your prettiest face forward.

If you're a guy, shower often. Studies show that pheromones—those love hormones the opposite sex responds to without consciously smelling them—can't be detected when they're hiding under gobs of sweat. Don't mask your pheromones. You're going to need them to attract a mate.

While you're in the process of cleaning up your appearance, remember to wear clothing that isn't spotted, soiled, or threadbare. Forgo the droopy shorts, low-rider jeans, and Birkenstocks. Don't show cleavage—either up at the chest level, down at the toe level, or anywhere in between. Leave much to the imagination.

Keep Up-To-Date on Your Field Research

You'd never waste your time looking for a job at company that wasn't hiring. Why squander valuable resources searching for a date in an area where 99 percent of the residents are married?

Synchronicity happens. But it will occur with even greater frequency when you put yourself in a place where you are likely to find success.

Study reports from the U.S. Census Bureau and any timely news items about "best places to live in the United States." *Forbes* magazine is a font of this type of information. the *New York Times* and *USA Today* often cite intriguing polls. To round out your research, check out *Sperling's Best Places* online.

In particular, direct your focus to information that reveals pertinent stats, such as male-to-female ratio, single-to-married ratio, and how economically healthy a region is, as expressed through statistics like unemployment or foreclosure figures. The lower they are, the healthier the region and the happier the people. (This makes them eminently more dateable.)

Recognizing that the numbers quoted here could change radically by the time of publication, I include them only to illustrate how acquiring some knowledge can help you in your quest. (Stay up-to-the-minute through the sources listed above.)

Today there are millions of millionaires living in the United States. How many, precisely? At last count, 9 million, or 2.8 percent of the population. And, by most guesstimates, that number will continue to rise. There are fewer billionaires—as of this writing, just slightly over twelve hundred of them—but that number is also trending upwards. In between the run-of-the-mill millionaires and the billionaires are the U.H.N.W.I.s—the Ultra High Net Worth Individuals—each with a net worth of at least $5 million. The bottom line? There are a lot of richlings out there and their number is expected to go up.

Statistically, this means that out of every 100 people you pass on the street today, two or three could be in your target group. With so many millionaires milling about, every day presents an opportunity to meet, greet, and befriend one of them.

If you're female, however, sorry to report that the numbers aren't always rosy. According to the U.S. Census Bureau, there are only 88 single men for every 100 single women over the age of 18. That's nothing to get depressed about. It just argues for portraying yourself in the most polished, poised, and presentable way imaginable whenever you do meet someone who's eligible. *Synchronicity happens. Be prepared.*

How can you improve your chances of meeting someone dateworthy? Go north, young woman! If you're willing to move, consider migrating to a city where the odds will tilt in your favor. In Boston, there are 52 percent women to 48 percent men, but the high ratio of singles to married folks helps make it an ideal spot for singles to mingle.

In Washington D.C., the stats are similar—slightly more women than men, but a proportionally high rate of singletons. Seattle, too, has almost equal numbers of men and women plus a high percentage of single people. In Austin, there are actually more men than women. (If you're just looking to hang out with upper-crusters, and you don't care whether or not they're married or working, Los Angeles; Orange County, California; and Cook County, Illinois, are excellent bets.)

However, beware: Sometimes statistics lie. Believe everything

To find eligible dates, move to an area where the male-to-female ratio helps advance your cause.

you read, and you'd think that the female-to-male ratio in Manhattan wasn't wildly out of wack. Yet anyone who lives here knows that in any given bar on any given weeknight, there will be eight or nine women to every guy. If you can find a straight, single man here, you can find one anywhere. (And by the time you do, you're so worn out from the search that you don't care how little money he has.)

Are you male? From a statistical standpoint, the big news is that dating up is no longer primarily a female pastime. Neither is marrying up. Current statistics cite that 40 percent of working wives outearn their spouses and a whopping 30 percent of married women have more education than their hubbies. What do men find sexiest now? Women with high-paying jobs. Guys can't stop drooling over those paycheck stubs.

Dating up: Men do it; women do it; everyone does it. Do you want to do it? Scout out a location where the ratio of men to women works in your favor, the rate of singletons is high, and the zip code is geographically desirable.

Thomas Jefferson once said, "I'm a great believer in luck, and I find the harder I work, the more

I have of it." If you're intent on hanging out with the Gucci'd class, scope out where members of the tribe live and work. Doing so will improve your chances of meeting one. And where there is one, there are millions.

DO YOUR HOMEWORK

You'd never dream of going on an in-person job interview without first investigating the interviewer. Doing your homework in preparation for a date is equally mission-critical.

The Internet and the explosion of new media make it a snap to research anyone on the planet. If someone tickles your fancy, try to do your homework before you let him or her give you a backrub.

There are three reasons why it's essential to dig up as much background information as possible. First, doing so can help you uncover new areas of synchronicity. Perhaps you both attended the same high school without actually being there at the same time. Or maybe, you both know people in common, collect esoteric snow globes, or have a hankering for beet milk shakes. Who knew? You would—if only you had done your homework! Researching your date in advance gives you exponentially more conversational fodder to pore through when you finally meet face-to-face.

Doing your homework will instill you with confidence. So will mentally rehearsing the conversational play-by-play once or twice in advance. That's right. Before you find yourself on a pressure-packed evening out with your prospect, imagine in your mind's eye how the conversation might progress. Visualization can help ease high-stress situations and allow you to relax just enough to perform at your best.

That said, you don't want to do so much research that your questions sound canned. It's always better to seem spontaneous and natural. Also, even if you've determined that you and your date have innumerable life experiences in common, vow to listen more than you talk. Dale Carnegie, author of the blockbuster *How to Win Friends and Influence People*, recognized that most people love nothing more than to chat about themselves. As a result, this super savvy salesman advised readers to listen hard, talk little, and take a sincere interest in others.

"You can close more business in two months by becoming interested in other people than you can in two years by trying to get people interested in you," he observed.

Lastly, and of no small significance, sometimes doing your due diligence can actually save you years of pain. For example, let's suppose that you look up someone's profile on Facebook and under relationship status, it says, "It's complicated." In that case, you'd be well advised to run as fast as you can in the opposite direction!

Today you no longer need to hire a private detective to discover everything you always wanted to know about someone but were afraid to ask. Start with Google, and tease out any articles about your potential love interest. Articles often offer the best glimpse into a target's personality because any quality reporter will take special care to make his subject come alive through the medium. Sometimes, a reporter will be able to reveal something about the person profiled that will add a color or nuance that's unlikely to surface elsewhere.

Does your date have a website? Visit it without delay. Learn what the prospect has to say in his defense. Has she ever appeared on YouTube? Watch any videos as if your future happiness depends on it. (It pretty much does.)

After you've exhausted Google, expand your search to LinkedIn, Facebook, and Twitter. On LinkedIn, in particular, you will often find extensive bios of people. However, rein in the urge to constantly check your date's bio to see if anything much has changed since the last time you checked it. Each time you look up someone, your name automatically shows up under the "Who's Viewed Your Profile" feature. And, even if you have your account set up in away that doesn't directly reveal your identity, eventually your name will show up under his or her "People You May Know Listing." Your prospect doesn't have to be a Sherlock Holmes to figure out that *you're the one* who's been researching his name over and over.

Both LinkedIn and Facebook automatically display any common connections that you and your target share. This helpful material is like conversational gossamer; you can spin it into silky smooth dialogue.

Once you have researched where your prospect works, his or her past places of employment, home and work address, political party, and religious affiliation, you should have more than enough conversational fuel to cruise through at least one date. However, be sure to keep the questions from your side of the table light, fun,

and noninvasive. Don't act like a district attorney on that first date even if you *are* a district attorney.

If the two of you hit it off, trust that there will be plenty of time to dig deeper.

ASK REVEALING QUESTIONS

You probably wouldn't stroll into a job interview without preparing a few questions in advance—just in case the opportunity arose. It's not a bad idea to prepare a couple of softball questions to toss at your date, as well.

When querying, the trick is finding the right balance. You want to seem curious rather than nosy. And since the idea is to prolong the conversation, it's often wiser to pose questions to which there are no right or wrong answers.

So much of the extant dating literature suggests that one should ask the most personal questions starting from the first face-to-face meeting. I can only assume that most of this advice was penned by lonely spinsters with no fewer than forty cats to keep them company!

Personally, I believe that you should stay *far away* from any disturbing topics—such as past relationships and why they failed, what you might expect from this relationship, or any time that you spent in prison. Unless your first date happens to coincide with Halloween, try not to scare the person. Keep the cocktail of meds that you take every day and your mother's foiled suicide attempt off the conversational menu tonight.

Here are five fail-safe first date questions. These should allow the conversation to flow without delving into anything too weird, too difficult to talk about, or too mentally draining.

1. If you could be any character from a book, movie, or play, who would it be?

Reveals: A window into your prospect's character.

Does he identify with the stuffy but upstanding Mr. Darcy from *Pride and Prejudice*? Or, like Huckleberry Finn, does he refuse to be "civilized"? Does she fancy herself to be as passionate as Jane Eyre? Or is she more like Scarlett O'Hara—fiery, flirty, and ultimately, uncontainable?

2. Who's your favorite real-life hero?

Reveals: A glimpse into your target's worldview.

Does your prospect think locally or globally? Does he admire a local fireman who saved a cat from burning building? Or is she more enthralled with larger-than-life figures who grace the world stage, such as American presidents and secretaries of state?

3. If you could be any animal, which one would you pick, and why?

Reveals: Attitude toward intimacy.

Does he gravitate to an animal that leads a solitary life, such as a polar bear? Or does he liken himself to a hippopotamus with a harem? Does she think of herself as a swan who mates for life? Or does she identify more with a fiercely territorial lioness?

4. Where did you grow up? Do you prefer the city or the country?

Reveals: Compatibility.

If your target grew up in the country and you grew up in the city, you may have to work harder at the relationship than if you were both raised in the suburbs.

5. What first attracted you to your field?

Reveals: Motivation. What excites your prospect? Is the primary driver greed, self-esteem, or wanting to make a difference in the world? Helpful dating tip: If your prospect is in the process of transitioning from something corporate and high-paying to something virtuous but low-paying, you may want to feign enthusiasm, at least until the end of the meal. Saying, "Ick! You'll never earn a penny as a journalist!" is not a statement of sympathy.

Here are some questions to shy away from: "What's the most embarrassing thing you've ever done?" (It's too early in the relationship to peel away the layers of the onion unless you really want to cry); "What do your parents do?" (Asking this could spark an alarm. Wow! She's asking me about my parents already?); plus any questions that lead to one-word answers, such as "What's your favorite cuisine?" ("Mexican.") Or "What's your favorite season?" ("Fall.") Monosyllabic responses are conversation killers. Use sparingly.

STAY TOP-OF-MIND

Smart interviewees don't leave the premises without knowing what the "next step" is. While it's not always possible to lock in on step two by the close of date one, you can certainly try to suggest a second meeting and assess the response.

Failing that, there are still ways to stay top-of-mind after your get-together. First, remember to tell the person that you had a nice time. Then follow up with an email and say it again. Communicating via email is especially useful because if you're lucky, your date will bang the email right back to you, and you'll be able to glean from the tone of the response whether the interest is mutual.

From a communication standpoint, you are now free to friend the person on Facebook, connect on LinkedIn, and become Twitter buddies. Some dates need to be gently pushed to commit to a second evening out, and staying in touch electronically can help you achieve your aim.

YOU ONLY NEED ONE

If you have ever looked for a job, you know that it's important to pursue every opportunity that arises, but at the end of the day, you only need one. This is equally true with finding someone financially sound to date.

If it's the right person, you won't need to play numerous games, wrest him or her from a loving spouse, or spend a great deal of time pretending to be someone you're not. I believe that love and marriage *should* go hand in hand. I do not advocate marrying anyone purely for the financial stability that he or she affords. It's not so much a moral issue as one of practicality. It's simply too darned time-consuming to be into someone just for the money. Assuming that you have a nine-to-five job, you will still have to spend 112 hours a week with your spouse. That's the equivalent of *three jobs' worth of time.* You'd better really like him or her. A lot. As my friend Charlie's grandmother once said,

"Marry for money, and you'll have to earn every penny of it."

That said, for most of Western history, marriage *was* more like a business arrangement. Love and marriage did not go together like the proverbial "horse and carriage."

But the horse, carriage, clothing, household goods, land, house, and tools did go with marriage. The fathers of the prospective couple-to-be would negotiate extensively about such matters prior to engagement. Most marriages resembled alliances between two families (or what today might be termed "marriages of convenience"). "Love," per se, didn't factor into the equation.

In the mid-1800s, marriage gradually morphed from an economic arrangement to one that was based on love and affection. And by most accounts, the institution of marriage enjoyed its greatest popularity during the post–World War II 1950s. Today, the trend has reversed and statistics claim that marriage is on the decline. In the United States, the number of singletons has never been higher. Married couples have fallen below half of all Amer-

ican households for the first time ever—down to 48 percent.

I believe that the downward trend is due less to demographic reasons (such as people marrying later, for example) than to everyone being infinitely smarter about their choices. We are living in the age of information, after all.

Today it's possible to amass an encyclopedia's worth of knowledge about the prospect before you waste one minute of actual "face time" together. In the old days, you'd have to be married to someone for at least a year and a half to learn all of the background information you can find out on Facebook or LinkedIn in five minutes! Having access to that knowledge is bound to save years of wasted time and heartache. And of course, if you're still not sure, you can always live with your paramour first as an experiment.

Whether you're into "love and marriage," or you're into love and marriage and the carriage with a Mercedes logo on it, by preparing in advance and then allowing synchronicity to do its job, there's no reason why you can't have it all.

YOU, ONLY RICHER

Your long, dry spell is over, and you've found someone eligible to date. Hallelujah! This morning, you do a rain dance in your shower (the faucet is working properly), and then dash downstairs to pay your landlord your check—on time for once.

In the lobby, you open your mailbox and extract a heavy, rectangular ochre envelope, addressed in gold calligraphy, and adorned with a postage stamp featuring an angel with a lute. The envelope looks so much like a piece of fine art that, for a moment, it takes your breath away, and you don't want to open it. You marvel at it the way one might appreciate a beautifully wrapped present. But this time, there is no surprise inside. You know exactly what it is, have been expecting it, even.

You whip out your brand-new mobile device and text your friend Hadley.

"Do you mind if I bring two guests?" you write, staring at the tiny ochre R.S.V.P. card and fishing out a Tiffany ballpoint pen from your jacket pocket.

"Two?" Hadley texts back.

"Yes—the lawyer and my parakeet."

Two seconds later, your cell phone rings. It's Hadley, of course.

"Your parakeet? You want to bring your PARAKEET as a guest to my wedding?"

"Well, Paulina gets really lonely when I'm away and ..."

"You'll just have to find her a parakeet babysitter," Hadley says with a laugh. "The lawyer, of course, is welcome to come."

That Hadley! What will you do without her companionship now that she's tying the noose?

As you exit the door of your tiny building, you spot a *Bergdorf Goodman* catalog that's been left behind on the top stoop. You kneel down and carefully scoop up the lustrous catalog—why just let it sit and collect dust? The gorgeous glossy pages will provide some inspiration for the new outfit you have to purchase even if you can't afford any of the clothing in the store. You have a wedding to attend!

A dark blue Mercedes 450 SL pulls up to the curb with a green-eyed lawyer perched in the driver's seat. You fling your Louis Vuitton duffle in the trunk of the car, then crouch low to the pavement, so as not to inadvertently frighten the parakeet on your shoulder. Then, gingerly, taking care not to shave the parakeet's head, you slide into the passenger seat and fasten your seat belt for the long and winding journey ahead. Hopefully, there won't be too many potholes to navigate or treacherous curves.

You have no idea whether your first weekend away together will lead to anything permanent, but you have three days off from work, a bird on your shoulder, a date in the driver's seat, and thirty days until your rent is due. You have

seventeen friends, three firm plans in the calendar, plus your best friend's wedding coming up.

You glance at yourself in the side view mirror and like the confident person staring back at you. Upon reflection, today is the first day, hopefully of many more to come, that you feel like a million dollars.

A NOTE OF CAUTION: A SIGNIFICANT OTHER IS NOT A RETIREMENT PLAN

A lot of bizarre surprises can come to light on the way to the altar. Maybe it will turn out that the significant other has a shoplifting addiction that can't be tamed. Maybe the person will be an alcoholic who disappears into rehab, only to emerge with a Frankenstein-like personality transplant. Maybe the two of you won't see eye to eye on expenditures and will end up forever sparring about money. Many couples do.

Barring that, marriage offers little in the way of disaster insurance. Depending on how you tabulate it, between 41 percent and 50 percent of first marriages in this country end in divorce. For better or worse, it's foolhardy to assume that *your* relationship will be immune. Suffice it to say that you don't want to put all of your eggs in your significant other's basket, no matter how much in love you are or how wealthy the person is.

You never want to feel obligated to stay with someone just because your own financial situation is tenuous. And, should you decide that the marriage is over, you don't want to be forced to marry someone else just to make ends meet!

Instead, set a goal of becoming financially independent. Aim high. Imagine yourself so comfortable that you won't need to rely on a second income or even a semimonthly paycheck. That's freedom—freedom from the stress of creditors pounding at your door.

That may seem like the impossible dream from your vantage point today. But with prudent planning, you can at least dig yourself out from a dismal hole and begin to put your financial affairs in order. Why not take this quick diagnostic to assess your financial personality, and then we'll pursue it from there.

WHAT'S YOUR FINANCIAL HOROSCOPE?

1. **You check your balance the day before payday and breathe a sigh of relief. You have:**

   a. $5.62 left, but hey, at least you're not overdrawn.

   b. $500 left, but there's this adorable sweater you've had your eye on for months . . .

   c. $1,000 left, so you sock it away in your passbook savings account.

2. **You don't make much money. But every summer you manage to take a few weeks off and vacation in the country because:**

   a. In the grand scheme of things, a few thousand dollars in the bank won't matter either way so you'd rather spend your meager savings on a summer share.

b. Meeting someone wealthy *is* your financial plan and you've heard the crème de la crème hang out in the country.

c. You're being paid to watch a country house while the owners are in Europe.

3. **Your idea of extra spending money is:**

a. The money you receive from Uncle Sam each year when you withhold too much money from your paycheck.

b. Aunt Agatha's generous birthday check to you: $500, *woo-hoo*!

c. The extra cash you earn from filling out surveys, sitting in focus groups, and persuading others to fill out the census.

4. **You haven't committed to your company's 401(k) plan (even though you're eligible for a company match) because:**

a. You still need your whole paycheck to live on.

b. You're waiting for your prince or princess to come and make those heavy financial decisions for you.

c. You have a lot of credit card debt to pay off first.

YOUR FINANCIAL PERSONALITY IS . . .

Answers: (Also see the discussion that follows.)

MOSTLY AS: SPENDTHRIFT

It's time to wake up and realize that you're not a kid anymore. Start saving something without delay. Look for simple cuts, and redirect every penny that you don't spend into a passbook savings account. Do you really require *both* a cell phone and a landline—when the only way you ever communicate is via text? Pull the plug. Eliminate your landline, save the hefty monthly charge, and repur-

Do you feel like every spare bit of cash burns a hole in your pocket? You may be a spendthrift.

Mostly Bs: Princess or Prince Wannabe

Once upon a time, in the not-so-distant past, you lived hand-to-mouth. Now you have enough money left over at the end of each month to either save or invest. But the items you're choosing to invest in aren't wise—unless Prince or Princess Moneybucks really is just around the next sand dune.

Instead of squandering your cash on yet more threads, stash the same amount each month into a savings account, or seek a low-risk investment that will help your money grow.

pose it towards your brand-new savings plan.

Must you order that second glass of wine? If not, that's $12 saved plus the tip. Splurge on sushi one night less per week and you'll save a small fortune by year's end.

Fact: Even squirreling away $50 a month will add up to thousands of dollars saved over time.

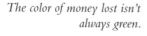

The color of money lost isn't always green.

MOSTLY Cs:
BARON-TO-BE

You recognize the importance of saving and approach the task with forethought and wisdom. Through prudent money management, you amass your nest egg slowly but steadily. Once you pay down your credit card debt, seek opportunities for wealth creation that will bring you to your goal faster.

SPEND TODAY, FOR
TOMORROW YOU MAY DIE

Saving money isn't something at which most Americans excel.

Nearly half of American workers live from paycheck to paycheck. And making more money doesn't necessarily help. Many who earn six-figure paychecks spend their way through them long before the next one arrives. Thinking about retirement? In our "live young" culture, many people don't participate in *any* retirement plans until it's too late. And people are living longer than ever too.

The spendthrift trend is reflected in other telling statistics as well.

For the first time since the Great Depression, we have a negative savings rate in this country. More than 40 percent of women have less than $500 in the bank. Thirty percent of people cash in their 401(k) plans whenever they leave a company (rather than rolling over the money into an IRA or their new employer's 401(k) plan).

Most Americans aren't saving now, never have, and never will.

That's scary, especially when you consider that each time the economy nosedives, millions of jobs are shed at the blink of corporate titan's eye. You could be unemployed for months without an emergency fund to tide you through. Even if you do land a new job quickly, you might be forced to take a substantial pay cut. Stranger things have happened.

Or you could be like my friend—let's call her "Penelope." She married for love, but divorced for money. When she and her husband split up, he allowed her to keep the large apartment—but only until their daughter went to college. Once that happened, Penelope was forced to vacate the premises pronto, and her lifestyle *still* hasn't recuperated from the nasty shock.

While there is nothing remotely sexy about enforced savings, it is prudent to force yourself to stash away some money each month. Go on an austerity diet if need be to kick-start your savings program.

Identify one or two monthly expenses you can live without and eliminate them outright. If that's seemingly impossible, keep a daily log of your expenses to note where you can shave some of them. Perhaps instead of indulging in a latte from Starbucks every day, you can purchase a bag of Starbucks coffee and brew it at home four days a week, but then treat yourself to the in-store experience on Friday

mornings. Did you circle mostly As and Bs on the quiz? You owe it to yourself to read about spendthrift economics so that you can avoid them at all costs.

SPENDTHRIFT ECONOMICS

If you inherited the spendthrift gene, chances are you think of *yourself* as an investment. Any money that you *do* manage to stash gets automatically reinvested in yours, truly. You believe that "you get what you pay for," and if something costs more, *you're* worth it. Somehow you manage to squirrel away enough money in the you-only-live-once fund for short-term goals, such as spas and ski trips. But when it comes to paying off your school loans or credit card bills, you're hopeless. At the rate you're burning cash, you will never escape from your rent-stabilized hellhole. Every raise you receive at the office just means there's more money to spend—on you.

It's hard for many spendthrifts to conquer their proclivity for lavish spending. But if you believe that those who don't pay attention to history are doomed to repeat it, then adopting a historical

Marie Antoinette's haughty disregard for thrift helped turn her country against her.

perspective might help. Did you know that during the nineteenth and twentieth centuries, a few states, such as Oregon and Massachusetts, experimented with laws whereby the family of the profligate could have him legally declared a "spendthrift" by a court of law? The wisdom at the time was that the spendthrift was legally incapable of entering into a binding contract. These laws made it harder for a spendthrift's family to end up in the poorhouse. Today, however, the old laws have been abolished in favor of modern bankruptcy laws (which are harsher for spendthrifts and their families).

Modern spendthrifts should learn from the fate that befell Marie Antoinette who was nicknamed "Madame Déficit" by her detractors in the summer of 1787. To compensate for a lack of attention from her husband, she frittered away money on gambling, clothing, shoes, pomade, and rouge.

Her renovation of the Petit Trianon during the early years of her marriage only fueled the rumors of her extravagance as her enemies claimed that she had "plastered the walls with gold and diamonds."

With heavily mounting debts that had been incurred during the Seven Years' War still unpaid and mounting pressure to support the colonists in America in their war against England (which would only lead France into further debt), Marie Antoinette's purchase of Château de Saint-Cloud for six million livres was ill-advised. The whole country soured on its spendthrift queen and her husband, and the monarchy was deposed. Off with their heads!

The moral: Paying down debt *must* take priority over maintaining a lavish lifestyle.

If you have multiple cards with high balances, here's a savvy way to shrivel the outstanding amounts down to $0. Start by listing your cards in order from the highest interest rate to the lowest. (Don't concentrate on the balances; just focus on the interest rates.) Take care of the most expensive debt first, that is, pay down the card with the highest interest rate. Keep paying the extra amount on the card with the highest interest rate until the balance disappears.

Once your first card is entirely paid off, use the money that you were paying towards that card and apply it to the card with the next highest interest rate, and so on.

While you're in the process of paying down one card, be sure not to rack up additional charges on your other cards. Also, always pay

Some cut their credit cards; other spendthrifts sometimes need to take other austerity measures.

your bills on time. Being consistently late or missing a month can wreak havoc on your credit score (which means you'll be subjected to even higher interest rates). It's in your self-interest to keep those interest rates as low as possible.

PRINCESS OR PRINCE WANNABE ECONOMICS

Did you mark mostly Bs in the quiz above? In that case, you are waiting to be financially rescued by a prince or princess. It's a pity that "Someday my prince(ss) will come" is not a sound financial plan with an absolute rate of return. First off, you may never meet your aristocrat with shiny lucre. Second, there could be stiff

competition for the person's hand in marriage. Third, what if (God forbid) you have to sign a prenup?

You can't afford to put off all intelligent economic planning while you wait. You are losing out on the real gains to be had by signing up for your company's 401(k) plan. And there's no time like today to seek the low-risk investments that can help you scrabble together a rainy day fund. Don't believe the myth that "it's as easy to fall in love with a rich person as a poor person." It may or may not be. Rich people can be ornery too!

Modern Princess or Prince Wannabes can learn a lot from the plight of poor King George IV. When he was Prince of Wales, he amassed so many debts from his profligate spending on booze, babes, horse stables, and house renovations, that his father, King George III, adamantly refused to aid his son unless he agreed to marry his cousin, Caroline of Brunswick. Even though George IV was in love with (and illegally married to) someone else at the time, he agreed to marry Caroline because if he contracted a marriage with an eligible princess, Parliament would increase his allowance.

The union, however, was a fiasco. On meeting his future wife for the first time, George was appalled by her tactlessness and talkativeness. Meanwhile, Caroline was flabbergasted by his overt flirtation with one of his numerous mistresses. At the marriage ceremony, George arrived drunk, and things only spiraled downwards from there.

The public vilified George for his wanton spending and adored his wife, Car-

One of the many castles King George IV built on someone else's dime.

oline, for her easy outspokenness. In time, the two separated. When George was appointed Regent, he restricted Caroline's access to their daughter. In revenge, his wife joined forces with a powerful Whig named Henry Brougham and launched an extensive propaganda campaign against her estranged husband.

The moral: Marrying for money is not a cogent financial strategy. Instead, look for "easy money" elsewhere.

"Easy money" is money that comes to you through no particular effort on your part. If you live in a rent stabilized building and your landlord absolutely insists on paying you money to leave the building so he can convert it into a co-op, that's a quick gain that could form part of the down payment on your first apartment or home. If your company has a 401(k) plan that will match, dollar for dollar, whatever you put into it, that's found money. (If you do end up marrying a prince or princess and your spouse-to-be forces you to sign a pre-nup, *that* money was gained relatively easily too—unless you stamp your feet and have a snit fit about the pre-

nup. You could secure your own apartment out of the deal if things don't work out.)

As a general tactic, stop borrowing expensive money from banks and credit card providers, and look for easy money instead. It's also smart to invest in long-term CDs, treasury bonds, and other relatively safe investments that will provide a small but guaranteed rate of return.

BARON-TO-BE ECONOMICS

If you marked mostly Cs on the quiz, you're on the right path. You scout for money-saving opportunities at every turn. You already know that if you received a tax refund this year, it means you overpaid Uncle Sam, so it's time to adjust your tax withholding. You're already aware that you *must* pay down expensive credit card debt before any true savings plan can manifest.

You take advantage of your company's 401(k) plan. Maybe you've even identified some creative ways to bring in a little extra cash through activities such as house-sitting for others (or walking their dogs). At this point, it may make sense to take a financial planning class so you can master some of the fine points of investing.

WHILE YOU'RE COUNTING TO TEN, TAKE OUT A $10 BILL

Whenever you are tempted to spend a great deal of money on something frivolous, it's a good idea to count to ten. It may also be effective to remove a $10 bill from your wallet and stare at the man gracing it: Alexander Hamilton. You don't have to be a Federalist to appreciate Hamilton, and his story is inspirational. He came from a humble background. He was an illegitimate orphan, working in St. Croix as a clerk. But eventually, this lowly clerk rose to become one our nation's Founding Fathers.

In addition to being the only New Yorker to sign the U.S. Constitution and the author of approxi-

mately 50 percent of *The Federalist Papers*, Hamilton became the nation's first secretary of the Treasury under President George Washington.

Hamilton consolidated the nation's debts and paid them off, established a modern economy that's still in place today, urged our country not to support the French Revolution (even though the French had supported the American Revolution) because doing so would incur more debt, and successfully argued for a strong federal government and a government-owned Bank of the United States. This was a person who understood the value of a solid financial footing and worked hard to achieve it for our country. With some scrimping and some forethought, you too can achieve financial stability. I have every confidence that you will.

A MORE POLISHED YOU

Congratulations. You now dress the part. Even if you can afford only a couple of classic pieces a year, they are the finest that money can buy. Naturally, you've created a clothing budget and skimp on other items that no one will notice anyway. You draw your fashion sensibility from elegant catalogs and your intellectual inspiration from your numerous hobbies and interests. You are as multifaceted as a diamond, and your conversation is as brilliant. Above all, you learned how to listen.

While you may not enjoy all of the trappings of privilege, you do feel privileged. You've got the richest hair and skin that money can't buy. You have amassed a $64,000,000 vocabulary. Your elocution would make Henry Higgins chortle with approval.

Perhaps, in the process of trying to better brand yourself as a success story, you changed your name, or developed a new interest or fostered an eccentricity. In any case, the very people who you most want to be with view you as a success, and someone they want to have seated next to them at the A-table.

Whether you have $1,000, $5,000, or $100,000 in the bank, you are well on your way.

NOTES

1. In all seriousness, check out www.gilt.com for elegant clothing on a shoestring.
2. For further reading, see "Diversifying the Literary Canon," Onward and Upward blog (July 2, 2008) at: http://calebteaches.wordpress.com/2008/07/02/diversifying-the-literary-canon/ (accessed May 10, 2011).
3. Dustin Lushing, "What CEOs Read Before They Lead," Newser (July 22, 2007) at http://www.newser.com/story/4613/what-ceos-read-before-they-lead.html#ixzz0xSeveYGE (accessed May 10, 2011).
4. Robert Frank, "The Billionaire Book Club: What the Rich Are Reading This Summer," The Wealth Report blog (June 11, 2010) at:http://blogs.wsj.com/wealth/2010/06/11/the-billionaire-book-club-what-the-rich-are-reading-this-summer/ (accessed May 10, 2011).
5. "Heights of Presidents of the United States and Presidential Candidates," Wikipedia, http://en.wikipedia.org/wiki/Heights_of_Presidents_of_the_United_States_and_presidential_candidates (accessed May 10, 2011).
6. Isaac B. Rosenberg, "Height Discrimination in Employment," *Utah Law Review*, No. 3 (February 16, 2009) at http://ssrn.com/abstract=1344817 (accessed May 10, 2011).
7. Sean Gregory, "Why Tall People Are Happier than Short People," *Time* magazine (July 29, 2009) accessed online at http://www.time.com/time/business/article/0,8599,1913256,00.html (accessed May 10, 2011).
8. Deborah Dunham, "Gray Hair Debate: Is it OK to Go Gray?" Stylelist (June 2, 2010) http://www.stylelist.com/2010/06/02/gray-hair-ok/ (accessed May 10, 2011).

9. "Beauty by Numbers, A Candidate to Dye For," Beauty Addict Blog Spot (Thursday January 10 2008). http://beautyaddict. blogspot.com/2008/01/beauty-by-numbers-candidate-to-dye-for.html (accessed May 10, 2011).

10. "Playing Cards," Classic Encyclopedia, http://www.1911 encyclopedia.org/Playing_Cards (accessed May 11, 2011).

11. Martha T. Moore, "Billionaires Bank on Bridge to Trump Poker," *USA Today* (12/19/2005) accessed online at http://www.usatoday.com/news/education/2005-12-19-bridge-schools_x.htm (accessed May 11, 2011). See also "Who Plays Bridge?" American Contract Bridge League website, http://www.acbl.org/about/Who-Plays-Bridge.html (accessed May 11, 2011).

12. Check out the U.S. Chess Federation website at http://main. uschess.org/content/view/7326 (accessed May 11, 2011).

13. For more information about boomerang throwing, see "Spreading the word about a modern sport with prehistoric roots," U.S. Boomerang Association brochure, http://www.usba.org/Resources/brochure/brochure2color.pdf (accessed May 11, 2011) and the U.S. Boomerang Association website, http://www.usba.org/FAQ/index.html (accessed May 11, 2011).

14. Shiri Lev-Ari and Boaz Keysar, "Why don't we believe non-native speakers? The influence of accent on credibility," *Journal of Experimental Social Psychology* (April 9, 2010). Accessed from the University of Chicago website, http://search.uchicago.edu/search?site=default_collection&client=default_frontend&output=xml_no_dtd&proxystylesheet=default_frontend&oe=utf8&ie=utf8&q=Why+don%27t+we+believe+non-native+speakers%3F&btnG.x=0&btnG.y=0&btnG=submit (accessed May 11, 2011). The study was also reported on in Science Daily, at http://www.sciencedaily.com/releases/2010/07/100719164002.htm (July 20, 2010) (accessed May 11, 2011).

15. NPR interview with Anthony LaPaglia (April 25, 2005) at: http://www.npr.org/templates/story/story.php?storyId= 4618648 (accessed May 11, 2011).

16. This study was referenced in Korin Miller, "What Do Your Shoes Say About You?" *Yahoo India* (reproduced from *Cosmopolitan* magazine, November 16, 2010) at http://realbeauty.yahoo.com/indulge-detail/post/dove_indulge/95/what-do-your-shoes-say-about-you.html (accessed May 11, 2011).

17. "Always buying sneakers? It's the sign of a leader: poll," *Reuters* (April 1, 2008) at http://www.dancehallareaz.com/forum/dhaz-street-journal/26109-always-buying-sneakers-its-sign-leader-poll. html (accessed May 11, 2011). This poll was also reported on in current.com at http://current.com/groups/art-and-style/88885707_always-buying-sneakers-its-the-sign-of-a-leader-poll.htm (accessed May 11, 2011).

18. John G. Havens and Paul G. Schervish, "Individual Giving Model," *The Center on Wealth and Philanthropy* at Boston College, Advancing Philanthropy, July 2010, accessed online on July 27, 2010 at http://www.bc.edu/research/cwp/

19. For further reading, see Emily Post, *Etiquette in Society, in Business, in Politics, and at Home.* New York: Funk & Wagnalls, 1922. (accessed online). http://www.bartleby.com/95/ (accessed May 12, 2011).

20. "Do You Know How to Behave?" *The American Magazine*, July-December 1921, New York: Crowell, 1921.

21. "Eccentricity, science definition," *The American Heritage Science Dictionary*, copyright 2010, Houghton Mifflin Harcourt Publishing Company, accessed online at http://science.yourdictionary.com/eccentricity (accessed May 15, 2011).

22. "Eccentricity," Dictionary.com Unabridged (Based on the Random House Dictionary copyright, Random House, Inc. 2011.) (accessed May 16, 2011).

23. "Eccentric," *Merriam Webster Collegiate Dictionary*, Eleventh Edition, Springfield: Merriam-Webster, 2009.

24. For more reading on eccentrics, see J. Frater, "Ten Incredibly Eccentric People," *Sun*, March 15, 2009 accessed online at: http://listverse.com/2009/03/15/10-incredibly-eccentric-people/ (accessed May 12, 2011). Also see: from Michael Myers, Thinking

and Writing about Literature, "Biography of Emily Dickinson," accessed online at http://www.vcu.edu/engweb/eng384/emilybio.html. Also, check out: Helen Gent, "Doris Duke, Billionaire Playgirl," Marie Claire, accessed online at http://au.lifestyle.yahoo.com/marie-claire/article/-/5887761/doris-duke-billionaire-playgirl/ (accessed May 12, 2011).

RECOMMENDED READING AND OTHER RESOURCES

BOOKS

1. Doonan, Simon. *Eccentric Glamour.* New York: Simon & Schuster, 2008.
2. Fadiman, Clifton and Major, John S. *The New Lifetime Reading Plan: The Classic Guide to World Literature, Revised and Expanded.* New York: HarperCollins, 1999.
3. Gladwell, Malcolm. *Blink: The Power of Thinking without Thinking,* New York: Little, Brown and Company, 2005.
4. Fussell, Paul. *Class: A Guide Through the American Status System.* New York: Touchstone, 1983.
5. Frank, Robert. *Richistan: A Journey Through the American Wealth Boom and the Lives of the New Rich.* New York: Three Rivers Press, 2007.
6. Hirsch Jr., E.D., and Kett, Joseph F. and Trefil, James S. *The New Dictionary of Cultural Literacy: What Every American Needs to Know.* Boston: Houghton Mifflin, 2002.
7. Oliver, Vicky. *301 Smart Answers to Tough Business Etiquette Questions.* New York: Skyhorse, 2010.
8. Post, Peggy. *Emily Post's Etiquette, 17th Edition.* New York: Harper-Resource. 2004.
9. Salk, Susanna. *A Privileged Life: Celebrating Wasp Style.* New York: Assouline, 2007.
10. Smith, Keith Cameron. *The Top 10 Distinctions Between Millionaires and the Middle Class.* New York: Ballantine, 2007.

WEBSITES

for business travelers
flyertalk.com
fbgolfclub.com

for chic threads
www.bluefly.com

to accumulate "common knowledge"—fast!
www.nytimes.com
www.openculture.com/freeonlinecourses.com

to enjoy nothing but good hair days
http://www.ivillage.com/beauty-hair

to see how your face will look with a different hair color or style
http://www.thehairstyler.com/virtual-hairstyler

to meet some new people offline
meetup.com—Go to Topic or Interest box and insert a hobby or sport.
foursquare.com

social networking
facebook.com
LinkedIn.com
twitter.com
instagram.com
www.pinterest.com

If you have a question or just need some friendly advice, you can email me once. I do promise to return your first email. So save it for a time when you could really use the help. Good luck with all of your business and social pursuits!
vicky@vickyoliver.com

Top Twenty Must-Have Catalogs (For best results, go to the store in person and ask how to order the catalog. Please be aware that information of this kind changes frequently, but friendly salespeople and customer service representatives should be able to help you.)

1. Banana Republic—Go to the store.
2. Bergdorf Goodman—Go to the store.
3. Bloomingdale's—Go to store.
4. Brooks Brothers—Request online. Enter "catalog" into search bar on website.
5. Coach—Go to store.
6. Donna Karan—Go to store.
7. H. Stern—Go to store.
8. J. Crew—Request online. Go to "The J. Crew Style Guide." Request one.
9. Jos. A. Bank—Go to store.
10. L.L. Bean—Request online. Go to customer service, then "Catalogs/Request a Catalog"
11. Land's End—Request online. Enter "catalog" into search bar on website.
12. Lily Pulitzer—Request online. Go to "request a catalog."
13. Michael C. Fina—Go to store.
14. Mikimoto—Go to store.
15. Neiman Marcus—Go to store. There may be a charge for the catalog.
16. Ralph Lauren—Go to store.
17. Saks Fifth Avenue—Go to store.
18. Scully & Scully—Go to website. Scroll to box that says "Our Current Catalogue." Hit the catalogue cover to request.
19. Tiffany & Co—Go to store and request.
20. Urban Outfitters—Go to store.

ACKNOWLEDGMENTS

My heartfelt thanks to the following people for their invaluable contributions, insights, and wisdom that helped make this book possible: Alec Fraser, Alexis Jacobs, Amy Li, Andrea Nierenberg, Bruce Blowman, Cammie Black, Elizabeth Jung, Gina Caulfield, Gordon Cohen, Jon Swan, Joseph Sverchek, Mark Dane, Mary Hoffman, Norm Scott, Phyllis Smith, Tony Lyons, and everyone in Cliff Hopkinson's most amazing writing class.

ABOUT THE AUTHOR

Vicky **Oliver's** savvy how-to advice has been featured in over 701 media outlets, including the *Wall Street Journal*, the *New York Post*, *L.A. Times*, *Esquire* magazine, *Forbes, Fortune*, New York 1, and Bloomberg TV.

She has won 17 literary awards, including the 2011 Paris Book Festival for How-To, the 2010 Eric Hoffer Award for Business, and both the 2009 and 2010 "Best Business Careers Book" in the National Best Books Award festival. Her books have also placed in the New England, London, San Francisco, L.A., Hollywood, and New York book festivals.

Live Like a Millionaire (Without Having to Be One) (Skyhorse, 2014) is Vicky Oliver's fifth book. Her first book, *301 Smart Answers to Tough Interview Questions* (Sourcebooks, 2005), is a national best seller now in its third printing. The book has been translated four times, is sold in fourteen countries, and is part of the job-hunting canon. Her second book is called *Power Sales Words: How to Write It, Say It, and Sell It with Sizzle* (Sourcebooks, 2006). Her third book, titled *Bad Bosses, Crazy Coworkers & Other Office Idiots* (Sourcebooks, 2008), swept the award shows and is now in its second printing. Her fourth book, *301 Smart Answers to Tough Business Etiquette Questions* (Skyhorse, 2010), now in its second printing, won seven literary awards and taught readers how to thrive in today's challenging professional environment.

When she's not writing books, Vicky Oliver teaches seminars. So far, she's given over 100 seminars on job-hunting, image presentation, and business etiquette for groups of 50–200. A Brown University alumna, she lives in Manhattan, where she helps people turn around their careers and their lives.